Swiss Contract Law

Swiss Contract Law

An Introduction for International Dispute Resolution Practitioners

Nino Sievi

Wolters Kluwer

Published by:
Kluwer Law International B.V.
PO Box 316
2400 AH Alphen aan den Rijn
The Netherlands
E-mail: lrs-sales@wolterskluwer.com
Website: www.wolterskluwer.com/en/solutions/kluwerlawinternational

Sold and distributed by:
Wolters Kluwer Legal & Regulatory U.S.
920 Links Avenue
Landisville, PA 17538
United States of America
E-mail: customer.service@wolterskluwer.com

ISBN 978-94-035-3437-4

e-Book: ISBN 978-94-035-3447-3
web-PDF: ISBN 978-94-035-3457-2

to my wife, Charlotte,
for her endless patience, her sharp wit and her gentle humour.

About the Author

Dr Nino Sievi is an international arbitration and litigation practitioner. He has been admitted to the bar in three jurisdictions – Switzerland, Germany and England & Wales (Barrister, non-practising). He holds an LLM in international law from the University of Cambridge and a PhD in Law from the University of Fribourg, Switzerland. For his doctoral dissertation, he was awarded the Joseph Vigener prize.

Today, Nino practices as a partner at Nater Dallafior Rechtsanwälte AG in Zurich representing clients in complex commercial disputes before arbitral tribunals (ICC, Swiss Rules, DIS, ad hoc) and Swiss courts, particularly in contracts, post-M&A, crypto/blockchain, technology, commodities, construction and banking matters. In 2024, Who's Who Legal recognised him as one of the top twenty most highly regarded arbitration practitioners under the age of 45 in the entire EMEA region. Besides his counsel work, Nino Sievi frequently sits as an arbitrator under Swiss, LCIA and ICC Rules and acts as an expert on Swiss law.

Table of Contents

Preface

Swiss contract law is among the most frequently chosen laws for commercial contracts. It offers parties a high degree of autonomy and authority over their agreements, surpassing the flexibility of most other legal systems. It is not bound by EU regulations or overly intricate rules concerning general terms and conditions. Simultaneously, Swiss contract law upholds the principle of good faith, safeguarding the parties' fair and reasonable expectations against any unethical practices. Its user-friendliness and predictability make it a cost-effective and logical option for parties seeking an impartial and practical legal framework.

Despite its popularity, there were no English text books on Swiss contract law until recently. The present book shall serve as a contribution to maintaining Swiss law's status in the world of international commerce. Parties shall feel confident in choosing Swiss law as the governing law of their contract, although they might not speak any of Switzerland's official languages.

As the title of the book suggests, this is an introduction to Swiss contract law. It is directed at dispute practitioners and thus puts an emphasis on topics and contracts that are frequently in dispute between commercial parties. I have avoided delving into scholarly debates about theoretical concepts of the law. Rather, I put the focus on case law as established by the Swiss Federal Supreme Court. The footnotes contain numerous (hyperlinked) references to decisions of that court and informal translations of the most important parts. This should equip practitioners with the understanding and sources to deal with most issues that might give rise to disputes.

In addition, I have taken a slightly atypical approach to depicting Swiss contract law. As a civil law system, it follows a rights-based approach, as opposed to a remedies-based approach typical to common law jurisdictions. Nonetheless, I have made an attempt to put the remedies at the centre of this book. While this might not be in line with prevailing theoretical concepts of Swiss law, I believe it makes my explanations more accessible to foreign practitioners, notably those with a common law background.

I have taken inspiration for this approach from an introductory remark in an article about the relationship between rights and remedies in private law:

> Remedies translate the abstract and lofty discourse of the law into the life-world of the disputants.[1]

1. Dedek, The Relationship Between Rights and Remedies in Private Law: A Comparison Between the Common and the Civil Law Tradition, in: Sharpe/Roach (eds), Taking Remedies Seriously, 2009, pp. 65 and 66.

CHAPTER 1

Introduction

1 This chapter addresses basic elements of Swiss private law. It builds the necessary foundation for understanding the subsequent chapters that deal in depth with Swiss contract law - a specific area of private law.

2 First, we will examine the statutory basis and system of Swiss private law, particularly the place that contract law holds within this system. Thereafter, the rules on interpretation of statutory law as well as the role of case law will be explained.

3 Further, we will consider the statute most relevant to contract law - the Code of Obligations (CO). The terminology of the CO as well as the specific role of contracts within the CO will be analysed.

I STATUTORY BASIS AND SYSTEM OF SWISS PRIVATE LAW

4 Swiss private law is based on two main statues: The Civil Code and the Code of Obligations. Further, there are many statutes dealing with specific aspects of private law. In addition, certain private sets of rules have developed that have gained wide acceptance.

5 The Code of Obligations is the statute most relevant to contract law. It sets the focus (as the name implies) on obligations. Such obligations can stem from four different sources: a tort, unjust enrichment, agency without authority and contracts. This concept of the Code of Obligations is fundamental for comprehending how the statute regulates contracts.

A The Relationship Between the Civil Code and the Code of Obligations

6 The Civil Code sets forth the basic principles of Swiss private law, such as the principle of good faith, legal capacity and the concept of legal persons. It also stipulates the rules of family, inheritance and property law.

7 The Code of Obligations deals with the law of obligations. It provides rules for obligations that exist between legal entities. It regulates their creation, performance, termination and enforcement.

8 While the Civil Code and the Code of Obligations form two separate statutes, they nevertheless form a unit on a substantive level.[2] Together they are the main statutory basis of Swiss private law. The two statues are also referred to as a *code unique*.

9 The connection of the two statutes resorts above all from their intertwined scope of application. The Code of Obligations applies to all areas of law covered by the Civil Code (Article 7 CC). Vice-versa, the provisions of the Civil Code apply to the Code of Obligations.

10 Further, several areas of law regulated by the Civil Code have a direct influence on certain aspects of the law of obligations. For example, while a sales contract is primarily governed by Articles 184 et seqq. CO, the provisions on property law contained in the Civil Code are of direct relevance for performing the seller's obligation under the sales contract, i.e., the obligation to transfer property of the good to the buyer.

B Fundamental Concepts of the Civil Code Relevant to Contract Law

11 While the Code of Obligations builds the main statutory basis of Swiss contract law, the provisions of the Civil Code remain relevant. Swiss contract law can only be fully comprehended by also considering the Civil Code. The general provisions of the Civil Code (Articles 1–10) set forth some of the most fundamental principles of Swiss private law that also apply to contracts.

1 The Principle of Good Faith and Prohibition of Abuse of Rights

12 Article 2(1) of the Civil Code set forth the principle that everyone must act in good faith in the exercise of his or her rights and in the performance of his or her obligations. This principle is of particular importance when dealing with the interpretation of contracts.[3]

13 In line with this principle, Article 2(2) of the Civil Code forbids the abuse of rights. The Swiss Federal Supreme Court has given some examples of behaviour that qualifies as abuse of rights:

> The assertion of a right is abusive if it contradicts earlier conduct and thereby disappoints [the opposing party's] legitimate expectations. However, contradictory conduct can also be seen without disappointment of legitimate expectations in

2. Tellingly, the official title of the Code of Obligations is 'Federal Act on the Amendment of the Swiss Civil Code (Part Five: The Code of Obligations)'.
3. *See* below, para. 215.

a current, in itself completely incompatible and therefore contradictory conduct. Furthermore, an abuse of rights is the exercise of rights without an interest worthy of protection or which would lead to a blatant disproportion of legitimate interests. An abuse of rights also exists if a legal instrument is used improperly for the pursuit of interests that do not lie within its scope of protection.[4]

2 *Burden and Standard of Proof*

14 Article 8 of the Civil Code sets forth the rules on the burden of proof. Unless the law provides otherwise, the burden of proving the existence of an alleged fact shall rest on the person who derives rights from that fact.

15 The burden of proof is discharged if the required standard of proof is met. There are generally three different types of standard of proof that may apply in contract law matters: the ordinary standard of proof (*Regelbeweismass*), the standard of predominant probability (*Beweismass der überwiegenden Wahrscheinlichkeit*) and the prima facie standard (*Glaubhaftmachung, simple vraisemblance, semplice verosimiglianza*).

16 In general, the ordinary standard of proof applies. Under this standard, an assertion is deemed proven if the court is convinced of the correctness of a factual assertion from an objective point of view. However, the degree of certainty must not meet a threshold of 100%. It is sufficient that any doubts that a judge might still have appear as insignificant.[5] Yet, it is not sufficient that there is merely a predominant probability that the alleged fact has materialised. Importantly, the enforcement of the law must not fail because the requirements for the standard of proof are too high or inconsistent.

17 Exceptions to the ordinary standard of proof arise on the one hand from the law; on the other hand, they have been established by case law and doctrine. A predominant probability is deemed sufficient where by the nature of the issue strict proof is considered impossible or a party cannot be reasonably expected to put forth such proof.[6] The easing of the standard of proof presupposes an 'evidentiary shortage' (*Beweisnot*). Such shortage does not exist where a party is merely unable to proof a fact, which by its nature would be readily accessible to direct proof. The issue in question must be of such a nature that requesting strict proof would appear unreasonable. Typically, this standard of proof applies where a party bears the burden of proof for a hypothetical fact (i.e., how events would have unfolded without the other party's breach of contract).

4. Decision of the Swiss Federal Supreme Court dated 5 March 2012, DSC 138 III 401, para. 2.2.
5. Decision of the Swiss Federal Supreme Court dated 12 February 2002, DSC 128 III 271, para. 2.b.aa: 'However, the realization of the fact need not be certain, but it is sufficient if any doubts appear to be insignificant. It is not sufficient, however, if there is merely a predominant probability that the alleged fact has materialized. The function of the standard of proof is to help the substantive law to prevail in the proceedings. The enforcement of the law must not fail because the requirements for the standard of proof are too high or inconsistent.'
6. Decision of the Swiss Federal Supreme Court dated 19 November 2014, DSC 140 III 610, para. 4.1.

18 Importantly, the standard of predominant probability must not be confused with the preponderance of probability test known in common law jurisdictions. The Swiss Federal Supreme Court applies a stricter test. The standard is only met if there are such weighty reasons for the correctness of the factual assertion from an objective point of view that other conceivable alternatives may reasonably be disregarded.[7]

19 In contrast, the prima facie standard is lower: 'A fact is deemed *prima facie* proven if certain elements speak in favour of its existence, even if the court still reckons with the possibility that it might not have materialized.'[8] This standard typically applies in Swiss civil proceedings that are subject to the rules of summary proceedings, e.g., requests for provisional measures.

20 In numerical terms, Swiss doctrine sums up the standards of proof as follows: the ordinary standard of proof requires a 90% certainty, the standard of predominant probability a 75% certainty, and the prima facie standard a 51% certainty.[9]

C Special Statutes and Private Sets of Rules

21 The statutory basis of Swiss private law is not confined to the Civil Code and the Code of Obligations. There are several special statutes dealing with specific aspects of private law. For example:

- Federal Act on Insurance Contracts
- Federal Act on Package Travel
- Federal Act on Liability for Products
- Federal Act against Unlawful Competition.[10]

22 Further, private sets of rules have developed over the course of the past decades.[11] While such private sets of rules do not have the power of law, parties may integrate them into their contractual relationship. Further, such private sets of rules (if sufficiently used in practice) may be considered to form part of trade custom which is relevant for the interpretation of a contract.[12]

D Structure of the Code of Obligations

23 The Code of Obligations does not only regulate contract law but also contains rules on torts law, unjust enrichment, company law and securities law. It is divided into five parts:

7. Decision of the Swiss Federal Supreme Court dated 19 November 2014, DSC 140 III 610, para. 4.1.
8. Decision of the Swiss Federal Supreme Court dated 28 August 2006, DSC 132 III 715, para. 3.1.
9. Leuenberberger/Uffer-Tobler, Schweizerisches Zivilprozessrecht, Bern 2016, N 9.159 et seqq.
10. For a more detailed list *see* the website of the Swiss Confederation, https://www.admin.ch/opc/de/classified-compilation/22.html#221.
11. For example, the SIA Norm 118 governing wide aspects of construction contracts.
12. *See* below para. 244.

(1) First Part: General provisions (Articles 1–183 CO).
(2) Second Part: The Individual Types of Contracts (Articles 184–551 CO).
(3) Third Part: Commercial Enterprises and the Cooperative (Articles 552–926 CO).
(4) Fourth Part: The Commercial Register, Business Names and Commercial Accounting (Articles 927–964 CO).
(5) Fifth Part: Securities Law (Articles 965–1186).

24 For contract law, primarily the first and second parts are of relevance. The first part contains the general rules on contract law (formation, interpretation and, performance of a contract). The second part contains detailed rules on specific contract types (e.g., sales contracts). The relation between the first and the second part is governed by the principle of '*lex specialis derogat legem generalem*'. Accordingly, the special provisions of the second part generally prevail over any conflicting provisions in the first part.[13]

E Contracts as a Source of an Obligation

25 At the centre of the first part of the Code of Obligations (the general provisions) is the legal concept of the obligation. The provisions of the code deal above all with the creation, performance (or failure thereof) and extinction of obligations.

26 There are four different bases on which an obligation can arise:

(1) Contracts (Articles 1–40 CO)
(2) Torts (Articles 41–61 CO)
(3) Unjust enrichment (Articles 62–68 CO)
(4) Agency without authority (Articles 419–424 CO).

27 Thus, a contract is first and foremost a source for an obligation. Fittingly, the first section of the Code of Obligations (Articles 1–40) is titled 'Obligations arising by Contract'.

28 The performance and extinction of the contractual obligation primarily follow the general rules, to which all obligations regardless of their source are submitted. Thus, many of the statutory provisions relevant to contract law, are not solely specific to contracts but also apply to obligations arising from torts or unjust enrichment.

29 Yet, there are certain provisions in the first part of the Code of Obligations that specifically only apply to contracts. For example, the rules on conditional obligations (Articles 151–157 CO) or on penalties (Articles 160–163 CO) apply by their nature only to contractual relationships.

13. *See* herein below para. 500.

30 The second part of the Code of Obligations (the individual types of contracts) contains special rules that solely apply to contracts. It sets forth the provisions that govern certain types of contracts. They sometimes deviate from the provisions of the first part regarding the formation and performance of a contract. To this extent, the obligation arising from a contract is treated differently from obligations arising from torts or unjust enrichment.

31 Summing up, a contract forms a basis for an obligation to arise. While the general provisions of the Code of Obligations contain general rules that apply to all obligations regardless of their ground for arising, there are many special rules that apply solely to obligations arising from a contract.

II INTERPRETATION OF STATUTORY LAW AND RELEVANCE OF CASE LAW

32 Swiss contract law is densely codified in the Code of Obligations. However, this dense codification does not prevent Swiss contract law from remaining dynamic and flexible.

33 First of all, courts have the power to concretise the meaning of the statutory provisions by interpreting them. Failing a specific rule in the Code of Obligations, a court may even develop a new rule of contract law. This enables courts to adapt Swiss contract law to new developments.

34 Second, parties may deviate from most provisions of the Code of Obligations, as they are generally of a non-mandatory nature. This leaves the parties a significant amount of autonomy when shaping their contractual relationship under Swiss law.

A Interpretation of Statutory Law

35 The Civil Code expressly stipulates the legitimacy of subjecting statutory provisions to interpretation:

> The law applies according to its wording or interpretation to all legal questions for which it contains a provision.[14]

36 The interpretation of statutory law follows the principle of pluralism of methods. Several methods of interpretation must be balanced when interpreting a statutory provision. The Swiss Federal Supreme Court refuses to install a hierarchy among the different methods:

> The law must first and foremost be interpreted out of itself, i.e., according to its wording, meaning and purpose as well as its underlying evaluations on the basis of a teleological method of understanding. The interpretation of the law must be

14. Article 1 CC.

guided by the idea that the provision is not merely the wording, but the statute as understood and specified by its application to sets of facts. What is required is the objectively correct decision in the normative structure, oriented towards a satisfactory result of the *ratio legis*. In doing so, the Swiss Federal Supreme Court follows a pragmatic pluralism of methods and refuses to subject the individual elements of interpretation to a hierarchical order of priority.[15]

37 In line with the practice of the Swiss Federal Supreme Court, courts primarily resort to the grammatical, historical, systematic and teleological methods of interpretation.[16]

38 The grammatical method of interpretation focuses on the wording of a provision. It is the starting point of any interpretation. If the wording is clear, departing from it requires good reasons.[17] When analysing the wording, the text of the provision in all three official languages must be considered. Further, also the titles, side notes and punctuation must be considered.

39 The systematic element of interpretation requires that a single legal norm is not understood in isolation but out of context. Thematically related norms as well as entire legal concepts form a systematic whole, laws are to be understood as a unit, and furthermore, the embedding of the norms in the entire legal system is to be taken into account

40 The historical element requires that the historical context of a provision is taken into consideration. The actual circumstances as well as the views and convictions at the time when the standard was created must be included in the interpretation. The materials, i.e., the documents produced in the drafting of a law, form the foundation of such analysis.

41 The teleological interpretation aims at dissecting the purpose of a provision. The legislator's intention when drafting the norm (*ratio legis*) shall be uncovered. The teleological interpretation is to some extent dependent on the grammatical, systematic and historical method, as the purpose of a rule becomes apparent from its wording, its systematic context and the legislative work from which it emerged.

42 The true meaning of any legal provision must be drawn from a combination of these four methods of interpretation. The methods are, however, not exhaustive. Also, other elements may be taken into account, such as comparative law aspects.

B The Role of Case Law in Swiss Contract Law

43 Courts are tasked to give specific meaning to the provisions of the Code of Obligations; they must interpret the provisions and thereby apply the law. When doing

15. Decision of the Swiss Federal Supreme Court dated 27 April 2015, DSC 141 III 195, para. 2.4.
16. For detailed explanations on methods of interpretation in Swiss law, *see*, *e.g.*, Hausheer/Jaun, Die Einleitungsartikel des Schweizerischen Zivilgesetzbuches, Bern 2003.
17. Decision of the Swiss Federal Supreme Court dated 21 March 2016, no. 9C_631/2015, para. 4.4.

so, a court 'shall follow established doctrine and case law'.[18] Thus, case law is of direct relevance for the interpretation of legal provisions and their application. Even though a line of judicial decisions establishing a particular legal practice does carry substantial weight, contrary to other legal systems, there is no strict rule on the binding nature of precedents (*stare decisis*).[19]

44 Further, the courts have the power to develop new rules of contract law complementing the Code of Obligations. Indeed, the Code of Obligations does not address all issues of contract law. Certain rules of Swiss contract law have been developed by the courts and do not find any explicit basis in the Code of Obligations. One prominent example of this is the liability for conducting negotiations in bad faith (*culpa in contrahendo*).[20]

45 When a court is called upon to decide on an issue not provided for in the Code of Obligations, it must find its decision 'in accordance with customary law and, in the absence of customary law, in accordance with the rule that it would make as legislator'.[21] A court shall distinguish structural elements of the case from atypical ones. Based on the former it shall develop an abstract rule (as a legislator would do) and then apply this rule to the case at stake.

46 Thus, case law is not only relevant for the interpretation of the Code of Obligations but also for its supplementation. It allows Swiss contract law to continue evolving and adapting to modern times.

C Non-mandatory Nature of Swiss Contract Law

47 Swiss contract law is densely codified. Yet, most of the provisions in the Code of Obligations are not mandatory. Thus, parties to a contract are free to deviate from these provisions. In this sense, the system provided by the Code of Obligations is a fall-back for issues not covered by a specific contract.

48 However, there are a few provisions that are considered mandatory in the sense that parties may not deviate from them. Any contractual clause contradicting such provision is considered void.[22] Mandatory provisions are often found in relation to contracts where the parties in question do typically not have the same bargaining

18. Article 1(3) CC.
19. Decision of the Swiss Federal Supreme Court dated 19 February 2007, DSC 133 III 335, para. 2.3: 'The change in case law requested by the claimant is not excluded from the outset. Courts are not precluded from changing a previously applied case law if they come to the realisation that a different application of the law better reflects the meaning of the law or changed circumstances. However, a change in case law must be based on serious objective reasons, which must be all the more weighty the longer the previous practice, which is no longer recognised as correct, has been followed.'
20. *See* below paras 193 et seqq.
21. Article 1(2) CC.
22. *See* Articles 19 and 20 CO.

power or where one of the parties is in particular need of protection (e.g., employment contracts). In commercial contracts, mandatory provisions are rare.

49 Whether a specific provision is mandatory must usually be determined by the aforementioned methods of interpretation. In this regard, it is imperative to consult the case law on a specific provision. At times, the Code of Obligations explicitly stipulates the mandatory nature of certain provisions.[23]

III TERMINOLOGY OF THE CODE OF OBLIGATIONS

50 For ease of understanding, a couple of terms used in the context of the Code of Obligations will be explained hereinafter. For clarity's sake, the term's German, French and Italian denomination is added in parentheses.[24] The list is in alphabetical order.

51 *Bilateral contract* (*zweiseitiger Vertrag, contrat bilateral, contratto bilaterale*): A contract in which both parties undertake an obligation to each other.

52 *Claim* (*Forderung, créance, credito*): The creditor's right under the law of obligations to demand performance from the debtor.

53 *Continuing contract* (*Dauervertrag, contrat de durée, contratto di durata*): The typical performance obligation is a continuing obligation meaning that it is not completed with one single act, but consists of repeated acts over a period of time (for example, a lease contract).

54 *Courtesy* (*Gefälligkeit, complaisance, cortesia*): A person gives a promise to perform a certain act without the will to be bound by this promise. In contrast to a contract, the promisor does not carry any enforceable duty to comply with its promise. Whether a certain promise constitutes a courtesy must be assessed by interpreting the circumstances of each individual case.[25]

55 *Debt* (*Schuld, dette, debito*): The obligation assumed by a debtor towards his creditor.

56 Defence (*Einrede, exception, eccezione*): A specific right of the debtor to refuse to fulfil his obligation, such as the defence on non-performance (Article 82 CO). Such right needs to be invoked by the debtor for otherwise, a court will not consider it.

57 *Duty* (*Pflicht, devoir, obbligo*): The rules of conduct imposed on a legal entity by law or contract.

23. *See, e.g.*, Articles 273c and 361 CO.
24. For a more detailed list of terms, *see* Müller, Swiss Contract Law in International Commercial Arbitration, 2023, pp. 685–714.
25. For some criteria that apply to such interpretation, *see* Decision of the Swiss Federal Supreme Court dated 20 October 2011, DSC 137 III 539.

58 *Expression of intent* (*Willenserklärung, manifestation de volonté, manifestazione della volontà*): Expression of a party's intention to establish, amend or terminate a right or legal relationship.

59 *Formative right* (*Gestaltungsrecht, droit formateur, diritto formatore*): The power to change the legal position of the parties by means of a unilateral, irrevocable expression of intent (for example, notice of contract termination).

60 *Legal transaction* (*Rechtsgeschäft, acte juridique, atto giuridico*): Any legal act based on an expression of intent which brings about a legal consequence.

61 *Liability* (*Haftung, responsabilité, responsabilità*): Duty of the debtor to answer for the failure to perform an obligation with his/her assets.

62 *Incumbency* (*Obliegenheit, incombance, incombenza*): An incumbency is a rule of conduct. Contrary to a duty, the other party cannot request performance from the party bearing the incumbency. Equally, failure to adhere to an incumbency does not give rise to a claim for damages. But the failing party may lose a right due to its non-performance of the incumbency.

63 *Objection* (*Einwendung, objection, obiezione*): Putting forth facts which inhibit the arising of a claim or extinguish an existing one. In contrast to the defence, a debtor must not explicitly invoke an objection.

64 *Obligation* (*Obligation, obligation, obbligazione*): The legal relationship between the creditor and the debtor. For example, a debtor is obliged to make a payment and the creditor is entitled to request such payment.

65 *Right* (*Recht, droit, diritto*): An entitlement bestowed upon a legal entity by the law or a contract.

66 *Synallagmatic contract* (*synallagmatischer/vollkommen zweiseitiger Vertrag, contrat bilatéral parfait/synallagmatique, contratto bilaterale perfetto/sinallagmatico*): A contract in which both parties undertake obligations that are in an exchange relationship (synallagma). For example, in a sales contract, the obligation to transfer ownership stands in an exchange relationship to payment of the purchase price.

67 *Unlawfulness* (*Widerrechtlichkeit, illicéité, illiceità*): The notion of unlawfulness is of particular relevance in connection with torts (Articles 41 et seqq. CO). In this context, an act is considered unlawful if it infringes upon an absolute legal right (e.g., property right or right to not be bodily harmed) or violates a legal provision whose purpose is to protect against the kind of damage that has occurred.

68 *Unilateral contract* (*einseitiger Vertrag, contrat unilatéral, contratto unilaterale*): A contract with two (or more) parties, but only one of them owes performance of an obligation to the other (for example, a gift contract).

CHAPTER 2

Concluding a Contract

I EXPRESSIONS OF INTENT: THE DRIVING FORCE OF CONTRACTUAL RELATIONSHIPS

69 Contracts are party-driven endeavours. All depends on their intent as expressed to the outer world. Expressions of intent build the driving force of contractual relationships. Only where the parties' expressions of intent overlap (meeting of the minds) a contract may arise. But, also during the lifetime of a contract, parties' expressions of intent become relevant (e.g., modification of contractual terms, termination of a contract). In light of their importance, some general rules relating to expressions of intent are explained.

70 Without explicit statutory provision to the contrary, an expression of intent is not bound to a specific form. An expression of intent may be given explicitly or impliedly.

71 Certain expressions of intent only become effective if and when received by the other party. If such expression is made in writing it is considered received by the other party once it has arrived in that party's sphere of control. It is, however, not necessary that the recipient has actual knowledge of the expression of intent.

72 Often, the precise content of an expression of intent is not fully clear. In such cases, the meaning of the expression of intent must be determined by means of interpretation.

73 If the receiving party understands an expression of intent as meant by the originator, no further interpretation is required. It is the actual intent of the originator as understood by the receiver that determines the content of the expression of intent. Even if the term used has a different objective meaning, the parties' common actual intent and understanding still prevail (*falsa demonstratio non nocet*).

74 If, however, there is no such common understanding between the parties the expression of intent's objective meaning must be uncovered by ways of interpretation.

Such interpretation must be carried out in accordance with the principle of trust (*Vertrauensprinip, principe de la confiance, principio dell' affidamento)*. Pursuant to this principle, an expression of intent must be interpreted as the receiver could and ought to have understood it in good faith.[26] Consequently, it is not the meaning that an uninvolved third party will ascribe to the expression of intent, but rather the perspective of the particular receiving party that matters. Accordingly, there is a subjective touch to the interpretation, as the specific characteristics of the receiver, such as expert knowledge of the industry, will be taken into account when interpreting the expression of intent.

II MEETING OF THE MINDS: CONSENT AS THE BASIS OF CONTRACTUAL OBLIGATIONS

75 Conclusion of a contract requires two coinciding expressions of intent: the offer and the acceptance. The two declarations must correspond to each other for there to be consent. The consent between the parties builds the cornerstone of any contract.

76 Further, there are certain requirements in relation to the parties making these expressions of intent. They must have the legal capacity to enter into a contract. Without such capacity, the declarations do not give rise to a contract.

A The Mutuality of the Expressions of Intent

77 Pursuant to Article 1(1) CO, the conclusion of a contract requires mutual expressions of intent by the parties. Whether and on which terms consent has been reached between the parties, must be determined by interpreting their mutual expressions of intent: the offer and the acceptance.[27]

1 The Offer

78 With the offer, the offeror submits to the offeree its intention to conclude a contract. For this expression of intent to have any legal effect, it must be received by the offeree.

26. Decision of the Swiss Federal Supreme Court dated 14 October 2002, DSC 129 III 118, para. 2.5: 'If the actual intent of the parties cannot be established or does not coincide, the judge must interpret the statements made and the conduct according to the principle of trust. He must therefore consider how a statement or conduct could be understood in good faith in the light of all the circumstances. ... . It should be recalled that the principle of trust makes it possible to impute to a party the objective meaning of his statement or conduct, even if it does not correspond to his actual intent.'
27. For the rules on interpretation of the parties' expressions of intent, *see* below paras 207 et seqq.

79 The offer must be sufficiently clear and precise to ensure that the offeree can conclude the contract by simply accepting it; a mere 'yes' must suffice. It must contain at least the objectively essential terms (*essentialia negotii*) of the contract.[28]

80 The offer does not have to be made explicitly. Article 1(2) CO states that the expression of intent may be implied. For an expression of intent to form an offer, the offeror must have the intent to be bound by its declaration. At times, it can be difficult to assess whether an expression of intent does, indeed, carry the required will to be bound. Whether an explicit or implied expression of intent qualifies as an offer, must be determined in accordance with the rules of contract interpretation.

81 The Code of Obligations does, however, regulate certain specific implied expressions of intent. Pursuant to Article 6a CO, the delivery of unsolicited goods does not constitute an offer. Equally, the sending of tariffs, price lists and the like does not constitute an offer.[29] By contrast, a display of merchandise with an indication of its price is generally considered to be an offer.[30]

82 Once an offer is made, the offeror remains bound by it for a certain duration. During that time the offer may not be withdrawn. The duration is dependent on the specific circumstances in which the offer is made.

83 If the offeror sets a deadline for acceptance of its offer, acceptance must have reached the offeror by the end of such deadline.[31] Importantly, such a deadline may also be implied from the circumstances.[32]

84 If the offeror does not set a deadline, a distinction must be made between an offer that is made with both parties present and an offer where the offeree is absent:

85 If the offer is made in the offeree's presence, the offeror is no longer bound by the offer if the offeree does not immediately accept the offer.[33] In practice, the offeror is considered bound by its offer as long as the parties are in the same room. Pursuant to Article 4(2) CO, contracts concluded by phone (or other means of immediate communication) are deemed to have been concluded in the parties' presence. Accordingly, the offeror is considered bound as long as the telephone call lasts.

86 If an offer is made in the offeree's absence (e.g., via letter or e-mail), it remains binding on the offeror until such time as he might expect a reply sent duly and promptly to reach him.[34] The time period includes the transport (back and forth) of the offer and acceptance as well as reasonable time for consideration. The adequate time for consideration depends among others on the complexity and economic importance of

28. *See* below para. 95.
29. Article 7(2) CO.
30. Article 7(3) CO.
31. Article 3 CO.
32. *See, e.g.*, Decision of the Swiss Federal Supreme Court dated 28 January 1924, DSC 50 II 13 (perishable goods).
33. Article 4(1) CO.
34. Article 5(1) CO.

the contract.[35] If the offeror deems an acceptance to have reached him late, he must immediately inform the offeree of this. Otherwise, the contract is deemed concluded.[36]

87 Finally, the binding nature of the offer ends before elapsing of the aforementioned time periods when the offeree rejects the offer. In such a case, the offeror is no longer bound by its offer.

88 The offeror may avoid the binding nature of the offer by reserving the revocation of its offer.[37] Such reservation may be made explicitly or arise from the circumstances or the particular nature of the transaction. By making such a reservation the offeror expresses that it is still lacking the final will to conclude a contract.

89 Furthermore, an offer is deemed not to have been made and thus without binding effect if its withdrawal reaches the offeree before or simultaneously with the offer itself. Equally, no binding effect arises where the withdrawal is communicated to the offeree before the offeree becomes aware of the offer.[38]

2 The Acceptance

90 With the acceptance the offeree informs the offeror that it agrees with the proposed terms for the conclusion of the contract. Same as the offer, the acceptance is an expression of intent in need of receipt.

91 The acceptance must cover all essential terms, subjectively and objectively.[39] It is not bound by a specific form. It may be expressed explicitly or impliedly.

92 The acceptance must consist of an unconditional 'yes'. Only then a contract is concluded. Anything else constitutes a rejection of the offer. Depending on the circumstances, it might be considered a counter-offer ('yes, but').

93 Generally, silence does not amount to acceptance.[40] Yet, pursuant to Article 6 CO, where the particular nature of the transaction or the circumstances are such that express acceptance cannot reasonably be expected, the contract is deemed to have been concluded if the offer is not rejected within a reasonable time. In such circumstances, silence may amount to acceptance. A typical example of such circumstances is a transaction which only benefits the silent party (e.g., a gift contract).[41]

35. Decision of the Swiss Federal Supreme Court dated 5 November 2008, DSC 134 II 297, para. 4.3.1.
36. Article 5(3) CO.
37. Article 7(1) CO.
38. Article 6(1) CO.
39. *See* below paras 94 et seqq.
40. For an exception, *see* Article 395 CO.
41. *See* decision of the Swiss Federal Supreme Court dated 15 May 1984, DSC 110 II 156. para. 2.d.

94 A withdrawal of acceptance underlies the same rules as the withdrawal of an offer.[42] Accordingly, withdrawal of an acceptance must reach the offeror before or at the same time as the acceptance itself.

95 Generally, a contract takes effect once acceptance is given. There are, however, two scenarios in which the entry into effect of the contract is backdated. First, where a contract is concluded in the parties' absence, it takes effect from the time acceptance is sent, not when it is received.[43] Second, where express acceptance is not required, the contract is deemed to take effect from the time the offer has been received.[44]

B The Required Scope of the Parties' Mutual Expressions of Intent

96 The mutual expressions of intent must cover all essential terms of the contract to be concluded. In this regard, a distinction is made between objectively and subjectively essential terms.

97 Objectively essential terms are the fundamental elements of a contract (*essentialia negotii*) without which there could be no contract. They are the indispensable core of the contract. For example, a sales contract requires consent on the price, the object of the sale and the transfer of property.

98 Subjectively essential terms are the provisions that are of such importance to the parties that they wish not to be bound unless an agreement has been reached on them. There is no objective limit on what may form a subjectively essential term. The parties can make the conclusion of the contract dependent on the agreement on any subjectively essential points (e.g., payment deadlines).

99 If a certain provision constitutes a subjectively essential term to only one of the parties, lack of agreement only prevents conclusion of the contract if the other party is or ought to be aware of the subjective essentiality. Otherwise, the contract is concluded despite lacking agreement on this term. The contract might in such case, however, be susceptible to supplementation by the judge[45] or to a challenge for mistake.[46]

100 In addition to essential terms, there are also ancillary terms. Lacking agreement on ancillary terms does not hinder conclusion of a contract. The contract remains silent on the issues covered by non-agreed ancillary terms. If a dispute should arise on such an issue, the court determines the content of the applicable contractual rule 'with due regard to the nature of the transaction'.[47]

42. Article 9(2) CO.
43. Article 10(1) CO.
44. Article 10(2) CO.
45. *See* below paras 241 et seqq.
46. *See* below paras 160 et seqq.
47. Article 2(2) CO. Regarding supplementing a contract, *see* below paras 241 et seqq.

101 With regard to the question of whether a particular provision is a subjectively essential or ancillary term, the Code of Obligations places the burden of proof on the party claiming that a particular term is essential. This is based on Article 2(1) CO.[48]

C Legal Capacity to Enter into a Contract

102 Even where there is a mutual expression of intent among the parties, no contract arises if one party lacks legal capacity to enter into a contract. A party's legal capacity is governed by the Civil Code.

103 A natural person is considered to have legal capacity to enter into a contract if he/she is of full age (age of 18 years[49]) and sound judgment.[50,51] Being of sound judgment entails several elements: the ability to recognise and assess one's surroundings as well as to build one's own will and direct one's actions after it.[52]

104 If a natural person lacks sound judgment, he/she is unable to enter into contractual relationships.[53] However, a person not of full age but of sound mind may enter into a contract despite its generally lacking capacity if their legal representative consents or if the relevant legal act pertains to their strictly personal rights.[54]

105 A legal person (such as a limited liability company) is considered to have legal capacity to enter into a contract once the governing bodies required by law and their articles of association have been appointed.[55] A legal person expresses its will through its governing body.[56]

III THE FREEDOM OF ENTERING INTO A CONTRACT AND CHOOSING ONE'S CONTRACTING PARTNER

106 The principle of freedom of contract is paramount in Swiss contract law. It states that everyone is permitted to enter (or not enter) into a contract with whom he pleases and to freely determine the content of such contract:

> The private law system is based on private autonomy. In the law of obligations, private autonomy is concretized by freedom of contract. The freedom of contract has various aspects (freedom to conclude a contract, freedom to choose a partner, freedom of content, freedom of form and freedom to annul). The freedom to conclude contracts and choose a partner as partial aspects of contractual freedom may be restricted by contracting obligations in exceptional cases. Such contracting

48. For details, *see* Berger, Allgemeines Schuldrecht, Bern 2018, N 643 et seqq.
49. Article 14 CC.
50. Article 16 CC.
51. Article 13 CC.
52. *See, e.g.*, Huguenin, Obligationenrecht, Zurich 2019, N 145.
53. Article 18 CC.
54. Articles 19–19c CC.
55. Article 54 CC.
56. Article 55(1) CC.

> obligations are based either on a contract (usually a precontract) or a statutory basis.[57]

107 While the principle is paramount, it is not without restrictions.[58] There are certain circumstances under which a person is legally bound to conclude a contract (with a specific person).

A Contractual Duty to Contract: The Precontract

108 In a precontract (*pactum de contrahendo*), one or both parties undertake the obligation to later enter into a contract - the main contract.[59] This constitutes a voluntarily imposed limitation of the freedom of contract. By entering into a precontract, each party is accorded the right to later request conclusion of the main contract.

109 The precontract must be distinguished from the mere agreement to enter into negotiations that do not entail an obligation to conclude a contract.[60] Whether a 'letter of intent' or a 'memorandum of understanding' qualifies as a precontract must be determined in each individual case by interpreting the terms of the agreement:

> The letter of intent in question must first be examined. The letter of intent is commonly used in the preparatory phase of a contract in commercial and financial matters of a certain complexity or economic importance. It is an expression of intent by which one party informs another that he is interested in concluding a contract and wishes to open negotiations to this end. Typically, the parties are not obliged to enter into a contract and have no claims against each other in this respect. The letter of intent thus differs from the pre-contract, governed by article 22 CO, which is an agreement by which both parties, or only one of them, undertake to conclude a specific contract in the future.
>
> The content of such an expression of intent varies from case to case and the delimitation with other institutions, such as the precontract or even the conclusion of a contract, must be analysed according to the circumstances of each individual case.[61]

110 The precontract in itself constitutes an ordinary agreement that is subject to the provisions of the Code of Obligations. Accordingly, the rules on the required scope of the parties' consent for a contract to arise[62] also apply to a precontract.[63] Certain scholars deduce from this that a precontract must include already the objectively

57. Decision of the Swiss Federal Supreme Court dated 7 May 2002, DSC 129 III 35, para. 6.1.
58. Regarding restrictions on the content of a contract, *see* below paras 229.
59. Article 22 CO.
60. *See* below paras 193 regarding a potential liability under the doctrine of *culpa in contrahendo*.
61. Decision of the Swiss Federal Supreme Court dated 21 March 2006, no. 4C.409/2005, para. 2.3.1.
62. *See* above paras 9 et seqq.
63. Decision of the Swiss Federal Supreme Court dated 6 March 1992, DSC 118 II 32.

essential terms of the main contract.[64] The Swiss Federal Supreme Court seems to be less strict. While a precontract does not have to contain all objectively essential terms of the main contract, their presence gives the parties an advantage: they may sue directly for performance of the main contract (instead of first suing for conclusion of the main contract, before launching a second claim for performance).[65]

B Legal Duty to Contract

111 Under certain circumstances the law prescribes that one must conclude a contract with another party. A legal duty to contract may arise under public or private law. However, due to the fundamental nature of the freedom of contract, such duties may only be assumed restrictively.[66]

112 Public law duties to contract exist, for example, for the Swiss Post.[67] Further, the owner of a motor vehicle is required to conclude a liability insurance.[68] In addition, Article 7(2) of the Cartel Act provides that a company in a dominant market position may be acting unlawfully when refusing to deal with another market participant (e.g., refusal to supply goods). A court may order a dominant company to conclude a contract with a third party on terms that are in line with the market or the industry standard.[69]

113 Also private law foresees certain statutory provisions dictating a party to conclude a specific contract. For example, under Article 694 CC, a landowner who does not have adequate access from his or her land to a public thoroughfare has the right to require his or her neighbours to grant him or her the necessary right of way in exchange for full compensation.

114 Further, a more general duty to contract may be deduced from the principle of protection of personality (Article 28 CC) or good morals (Article 20 CO). Based on Article 28 CC a duty to contract may arise if a seller publicly offers certain goods for sale but denies sale to certain persons based on characteristics such as race, religion or

64. *See* Schwenzer/Fountoulakis, Schweizerisches Obligationenrecht – Allgemeiner Teil, Bern 2020, N 28.05 et seqq. *Contra*: Herzog, Der Vorvertrag im schweizerischen und deutschen Schuldrecht, Zurich 1999, N 240 et seqq.
65. Decision of the Swiss Federal Supreme Court dated 6 March 1992, DSC 118 II 32, para. 3.c. Also *see* decision of the Swiss Federal Supreme Court dated 28 March 2003, DSC 129 III 264.
66. Decision of the Swiss Federal Supreme Court dated 7 May 2002, DSC 129 III 35, para. 6.3: 'It is now generally accepted that a contracting obligation is not limited to cases where there is an explicit legal basis. Rather, a duty to contract may also arise from general principles of private law such as the prohibition of immoral conduct. In order to concretise this principle, however, it must first be noted that freedom of contract – and thus also the freedom to conclude contracts – as an element of private autonomy has an extraordinarily high status in the private law system. Since restrictions on the freedom to conclude contracts already result in large numbers from explicit – usually public law – legal provisions, contractual obligations outside of explicit statutory basis are of an exceptional nature and can only be accepted with great restraint.'
67. Articles 2 et seqq. Postal Act.
68. Article 63 Road Traffic Act.
69. Article 13(b) Cartels Act.

gender.[70] Good morals mandate conclusion of a contract if four conditions are fulfilled: (i) the goods or services must be offered publicly; (ii) the goods or services must form part of normal consumption;[71] (iii) the offeror must have such a strong position in the market that the other party lacks any viable alternative provider; and (iv) there are no objective reasons for declining conclusion of a contract.[72]

IV SIMULATING A CONTRACT

115 Simulation describes the case when parties deliberately choose a false denomination of the contract and its terms to hide their true intention. For example, they include a purchase price in their contract that is lower than the actually agreed and paid price in order to decrease any tax liability arising out of the transaction.

116 In terminological terms, the following applies: Depending on whether the simulation refers to the whole transaction or only to a part of it, it is called full or partial simulation. The fictitious contract is called simulated whereas the actually intended contract is referred to as dissimulated.

117 According to Article 18(1) CO, the simulated transaction is ineffective because it does not reflect the parties' true intentions. The simulated contract is generally also ineffective against third parties. However, an exception is made for a third party that acquires a claim based on a written acknowledgement of debt.[73]

118 If a dissimulated contract – often an oral one – exists 'behind' the simulated one, this transaction enters into effect. However, the dissimulated contract will be invalid if any applicable form requirements have not been observed.

V CONCLUDING A CONTRACT VIA A THIRD PARTY: AGENCY

119 The general rule is that one may only enter into obligations for oneself. Agency, as regulated in Articles 32 et seqq. CO, allows for an exception to that rule. The agent may act on behalf of another (the principal) to create legal relations with a third party. The agent may give expressions of intent (active agency) as well as receive expressions of intent (passive agency) on behalf of the principal.

120 Article 32 CO makes a distinction between direct and indirect agency. The former constitutes the typical form of agency where the agent indicates that it is acting on behalf of another person. In contrast, an indirect agent does not make such an indication to the third party.

70. Huguenin, Obligationenrecht, Zurich 2019, N 163.
71. Goods or services that are available to everybody and are used in everyday life.
72. Decision of the Swiss Federal Supreme Court dated 7 May 2002, DSC 129 III 35, paras 6.3–6.5.
73. Article 18(2) CO.

A Direct Agency

121 Direct agency requires that the agent acts on behalf of the agent and has the authorisation to do so. If these conditions are met, the contract concluded by the agent's expression of intent enters into effect between the third party and the principal.

1 Authorisation (Power of Attorney)

122 The agent must be authorised to act on behalf of the principal and to engage the principal in legal obligations. Such authorisation may be based on an expression of intent by the principal or a statutory provision.[74]

123 By a power of attorney (*Vollmacht, procuration, procura*) the principal declares to the agent that the latter is authorised to represent him vis-à-vis third parties. The power of attorney constitutes a unilateral legal transaction which requires receipt by the agent but is separate from the underlying legal relationship between the principal and the agent (e.g., mandate agreement).

124 Generally, the power of attorney is not subject to any form requirement.[75] It may also be given impliedly. This even holds true if the power of attorney is used for the conclusion of a contract to which a form requirement applies.[76] Depending on the underlying legal relationship an implied power of attorney may even be presumed.[77]

125 There are two specific cases where an authorisation may even be based on the principal's inaction. If the principal is aware that someone else is acting on its behalf without authorisation and yet the principal does not raise any objections to this involuntary agency, then a situation of agency by estoppel (*Duldungsvollmacht, procuration par tolerance, procura apparente*) arises. If the principal is not aware of the representative's conduct but could have been aware of it and prevented it if he had paid due attention, there is an agency by apparent authority (*Anscheinsvollmacht, procuration apparente, procura apparente*). In both cases, a third party may only rely on such an agency if it could in good faith assume the agent's implied authority.[78]

74. *See, e.g.*, Article 304(1) CC authorising parents to act on behalf of their children.
75. However, there are certain statutory exceptions to this. *See, e.g.*, Article 348b(1) CO or Article 493(6) CO.
76. Decision of the Swiss Federal Supreme Court dated 24 September 1986, DSC 112 II 330, para. 1.a. However, some scholars disagree with this position, *see, e.g.*, Huguenin, Obligationenrecht, Zurich 2019, N 1068 et seqq., with further references.
77. *See, e.g.*, Article 396(2) CO for mandate agreements.
78. Decision of the Swiss Federal Supreme Court dated 2 November 2020, no. 4A_360/2020, para. 5.2: 'The only decisive factor is whether the actual conduct of the represented party in good faith indicates an intention to communicate. This behavior can consist of a positive action, but also of a passive behavior, a conscious or normatively attributable omission or acquiescence. If the represented party is aware of the representative's conduct, but does not intervene against it, he is deemed to have agency by estoppel. If he is not aware of the representative's conduct, but could have been aware of it and prevented it if he had paid due attention, there is an agency by

126 The scope of the authorisation must be determined in accordance with the content of the power of attorney or the extent of the principal's inaction.[79] The power of attorney must be interpreted with the usual rules that apply to expressions of intent.[80] In line with these rules, any action by the agent that obviously contradicts the interests of the principal must be deemed outside of the power of attorney. When determining the exact scope of the authorisation the underlying legal relationship between the agent and the principal will also have to be taken into consideration. Often, the principal gives clear instructions to the agent on how the power of attorney is to be used. Such instructions limit the power of attorney's scope.

127 Certain powers of attorney are specifically regulated in the Code of Obligations.[81] In these instances, the scope of the power of attorney is set forth by law. Although these statutory provisions are not of a mandatory nature, meaning that the principal is free to deviate from the prescribed scope of the power of attorney, a party acting in good faith may rely on the scope of the power of attorney as defined by law.[82]

128 However, if the principal has informed the third party about the power of attorney, the scope of the power of attorney is determined in accordance with that communication.[83] Such communication may also result from the commercial registry.[84]

129 The principal may at any point in time withdraw the power of attorney and put an end to the authorisation of the agent.[85] If the principal has informed the third party about the power of attorney, the latter must also be informed of the withdrawal.[86] Otherwise, the third party when acting in good faith may rely on the power of attorney despite the principal's revocation.

130 The power of attorney also ends if the agent waives his powers of representation. Furthermore, Articles 35(1) and 35(2) CO assume the expiry of the power of attorney in certain situations (e.g., death of the agent).

131 Despite the expiry of the power of attorney, the actions of the agent may still bind the principal in some instances. This holds true for the agent that has in good faith not become aware of the expiry of his power of attorney. As long as the third party has not

---

apparent authority. Finally, representation without power of attorney only has an effect if the third party is acting in good faith.'

79. Article 33(2) CO.
80. *See* above paras 3 et seqq.
81. For example, Article 459 CO (registered power of attorney) or Article 462 CO (commercial agency).
82. *See, e.g.*, Article 460(3) CO.
83. Article 33(3) CO.
84. However, only the registered power of attorney (Article 459 CO) is capable of being registered in the commercial registry. In addition, the commercial registry contains information on the scope of the director's authorisation to act for their company (e.g., single signature or joint signature at two). Also *see* Article 933 CO, pursuant to which third parties are deemed to be aware of the commercial registry's content.
85. Article 34(1) CO.
86. Article 34(3) CO.

become aware that the agent's authority has ceased, the agent's actions still bind the principal.[87]

2 Acting in the Name of Another Person

132 The agent must indicate to the third party that he acts on behalf of the principal for the latter to become a party of the contract with the third party. The required declaration by the agent may be made explicitly or impliedly. Pursuant to Article 32(2) CO, it is sufficient that based on the circumstances the third party ought to be aware of the agency.

133 An exception is made for cases where the third party does not care with whom he concludes the contract. In such cases, the principal may become party to the contract even if the agent has failed to declare that he is acting on behalf of the principal.[88] Contracts typically covered by this exception are the dealings of everyday life (e.g., grocery shopping). But, the Swiss Federal Supreme Court significantly widened the scope of application of the exception. It is sufficient that the third party would have been willing to also conclude the contract with the principal.[89]

B Indirect Agency

134 Indirect agency occurs where an agent enters into a contract on behalf of the principal (for the accounts of the principal) but fails to disclose (explicitly or impliedly) this to the third party.[90] In accordance with Article 32(3) CO, it is generally the agent that is bound by such contract and not the principal. Thus, the agent himself becomes party to the contract with the third party. For the principal to become a contracting party, the contract must be transferred to the principal meaning that claims must be assigned and debts assumed in accordance with the principles governing such measures.[91]

C Agent Acting Without Proper Authorisation

135 An agent acts without authorisation when lacking any authorisation or when concluding a contract outside the scope of the authorisation granted (e.g., power of attorney).

87. Article 37 CO.
88. Article 32(2) CO.
89. Decision of the Swiss Federal Supreme Court dated 25 October 1991, DSC 117 II 387, para. 2.c: 'The personality of the contracting party is indifferent to the third party if the latter, instead of concluding the contract with the person who presented himself to him without mentioning the existence of an agency relationship, would also have concluded the contract with another person.'
90. Also, the exception detailed in para. 132 must not apply.
91. *See* below paras 484 et seqq.

136 A special case of an agent acting without authorisation is so-called self-dealing (*Insichgeschäfte, auto-contrat, contratto con se stesso*). An agent engages in self-dealing if the agent concludes a contract with himself, either by acting as agent to both parties (double representation, *Doppelvertretung, double representation, doppia rappresentanza*) or by being one of the contracting parties (self-contracting, *Selbstkontrahieren, contrat avec soi-même, contrato con se stesso*).

137 Self-dealings are generally prohibited as they inevitably lead to a conflict of interest.[92] Thus when engaging in self-dealing, an agent is deemed to act outside of his authorisation. Yet, there are two scenarios in which self-dealings are permitted. First, the agent may have been given special authorisation for the specific contract. Such authorisation may also be granted retroactively by ratifying the contract in question.[93] Second, if it can be excluded that the self-dealing yields any disadvantage to the principal, a self-dealing is permissible even without special authorisation.[94] For example, no disadvantage will occur where the price is determined in accordance with a market price.

138 Pursuant to Article 38(2) CO, the principal is generally[95] not bound by a contract that the agent has concluded without proper authorisation. However, the third party with whom the agent has concluded the contract remains at first bound by the contract. The principal is given the opportunity to ratify the contract for which the agent lacked the necessary authority. Such ratification may also be given impliedly, e.g., by performing said contract.[96] The ratification has retroactive effect and the contract is deemed concluded as if the agent had had the required authorisation. The third party may set the principal a reasonable deadline within which the principal must declare ratification.[97]

139 If the principal rejects the contract or fails to make any declaration within the deadline set by the third party, the contract becomes void. Any payments made or goods transferred may be reclaimed in accordance with the principles of unjust enrichment[98] or property law.[99]

---

92. *See* decision of the Swiss Federal Supreme Court dated 16 December 1986, DSC 112 II 503, para. 3.b. Also *see* Huguenin, Obligationenrecht, Zurich 2019, N 1079, with further references.
93. Decision of the Swiss Federal Supreme Court dated 19 November 2002, no. 4C.212/2002, para. 3.2.
94. Decision of the Swiss Federal Supreme Court dated 2 May 2001, DSC 127 III 33, para. 2.a: 'According to the established case law of the Swiss Federal Supreme Court, self-dealing is inadmissible in principle because an agent contracting with himself regularly leads to conflicts of interest. Self-dealing therefore results in the invalidity of the legal transaction in question, unless the risk of disadvantaging of the principal is excluded by the nature of the transaction or the principal has specifically authorised the agent to conclude the contract with himself or has subsequently ratified the transaction. The same rules apply to the double representation of two contracting parties by one and the same agent as well as the legal representation of legal persons by their organs. Also in these cases a special authorisation or subsequent ratification by a superior or ancillary body is required if there is a risk of discrimination.'
95. But *see* hereinabove paras 61 et seqq. for some exceptions to this general rule.
96. Decision of the Swiss Federal Supreme Court dated 3 July 1975, DSC 101 II 222, para. 6.b.bb.
97. Article 38(2) CO.
98. Articles 62 et seqq. CO.

140 The agent acting without authorisation is not bound by the contract. However, the agent may be liable to the third party. Pursuant to Article 39(1) CO, where the principal refuses ratification of the contract, the agent is liable to the third party for any damage arising out of the extinction of the contract unless the agent can prove that the other party knew that he lacked proper authority. If the agent was not but ought to have been aware of the lacking authority, the court may reduce the amount of the compensation.[100] If the agent is found to have been at fault, the court may order further damages on grounds of equity.[101]

141 The principal only becomes liable to the third party if it has failed to insist on the returning of the instrument setting out the agent's authority (e.g., written power of attorney) after having withdrawn such authority.[102] If the third party has entered into a contract with the agent based on such instrument and the principal refuses to ratify the contract in question, the principal is liable to the third party (acting in good faith) for any damage arising from that omission.[103]

142 In many cases, the agent by acting outside of his authority will become liable to the principal based on the contractual relationship between the agent and the principal.

VI FORM REQUIREMENTS FOR CONCLUSION OF A CONTRACT

143 Pursuant to Article 11(1) CO, contracts are generally not subject to any form requirements. This general principle is in line with Article 1(2) CO which already foresees that expressions of intent may be given implicitly.

144 Exceptions to this general rule may either follow from an explicit provision in the law or from the parties' agreement.

A Statutory Form Requirements

145 Swiss statutory law sets forth form requirements for certain transactions. The rationale behind such form requirements varies. Often, the form requirement shall protect the parties from overhasty acts and establish legal certainty between the parties.

146 There are three different kinds of form requirements in the Code of Obligations:[104] simple written form, qualified written form and public deed.

99. Articles 642 et seqq. CC.
100. Decision of the Swiss Federal Supreme Court dated 18 December 1990, DSC 116 II 689. The Swiss Federal Supreme Court departs from the wording of Article 39(1) CO in this respect.
101. Article 39(2) CO.
102. The basis for requesting the return of such instrument lies in Article 36(1) CO.
103. Article 36(2) CO.
104. Swiss procedural law knows a fourth form requirement: text form. For example, jurisdiction agreements are required to be in text form (Article 17 of the Swiss Civil Procedure Code, i.e., the agreement must be reproducible as text; e.g., an email).

147 Where the written form requirement applies, the contract must be signed by all persons on whom it imposes obligations.[105] Generally, the signature must be made by hand meaning that a mere photocopy or scan of the signature is insufficient.[106] Only a qualified electronic signature[107] is deemed equal to one made by hand.[108] Typical examples of transactions with written form requirements are assignments of claims,[109] gift contracts,[110] and non-compete clauses in labour contracts.[111]

148 The qualified written form does require an additional element to the parties' signature. For example, under certain conditions, a surety requires a handwritten indication of the amount for which the signing party is liable.[112]

149 Where the law requires a public deed, the transaction must be authenticated by a notary public. The cantons regulate the manner in which public deeds are to be drawn up on their territory.[113] Examples of transactions requiring public deeds are sale of immovable property,[114] contract of surety[115] and deed of incorporation.[116]

150 The scope of a form requirement is only rarely explicitly stated in the statute.[117] Without any such explicit provision, all terms that are either objectively or subjectively essential must comply with the form requirement.[118] However, for subjectively essential terms the form requirement only applies if by its nature it forms a usual element of the contract in question.[119] Thus, a term that does not directly concern the main obligations of the type of contract in question does not need to comply with the form requirement, even if it is subjectively essential to a party.[120]

---

105. Article 13 CO.
106. Article 14(1) CO. *See* decision of the Swiss Federal Supreme Court dated 4 September 1986, DSC 112 Ia 173, para. 1.
107. In the sense of the Federal Act on Certification Services in Relation to Electronic Signature of 19 December 2003.
108. Article 14(2bis) CO.
109. Article 165(1) CO.
110. Article 243(1) CO.
111. Article 340(1) CO.
112. Article 493(2) CO.
113. Article 55 CC (Final Title).
114. Article 216(1) CO.
115. Article 493(2) CO.
116. Article 629 CO.
117. For example, *see* Article 493 CO (surety).
118. Decision of the Swiss Federal Supreme Court dated 16 June 1987, DSC 113 II 402, para. 2.a.
119. Decision of the Swiss Federal Supreme Court dated 26 January 1993, DSC 119 II 135, para. 2.a: 'Objectively non-essential but subjectively essential points are subject to the requirement of public deed if, because of their nature, they constitute an element of the relevant contract.'
120. Decision of the Swiss Federal Supreme Court dated 16 June 1987, DSC 113 II 402, para. 2.a: 'Thus, objectively non-essential terms only fall under the form requirement due to being subjectively essential if they are by their nature covered by the framework of a sales contract. Two conditions must be fulfilled: On the one hand, the commitment entered into must have its legal basis in a claim which is not outside the natural content of the agreement in that the promised performance is the consideration for the price or for the transfer of ownership. On the other hand, the obligation must fall within the framework of a sales contract, influence the legal situation of the object of sale and directly affect the content of the transaction. From the outset, therefore, only those terms which affect the relationship between performance and consideration of the purchase contract may fall under the form requirement.'

151 Article 12 CO clarifies that where the law prescribes the written form or another form requirement,[121] such form requirement also applies to any amendments to the respective agreement unless the amendments only concern supplementary terms that do not contradict the terms of the original contract. For terms that are neither objectively nor subjectively essential, an amendment is not subject to the form requirement, even if it conflicts with the original contract.[122] In addition, precontracts[123] must comply with the form requirement that applies to the main contract envisaged by the precontract.[124]

152 If the form requirements are not complied with, the contract is deemed concluded, but invalid.[125] The invalidity renders a contract null and void which a court must consider even if none of the parties raised the issue. Accordingly, any performances already rendered may be reclaimed based on property law and the law of unjust enrichment. However, if the invocation of the invalidity is deemed abusive (in particular, if the contract has already been fully performed[126]), the nullity is disregarded and the contract is treated as valid.[127]

153 Finally, it is possible to convert a transaction, which fails to comply with the form requirement, into a transaction that is not covered by any form requirement. However, such conversion may only be assumed if it complies with the parties' hypothetical will

121. Decision of the Swiss Federal Supreme Court dated 17 December 1969, DSC 95 II 419, para. 2.b: 'Article 12 CO states that if the written form is required by law for a contract, this provision also applies to any amendment, with the exception of supplementary ancillary provisions which do not conflict with the document. According to established doctrine, this provision is to be applied *mutatis mutandis* to contracts which must be made by public deed.'
122. Decision of the Swiss Federal Supreme Court dated 7 January 1997, DSC 123 III 97, para. 2.
123. *See* above paras 107–109.
124. Article 22(2) CO.
125. Article 11(2) CO.
126. Decision of the Swiss Federal Supreme Court dated 1 November 1966, DSC 92 III 323, para. 3: 'However, as the Swiss Federal Supreme Court further ruled in the above-mentioned case law, invalidity due to lack of form is irrelevant in the relationship between the parties and inadmissible to invoke it if it is contrary to good faith and therefore constitutes a manifest abuse of rights within the meaning of article 2(2) CC. [...]. Among the circumstances to be taken into account, the voluntary performance of the purchase contract by the parties is of paramount importance. It does not necessarily exclude the consideration of the invalidity of the contract, the invocation of a defect of form appears to be an abuse of law unless an assessment of all the other circumstances, in particular the conduct of the parties during and after the conclusion of the contract, clearly leads to the opposite conclusion from the point of view of good faith.'
127. Decision of the Swiss Federal Supreme Court, DSC 98 II 313, para. 2: 'However, according to case law, invalidity due to lack of form is irrelevant in the relationship between the parties if taking it into account would be contrary to good faith; this question must also be examined ex officio. Among the circumstances which must not be overlooked in this context is in particular the voluntary performance of the contract by the parties. ... . The defendant then admitted the claims, at least in part, and included them in the collocation plan, and consequently also assumed that the contract was valid; it could not, on the one hand, declare the contract null and void and, on the other hand, derive advantages in favour of the bankruptcy estate from it. This approach by both parties to the proceedings rules out any subsequent invalidity appeal. The contract must therefore be treated as if it were valid.'

(i.e., if they had been aware of the form requirement). The replacement transaction must not go further than the original transaction and must serve a similar purpose.[128]

B Contractual Form Requirements

154 Parties to a contract are free to agree on certain form requirements even for a contract that is in principle not subject to any such requirements. The agreement of such requirement is itself not subject to any form requirement and can therefore also be impliedly agreed on. Often commercial contracts contain a specific clause foreseeing the written form requirement for any amendment to the contract, e.g., 'no amendment to this contract shall be valid, unless made in writing'.

155 The parties are free in determining the type of form requirement and are thereby not bound by the three statutory requirements set forth in the Code of Obligations. They may invent a new type of form requirement. Pursuant to Article 16(2) CO, where the parties stipulate a written form requirement without elaborating further, the provisions of the Code of Obligations governing the written form (i.e., Articles 13–15 CO) apply.

156 Further, the parties may also determine the consequences of non-adherence to the form requirement. Generally, three options are conceivable:

- non-compliance shall lead to invalidity of the transaction;
- non-compliance shall mean that the contract has not even been concluded;[129] or
- the agreed form shall merely serve an evidentiary function.

157 Pursuant to Article 16(1) CO, there is a presumption that the parties intended that non-compliance with the form requirement means that the contract has not been concluded. Thus, it is presumed that the parties do not wish to assume any obligations until such time as the form requirements are satisfied.

158 Conversely, a contractual form requirement may be annulled by an agreement that does not comply with said form requirement (e.g., oral agreement or implied agreement).[130] In particular, if the parties perform their amended obligations although

128. Decision of the Swiss Federal Supreme Court dated 12 February 1998, DSC 124 III 112, para. 2.b.bb: 'Such a conversion of an invalid, void legal transaction into a legal transaction in conformity with the law is basically possible. In place of the void legal transaction, the other one is considered to have come into existence if it can be assumed that it would have been intended if the voidness of the intended transaction had been known. According to the case law of the Federal Supreme Court, the content of the replacement transaction must be included in the transaction that fails to comply with the form requirement. It may not then go further than the transaction intended by the parties and may not impose more stringent obligations on either party. Finally, it must pursue a similar purpose and success as the invalid transaction.'
129. This means that the issue of abusive invocation of the invalidity disappears, *see* hereinabove para. 181.
130. Article 12 CO only applies to statutory form requirements.

the form requirement has not been observed, it is assumed that the parties have waived the contractual form requirement.[131] Parties wishing to avoid such a situation must specifically agree in their contract that the form requirement also applies to any amendments to that form requirement.[132]

VII RENDERING A CONCLUDED CONTRACT INEFFECTIVE: DEFECTS IN CONSENT

159 A party may be able to withdraw from a contract if its consent is defective. For consent to be defective, either the formation or the expression of the party's intent must have been tainted. The Code of Obligations determines in Articles 23–31 the conditions under which a contract may be rendered ineffective for defective consent. There are generally three scenarios: (i) mistake; (ii) deceit; or (iii) duress.

A Mistake

160 A mistake in the sense of Articles 23 et seqq. CO concerns a misconception of the facts. However, as results from Article 23 CO, not every misconception is sufficient to render a contract ineffective, only a fundamental mistake will do so. Whether there was a mistake is a question of fact; whether such mistake was fundamental is a question of law.

161 Article 24 CO defines which mistakes are considered fundamental and makes a distinction between mistakes concerning the expression of the party's intent (*Erklärungsirrtum, erreur de déclaration, errore nella dichiarazione*) and mistakes concerning the formation of the party's intent (*Grundlagenirrtum, erreur de base, errore essenziale*). Whether the mistake must be attributed to the mistaking party's fault is irrelevant to this question.[133] However, a mistake may only be invoked if such invocation is in compliance with good faith.

1 Mistake Concerning the Expression of the Party's Intent

162 A mistake concerns the expression of intent when a party expresses something that does not correspond to its intention (e.g., offering a price of CHF 1,000 instead of

131. Decision of the Swiss Federal Supreme Court dated 6 February 1979, DSC 105 II 75, para. 1: 'A waiver of the written form is to be assumed if the contractual services are provided and received without reservation despite non-compliance with the form; because such conduct invalidates the presumption of article 16(1) CO.'
132. *See* Gabriel, Formvorbehalt für Vertragsänderungen, SJZ 2010, pp. 533 et seqq.
133. However, *see* below para. 172 regarding the mistaking party's liability for an avoidable mistake.

CHF 10,000[134]). This becomes an issue where the other party does not understand the expression as it was meant by the originator and was in good faith not required to understand it that way. In such a scenario, an interpretation in line with the principle of trust leads to an attributable expression of intent that deviates from the party's actual intention. Thus, a party is bound by an expression of intent that does not correspond with its actual intention.

163 Pursuant to Article 24(1)(1)–(3) CO, there are generally three mistakes of expression that are considered fundamental:

- where the mistaking party intended to conclude a contract different from that to which he consented (e.g., sale instead of lease) (*error in negotio*);
- where the mistaking party has concluded a contract relating to a subject matter or a person other than the one he intended (*error in objecto vel in persona*); and
- where the mistaking party has promised to make a significantly greater performance or has accepted a promise of a significantly lesser consideration than he intended (e.g., price of CHF 1,000 instead of CHF 10,000) (*error in quantitate*).

164 Importantly, the scenarios outlined in Article 24(1) CO are not exhaustive. Further, it is possible for a court to come to the conclusion that a mistake as outlined in said provision might not be fundamental in a particular case.[135] A mistake is fundamental if the mistaking party would not have concluded the contract in question (or at least not with the same terms) if it had been aware of its mistake. In addition, the discrepancy between the objective meaning of a party's expression and its actual intention must reach a certain level of seriousness. Mistakes about minor details do not justify rendering a contract ineffective.[136]

165 A special case of a mistake is the calculation error. A calculation error exists if the parties have incorporated the individual calculation elements into the contract, but have made a mistake in the calculation of the end result (e.g., wrong addition of two price elements, thus rendering the total price incorrect).[137] Pursuant to Article 24(3) CO, calculation errors do not render a contract ineffective but must be corrected.

134. *See, e.g.*, Decision of the Swiss Federal Supreme Court dated 20 February 1979, DSC 105 II 23, para. 2.
135. This is controversial in doctrine. *Pro*: Schwenzer/Fountoulakis, commentary on Article 24, in: Basler Kommentar, OR I, N 9; *Contra*: Dasser, commentary on Article 24 CO, in: Kurzkommentar Obligationenrecht, N 2.
136. Decision of the Swiss Federal Supreme Court dated 1 February 2021, no. 4A_571/2019, para. 7.2: 'For a fundamental mistake to arise, the other party must first of all be able to realise in good faith that the other party's mistake relates to a fact which was objectively such as to determine him to conclude the contract or to conclude it on the agreed terms; it must also be possible, from the point of view of the mistaken party, to accept subjectively that his mistake actually caused him to conclude the contract or to conclude it on the agreed terms.'
137. *See, e.g.*, decision of the Swiss Federal Supreme Court dated 23 May 2014, no. 5A_99/2014, para. 4.1: 'The miscalculation referred to in article 24(3) CO is based on the hypothesis of a common mistake by both parties, resulting from pure inadvertence in the arithmetic operations, when in reality they agree on the price due, so that these false calculations must be

2 *Mistakes Concerning the Formation of the Party's Intent*

166 Also mistakes concerning the formation of a party's intent are only relevant if they are fundamental in nature. If a mistake relates solely to the reason for concluding the contract (*Motivirrtum, erreur sur les motifs, errore sui motivi*), it is not fundamental.[138] The mistake must relate to specific facts which the mistaking party considered in good faith to be a necessary basis for the contract (*Grundlagenirrtum, erreur de base, errore essenziale*).[139]

167 At the time of conclusion of contract, the mistaking person must consider the facts to which the mistake relates as a necessary basis of the contract; they must be *conditio sine qua non* for the conclusion of the contract. If the person had not been mistaken about these facts, the contract would not have been concluded at all or not with the content in question. In addition, from an objective perspective, it must be reasonable that the mistaking person considered the facts a necessary basis of the contract.[140] Finally, the significance of the mistaken facts must be apparent to the other party.[141] This is in particular the case if the mistaken fact is of high importance to the contract as a whole.

168 A mistake about the future does only constitute a fundamental mistake under exceptional circumstances. Both parties must have been sure of the occurrence of the relevant fact in the future. Alternatively, it is deemed sufficient that only the mistaking party has been sure, but the other party ought to have been aware that the mistaking

---

corrected because the parties have in fact agreed on the result of their arithmetic reasoning, which, according to article 18 CO, must give way to the actual and common will of the parties. Article 24(3) CO is therefore a genuine rule of consensus; in particular, it states that the mathematical reasoning that gives concrete form to the will of the parties takes precedence over the clearly expressed final result. The term calculation error used in the law is to be understood in a broad sense; this rule therefore applies when a clause in an agreement is incorrectly inferred from other elements of the contract. The application of this provision presupposes, however, that the basis of calculation and the elements from which the erroneous final result is deduced form an integral part of the contract and that it is an open mistake on the part of both parties, not an internal mistake of assessment, i.e., a simple mistake, made by one of the parties when drawing up the instrument, which is not recognisable to third parties.'

138. Article 24(2) CO.
139. Article 24(1)(4) CO.
140. Decision of the Swiss Federal Supreme Court dated 10 February 1987, DSC 113 II 25, para. 1: 'A contracting party may invoke such a right if he has made a mistake about a legal situation or about a particular fact which he could have considered in good faith as a necessary basis for a contract. In the case of synallagmatic or bilateral contracts it is therefore not sufficient that he has been mistaken about the content or scope of the mutual performance or merely about the effects of the contract; what is required is rather a misconception which necessarily both parties have consciously or unconsciously shared and which, from an objective point of view, has been an indispensable prerequisite for the conclusion of the contract.' For an overview of the relevant case law on which facts pass this objective test, *see* Gauch/Schluep/Schmid, Schweizerisches Obligationenrecht, Zurich 2020, N 793.
141. Decision of the Swiss Federal Supreme Court, DSC 132 III 737, para. 1.3. However, this is controversial in doctrine, *see, e.g.*, Huguenin, Obligationenrecht, Zurich 2019, N 513.

party without being sure about the future occurrence of the fact would not have concluded the contract.[142]

3 *Invocation of Mistake Must Not Violate Good Faith*

169 Pursuant to Article 25(1) CO, a party may not invoke a mistake in a manner contrary to good faith. This is, in particular, the case if the mistaking party simply did not care to clarify the point in question when entering into the contract, so that the other party could assume that the point was irrelevant to its counterpart.[143] Equally, a party is barred from invoking a mistake based on the foreign language of the contract if the party had the opportunity to obtain a translation.[144]

170 In line with this principle, a party is precluded from invoking a mistake if the other party is willing to accept the contract in a manner that complies with the counterpart's original, unvitiated intention.[145] In such a case, the contract stands as intended by the mistaking party.

---

142. Decision of the Swiss Federal Supreme Court dated 5 May 1992, DSC 118 II 297, para. 2.b: 'In this decision [DSC 109 II 105], the Federal Supreme Court does not rule out the possibility of a mistake regarding a future situation if both parties to the contract consider its realisation to be certain, but from the outset rejects it in the face of mere hopes, exaggerated expectations and speculation. … . A fundamental mistake can, however, also be present if only the party relying on the mistake erroneously assumed that a future event was certain, but the other party should also have recognised in good faith that such certainty was a contractual requirement for the other party.'
143. Decision of the Swiss Federal Supreme Court dated 11 July 1991, DSC 117 II 218, para. 3.a: 'However, the claimant is right when pointing out that for a challenge according to article 24(1)(4) CO it does, in principle, not matter whether the party relying on the mistake has erred merely by negligence. However, the claimant fails to recognize that a party to a contract does not have to expect the other party to act carelessly. The actions of one party give rise to certain conclusions in good faith. If someone does not take care to clarify a certain question when concluding a contract, although it is obvious that this question will arise, the other party may in principle conclude from this that this point is not important to the other party with regard to the conclusion of the contract. The behaviour which in retrospect turns out to be merely negligent can thus have the effect that a certain circumstance could not be considered in good faith by the mistaking party as a necessary basis of the contract.'
144. Decision of the Swiss Federal Supreme Court dated 16 November 2017, no. 5A_177/2017, para. 3.1: 'It would be up to her [the party relying on the mistake] to react in case of ambiguities or linguistic difficulties of understanding. The situation could be different if the accusation of deception was well-founded, which – as already mentioned – is not to be dealt with in this case. If she really did not understand the content of the contracts in 2008, but then invested large sums of money (deposits) in B.________ AG for years, whereby its financial difficulties must have been a constant topic, only to sign another allegedly misunderstood letter of subordination in 2012, then such behaviour – as the High Court has already considered – does not deserve legal protection (article 25(1) CO). There would have been sufficient time to inform oneself about the content of the contracts entered into and the legal significance of a subordination agreement.'
145. Article 25(2) CO.

4 *The Mistaking Party's Fault*

171 The mistaking party's fault is generally irrelevant to the question of whether it may rely on the mistake in order to be released from the contract. In particular, the mistaking party's fault does in itself not render the invocation of the mistake contrary to good faith.[146]

172 However, a mistaking party that invokes the mistake in order to be released from a contract is liable for any damage arising from the nullity of the agreement if the mistake is attributable to his own negligence unless the other party knew or should have known of the mistake.[147] In the interests of equity, the court may award further compensation to the person suffering damage.[148]

B Deceit

173 A party induced to enter into a contract by the deceit of the other party is not bound by the contract even if its mistake is not fundamental.[149] A deceit may consist of actively representing wrong facts and thereby inducing a mistake or knowingly exploiting an existing mistake of the other party. In any case, there must be a causal link between the mistake and the conclusion of the contract. Without the mistake, the mistaking party would not have concluded the contract, or at least not with the same terms.

174 The failure to disclose a fact only constitutes deceit if there is a duty of information owed to the other party. Such duty may result from a special legal provision, a contract or the principle of good faith.[150] Whether a duty exists must be determined based on the individual circumstances of each case. However, there is no general obligation to inform the contracting party about circumstances that might be important to that party.

---

146. Decision of the Swiss Federal Supreme Court dated 20 February 1979, DSC 105 II 23, para. 2.b: 'Finally, this is also the line taken by a more recent decision [DSC 91 II 275], in which it is argued that the mere fact that the mistaking person is to blame for the mistake due to his own negligence does not make the invocation of the mistake abusive within the meaning of article 25 CO; otherwise article 26 CO, which obliges the person in mistake through negligence to compensate for the damage resulting from the cancellation of the contract, would lose its meaning.'
147. Article 26(1) CO.
148. Article 26(2) CO.
149. Article 28(1) CO.
150. Decision of the Swiss Federal Supreme Court dated 22 May 1990, DSC 116 II 431, para. 3.a: 'A deceptive conduct in the sense of article 28 CO consists in the pretence of false facts or the concealment of facts. The concealment of facts is only frowned upon if there is an obligation to disclose the facts; such an obligation may arise from a special legal provision and from a contract, or if a disclosure is required in good faith and in accordance with the prevailing opinions. When this applies is to be determined in the specific individual case. There is no duty of disclosure if the seller was entitled to assume in good faith that the other party would easily recognise the correct facts of the case.'

In particular, there is no duty of disclosure if a party is entitled to assume in good faith that the other party is able to easily recognise the correct facts.

175 Deceit requires that the non-mistaking party had the intention to deceive. This includes, on the one hand, knowledge of the untruth of the assertions made or of the incorrect perception of the mistaking party and, on the other hand, the intention to entice the mistaking party to conclude a contract. It is not necessary that the non-mistaking party intends to harm the other party or gain a financial advantage.

176 If a third party is responsible for the deceit, the contract may only be rendered ineffective if the non-mistaking contracting party was or ought to have been aware of the deceit at the time of conclusion of contract.[151]

C Duress

177 Where a party has entered into a contract under duress from the other party or a third party, he is not bound by that contract.[152] A party is under duress if, in the circumstances, he has good cause to believe that there is an imminent and substantial risk to his own life, reputation or property or to those of a person close to him.[153] Where the other party threatens to enforce a legitimate claim, duress may only be assumed if the straitened circumstances of the party under duress have been exploited in order to extort excessive benefits from him.[154] In this context, threatening to file a criminal complaint is only considered to constitute duress if there is no connection between the threatened criminal complaint and the requested action (e.g., threatening to report for tax evasion unless a contract of sale is concluded).[155]

178 The duress may also originate from a third party. However, if the other contracting party neither knew nor should have known of the duress, a party under duress who wishes to be released from the contract must pay compensation to the other party where equity so requires.[156]

151. Article 28(2) CO.
152. Article 29(1) CO.
153. Article 30(1) CO.
154. Article 30(2) CO.
155. Decision of the Swiss Federal Supreme Court dated 3 September 1999, DSC 125 III 353, para. 2: 'The threat of a criminal complaint is unlawful if there is no internal connection to the intended purpose, for example, if a complaint of tax evasion is threatened in order to persuade the threatened person to conclude a purchase contract. However, if the threatened report concerns offences which have caused damage to the threatening party or a person close to it, the threat is permitted as long as the threatening party does not wish to obtain more than he is entitled to as compensation for damages. In the present case, the threat of criminal proceedings served to enforce claims for damages which the claimant derived from those acts of the defendant which it considered criminal. The internal connection to the intended purpose is thus given. The admissibility of the threats made therefore depends on whether the amount of the forced acknowledgements of debt is within the scope of the compensation claims to which the claimant is actually entitled.' *See also* decision of the Swiss Federal Supreme Court dated 2 February 1994, DSC 120 IV 17, para. 2.a.bb.
156. Article 29(2) CO.

D Negation of Defect in Consent by Ratification of the Contract

179 A party that has entered into a contract under mistake, deceit or duress is free to ratify the contract and thereby cure the defect in its consent. Such ratification may be expressed explicitly or implicitly. Ratification requires a clear indication that a party has accepted the contract, which presupposes knowledge of the defect.[157]

180 Nonetheless, silent ratification is possible. Pursuant to Article 31(1) CO, a contract is silently ratified by neither expressing to the other party that one intends not to honour the contract nor seeking restitution for the performance made within one year. The one-year period runs from the time that the mistake or the deceit was discovered or from the time that the duress ended.[158] An error or deception is only considered to be discovered when such mistake or deceit can be assumed with certainty.[159]

181 The declaration is not subject to any form requirements. However, it must clearly indicate that the party wishes not to be bound by the contract. The declaration may generally not be made subject to any conditions.[160]

E Legal Consequences of Defect in Consent

182 Defects in consent make a contract non-binding for the party suffering from the defect (e.g., the mistaking party). The party not suffering from the defect, however, remains bound by the contract.

183 Pursuant to the case law of the Swiss Federal Supreme Court, the contract is deemed to be made under the condition precedent that the party suffering from the defect in consent ratifies the contract (e.g., by not declining the contract within the time limit of Article 31 CO). Only after such ratification the contract enters into effect.[161] If

157. Decision of the Swiss Federal Supreme Court dated 22 June 1982, DSC 108 II 102, para. 2.a: 'This [a ratification of the contract] can already be assumed during the one-year period if the person entitled to contest clearly indicates by positive action or by an explicit expression of intent that he has accepted the defective contract. Ratification is still possible even after invoking the mistake if the other party agrees that the contract remains in force. In either case, however, the ratification presupposes a certain knowledge of the mistake; mere indefinite, unproven doubts are not sufficient. In the case of deception, in addition to the discovery of the mistake, the knowledge that the defect was caused by deliberate false pretence is also required. In the absence of an explicit expression of intent, in view of the scope of the waiver of rights that lies in a ratification, namely in the case of deliberate deception, it may not be concluded lightly that unconditional ratification has been given. Whether a certain act of the person entitled to challenge is to be understood as an unambiguous expression of a ratification is to be examined according to the principle of trust. The burden of proof for the alleged ratification lies with the non-mistaking party; this includes the proof that the mistaking party discovered the mistake before the act claimed to constitute the mistake.'
158. Article 31(2) CO.
159. Decision of the Swiss Federal Supreme Court dated 22 June 1982, DSC 108 II 102, para. 2.a.
160. Decision of the Swiss Federal Supreme Court dated 30 October 2001, DSC 128 III 70, para. 2.
161. Decision of the Swiss Federal Supreme Court dated 7 June 1988, DSC 114 II 131, para. 3.b. However, there are some scholars arguing that the contract enters into effect as of its

the party suffering from the defect declares within the required time limit that it wishes no longer to be bound by the contract,[162] the contract becomes void *ex tunc* (i.e., as if it had never been concluded). Only if such a declaration is made, the parties are released from their contractual obligations.

184 The party not suffering from the defect in consent is barred from declaring that it wishes to be released from the contract, it is to this extent dependent on the decision of the other party. However, if the other party is aware of its mistake and waits an unreasonably long period of time to decide about the ratification, that party might violate the principle of good faith which would bar any invocation of the mistake.[163]

185 If the party suffering from the defect has successfully invoked the non-binding nature of the contract, duties that have not yet been discharged need no longer be discharged. Performances already rendered must be returned. The assertion of claims for restitution is based on property law (Article 641(2) CC) and subsidiarily on the law of unjust enrichment (Articles 62 et seqq. CO).[164] Where both parties have already performed their obligations under the contract, the reversal must be carried out simultaneously quid pro quo.[165]

VIII RENDERING A CONCLUDED CONTRACT INEFFECTIVE: UNFAIR ADVANTAGE

186 Pursuant to the principle of freedom of contract, parties are generally free in determining the content of their contract. However, in exceptional circumstances, a party is enabled to void an unfair contract.

187 Where there is a clear discrepancy between performance and counter-performance under a contract and one party has exploited the other party's straitened circumstances, inexperience or thoughtlessness, the other party may declare that he will not honour the contract and demand restitution of any performance already made under the contract.[166] The necessary declaration must be made within one year after conclusion of the contract.[167]

188 Whether a clear discrepancy between performance and counter-performance in the contract exists, must be assessed based on the objective value of the promised

---

conclusion, but is voidable by the party suffering from the contract (*see, e.g.*, Schmidlin, commentary on Article 23 CO: in: Berner Kommentar, N 127 et seqq.).

162. *See* hereinabove para. 180.
163. Article 25(2) CO. *See* Decision of the Swiss Federal Supreme Court dated 22 June 1982, DSC 108 II 102, para. 2.a.
164. Concerning the start of the prescription period, *see* decision of the Swiss Federal Supreme Court dated 7 June 1988, DSC 114 II 131 (period begins running at the moment of performance).
165. Decision of the Swiss Federal Supreme Court dated 21 February 2003, DSC 129 III 320, para. 7.1.2.
166. Article 21(1) CO.
167. Article 21(2) CO.

performances.[168] As the underlying reason of Article 21 CO is to sanction the exploitation of a weak party, the threshold for the discrepancy must not be set too high.[169]

189 The disadvantaged party must have been in an exceptional position that precluded him from freely negotiating the terms of the contract and led him to make extraordinary decisions. The enumeration of exceptional situations in Article 21 CO is only of exemplary nature. The influence of alcohol, drugs or medication as well as states of exhaustion, dependencies or surprise may constitute exceptional situations envisaged by Article 21 CO.

190 The other party must have deliberately taken advantage of the decision-making weakness in order to conclude the contract with an unbalanced content.[170] Mere awareness of the other party's weakness and the unbalanced nature of the contract are not enough. It must have (knowingly) exploited the other party's weakness; i.e., it must have abused it in order to obtain a disproportionate advantage.[171]

191 If the conditions of Article 21 CO are met, the contract is one-sidedly non-binding for the disadvantaged party.[172] The disadvantaged party may declare within one year of conclusion of the contract that it wishes no longer to be bound by the contract and to claim back what has been performed under the contract. The disadvantaged party does, however, also have the option to not declare the entire contract void, but to request that the contract be amended to become more balanced.[173]

192 In addition, the disadvantaged party may be able to request compensation for any damage suffered due to the advantaged party's exploitation of its situation on the basis of *culpa in contrahendo*.[174]

168. Decision of the Swiss Federal Supreme Court dated 26 June 1997, DSC 123 III 292, para. 6.a: 'Performance and counter-performance are to be compared according to their objective value at the time of conclusion of the contract, which in the case of performance in kind corresponds to the market value at that time, the "*communis aestimatio*", the "*valeur courante*". The market price of the same or at least a comparable performance is the relevant parameter, in the absence of a market price one must turn to recognised valuation standards for corresponding performances, as long as an objective value determination is still possible on the basis of reasonably assured parameters.'
169. Gauch/Schluep/Schmid, Schweizerisches Obligationenrecht, Zurich 2020, N 734.
170. Decision of the Swiss Federal Supreme Court dated 26 June 1997, DSC 123 III 292, para. 7: 'If the obvious disproportion of the exchange services continues to be affirmed, the Higher Court will also have to examine whether the element of exploitation can also be affirmed under the new circumstances, i.e., whether the defendant "abused" the claimant's weakness in the knowledge of the obvious inequivalence of the performances.'
171. Decision of the Swiss Federal Supreme Court dated 14 January 2016, no. 4A_491/2015, para. 4.3.2; 'It is not enough simply to know that the disadvantaged party is weakened (in this case, inexperience) and that the benefits are disproportionately high. The injured party's contractual partner must have (knowingly) exploited his weakness, i.e., abused it to obtain a disproportionate advantage. It is for the disadvantaged party to prove the circumstances which, where appropriate, constitute an exploitation of weakness. According to the case law of the Federal Supreme Court, the exploitation of inexperience should not be easily admitted.'
172. *See* above para. 182.
173. Decision of the Swiss Federal Supreme Court dated 26 June 1997, DSC 123 III 292, para. 2.
174. *See* below paras 193 et seqq.

IX LIABILITY FOR LACK OF GOOD FAITH IN CONTRACT NEGOTIATIONS (*CULPA IN CONTRAHENDO*)

193 If a party violates duties of good faith in contract negotiations, it is liable to the other party for the damage caused (*culpa in contrahendo*). The aggrieved party must be put in the financial situation as if the negotiations had never taken place (so-called negative damages[175]).[176]

194 The principle of good faith entails in particular the duty to negotiate seriously and the prohibition to deceive. Based on the duty to negotiate seriously, negotiating contracts without the intention to conclude such a contract may cause a liability for losses (useless travel costs, missed other opportunities to contract) of the negotiation partner.[177] Further, under certain circumstances, non-disclosure of information can also constitute a basis for liability:[178]

> Liability from *culpa in contrahendo* is based on the principle that the parties must act in good faith during the contract negotiations. Certainly, there is no obligation to continue negotiations that have already begun; each party may, on the contrary, break them off and has not to give account to the others either. When entering into negotiations, however, mutual obligations inevitably arise. This includes in particular that the parties conduct negotiations in accordance with their real intentions and inform each other to a certain extent of facts which may influence the other party's decision on the conclusion of the contract or its conditions. The extent to which the parties must inform each other does not depend on a general rule, but on the circumstances of the individual case, namely the nature of the contract, the way in which the negotiations are conducted, and the intentions and knowledge of the parties. Contrary to the opinion of the defendant, however, liability from *culpa in contrahendo* does not presuppose fraudulent conduct. Anyone who initiates and continues negotiations but does not draw attention to circumstances of which the other party cannot and need not be aware, is rather liable even in the case of negligent breach of the duty of disclosure. This is particularly obvious if he should observe this obligation in his own interest, e.g., to prevent a non-binding promise.

195 Claims based on *culpa in contrahendo* are qualified as quasi-contractual claims. The prescription period for claims based on *culpa in contrahendo* is nonetheless the one that applies to actions based on torts law; i.e., three years.[179,180]

---

175. *See* below para. 398.
176. Decision of the Swiss Federal Supreme Court dated 11 March 2014, DSC 140 III 200, para. 5.2. In doctrine, some authors argue that further remedies such as positive damages or rescission should be available, *see, e.g.*, Schwenzer/Fountoulakis, Schweizerisches Obligationenrecht – Allgemeiner Teil, Bern 2020, N 47.14.
177. Decision of the Swiss Federal Supreme Court dated 2 February 1954, DSC 80 II 26, para. 4.c.
178. Decision of the Swiss Federal Supreme Court dated 6 February 1979, DSC 105 II 75, para. 2.a.
179. Article 60 CO.
180. Decision of the Swiss Federal Supreme Court dated 13 May 2008, no. 4A_499/2007, para. 4.3.

X LIABILITY FOR EVOKED TRUST

196 Liability for evoked trust is an extraordinary concept under which one may become liable for having disappointed another person's expectation although there was no contractual undertaking given towards that person. Merely, by one's behaviour, a legitimate expectation was created. This expectation was then unduly disappointed.

197 In 1994, the Swiss Federal Supreme Court accepted for the first time the concept of liability for evoked trust. In essence, the case concerned an underfunded subsidiary that had created the appearance of a close relationship with its parent company in its communication documents. When the subsidiary eventually went bankrupt and its business partners were harmed, the parent company became liable for tolerating its subsidiary's confidence-inspiring statements.[181] In subsequent decisions, the Swiss Federal Supreme Court confirmed this case law setting forth three conditions under which liability for evoked trust arose:

- there must exist a special relationship of trust (*Sonderverbindung*) between the person creating and the person relying on the expectation;[182]
- the person whose liability is contemplated must have acted in a way to create specific legitimate expectations on the part of the aggrieved party;[183]
- in reliance on the evoked trust, the aggrieved party makes certain dispositions that turn out to be disadvantageous due to the damaging party unduly disappointing the evoked trust.[184]

198 In 2007, the Swiss Federal Supreme Court amended its practice and significantly limited the scope of liability for evoked trust. It reasoned that 'the expectation that the partner will provide a service without a contractual obligation is in principle not worthy of protection since it is generally reasonable for the relying party to protect himself by concluding a corresponding contract'.[185] Liability for evoked trust therefore presupposes that conclusion of a contract with the damaging party was not possible

181. Decision of the Swiss Federal Supreme Court dated 15 November 1994, DSC 120 II 331.
182. Decision of the Swiss Federal Supreme Court dated 23 December 2003, DSC 130 III 345, para. 2.2: 'Such a special connection arises from conscious or normatively attributable conduct of the person claimed against. In contrast, an accidental and unintentional collision, as is usually inherent in tort liability based on negligence, does not create such a special connection. Thus, the personal liability of a vicarious agent can only be considered if he himself was in close personal relations with the client of his principal or if he offered him, due to his entire conduct, a personal guarantee for the success of the assumed business.'
183. Decision of the Swiss Federal Supreme Court dated 23 December 2003, DSC 130 III 345, para. 2.1: 'Trust worthy of protection presupposes conduct on the part of the damaging party that is capable of giving rise to sufficiently concrete and specific expectations on the part of the injured party.'
184. Decision of the Swiss Federal Supreme Court dated 23 December 2003, DSC 130 III 345, para. 2.1: 'If the injured party makes dispositions that prove to be disadvantageous, the damaging party shall be liable for the damage if and to the extent that the unrealized expectation was adequately responsible for it.'
185. Decision of the Swiss Federal Supreme Court dated 12 June 2007, DSC 133 III 449, para. 4.1.

and that foregoing the transaction could not have been reasonably expected from the aggrieved party.[186]

199 There are only very few cases conceivable where this additional condition will be met. To date, the Swiss Federal Supreme Court has not found anybody liable for evoked trust under this new case law.

186. Decision of the Swiss Federal Supreme Court dated 12 June 2007, DSC 133 III 449, para. 4.2.

CHAPTER 3
Establishing the Content of a Contract

200 Freedom of contract is the fundamental principle of Swiss contract law. Besides the freedom to choose whether and with whom to enter into a contract,[187] it also includes the principle of freedom of content. Pursuant to that principle, parties are free to determine the content of their contract. In particular, they may agree on contracts that do not correspond to any of the types of contracts in the special part of the Code of Obligations (Articles 184 et seqq.), so-called innominate contracts.[188]

201 However, the freedom of content is not limitless. The law establishes certain outer limits that every contract must respect. There are certain fundamental considerations of justice, often for the sake of protecting the weaker party, that any contract must comply with. These limits will be elaborated on in section II. Any term contradicting these considerations cannot bind the parties and can thus not form part of a contract's content.

202 In order to determine whether a specific contract violates such fundamental considerations of justice, first the specific content of the contract must be established. This is done by interpreting the terms of the contract. The rules that apply to such interpretation are dealt with in section I.

203 At times, even after interpreting all the terms of a contract, a certain issue may remain unaddressed by the terms of a contract. Here, the contract must be supplemented by non-mandatory provisions of the Code of Obligations and if gaps (*lacuna*) remain, by the judge. This issue will be analysed in section III.

204 Although the principle of *pacta sunt servanda* is well established in Swiss contract law, certain exceptional circumstances may give rise to the right to have a contract amended in order to restore the balance of the bargain. The doctrine of *clausula rebus sic stantibus* will be addressed in section IV.

---

187. *See* above paras 106 et seqq.
188. *See* below paras 513 et seqq.

205 The majority of contracts concluded today are not negotiated term by term but are rather template contracts that a party uses for a multitude of its contractual relationships. These template contracts are usually referred to as general terms and conditions. The special rules applying to general terms and conditions will be elaborated on in section V.

206 Finally, a contract often contains conditional promises. The Code of Obligations contains specific rules applying to such conditions. They will be analysed in section VI.

I INTERPRETATION OF A CONTRACT

207 The driving force behind a contract is the parties' expressions of intent.[189] Only the terms covered by the parties' mutual expressions of intent form the content of a contract. Accordingly, a contract's content must be established by interpreting the parties' expressions of intent.

208 Above all, the parties' actual intent is decisive in establishing the content of the contract. If no such actual common intention of the parties can be established - and only then - an interpretation governed by the principle of trust (*Vertrauensprinzip, principe de la confiance, principio dell' affidamento*) is required, in order to determine a contract's content. In this sense, Swiss law follows a two-step procedure for contract interpretation.[190]

209 The purpose of contract interpretation is to determine what the parties intended at the time of the conclusion of the contract, i.e., to establish the content of the contract. However, if the parties are in dispute about whether there has been any consensus about an objectively or subjectively essential term, the dispute rather relates to the question of whether a contract has been concluded at all.

A Priority of the Parties' Actual Intent (Subjective Interpretation)

210 Pursuant to Article 18(1) CO, the parties' real and common intent (*tatsächlicher Konsens, accord de fait, consenso di fatto*) at the time of concluding the contract is decisive for establishing the contents of the contract. It takes priority over any objective interpretation of a contract.

211 The contents of a party's actual intent is a question of fact, not of law.[191] Thus, the parties are to bring forth evidence supporting any assertion as to their and their contracting partner's actual intention when concluding the contract in question.

---

189. *See* above paras 64 et seqq.
190. *See* Sam Moss, Swiss Law vs. English Law on Contract Interpretation: Is Swiss Law Better Suited to the Realities of International Construction Contracts?, International Construction Law Review, 2015, p. 470 et seqq.
191. Decision of the Swiss Federal Supreme Court dated 30 January 2019, no. 4A_359/2018, para. 3.1: 'The aim of the interpretation of the contract is primarily to establish the real and common

212 In order to determine a party's actual intent a tribunal must assess circumstantial evidence giving insight into a party's intent:

> In proceedings, therefore, the judge must first ascertain the real and common intention of the parties (subjective interpretation), if necessary empirically, on the basis of circumstantial evidence. Circumstances in this sense are not only the content of the expressions of intent – whether written or oral – but also the general context, i.e., all the circumstances that make it possible to discover the real intention of the parties, whether they were expressed prior to the conclusion of the contract or as a result of facts subsequent to it, in particular the subsequent conduct of the parties, which establishes what the contracting parties' own conceptions were at the time.[192]

213 Although clear wording is an important point of reference for ascertaining the actual intention, it is not the sole relevant factor. Further relevant circumstances include the parties' declarations before the conclusion of the contract, draft contracts and any correspondence leading up to the conclusion of the contract. Finally, a party's conduct after conclusion of the contract often reveals its actual understanding of the contractual terms.[193]

B Interpretation under the Principle of Trust (Objective Interpretation)

214 If no actual and common intent can be established – and only then – the parties' objective intent, must be examined. For this, the parties' expressions of intent must be interpreted in accordance with the principle of trust.[194] In contrast to the actual intent, establishing the objective intent is a question of law – and thus open to the full examination by the Swiss Federal Supreme Court.[195]

---

intention of the parties (*see* article 18(1) CO). This subjective interpretation of the contract is based on the assessment of evidence, which is not subject to review by the Federal Supreme Court, subject to the exceptions of articles 97 and 105 Swiss Federal Supreme Court Act. If a real and common intention is established, there is no room for an interpretation according to the principle of trust. Only if a real and common intention remains unproven are the expressions of the parties to be interpreted on the basis of the principle of trust as they could and had to be understood according to their wording and context as well as the overall circumstances in order to determine the presumed will of the parties.'

192. Decision of the Swiss Federal Supreme Court dated 22 January 2018, DSC 144 III 93, para. 5.2.2.
193. Decision of the Swiss Federal Supreme Court dated 13 February 2020, no. 8C_14/2020, para. 4.4: 'For the actual understanding of the parties' will, the wording alone is not decisive; rather, the entire circumstances under which the expressions of will were made indicate the inner will of the parties. The subsequent conduct is to be taken into account insofar as it permits inferring what the parties actually intended with their respective declarations.'
194. Decision of the Swiss Federal Supreme Court dated 14 July 1992, DSC 118 II 365, para. 1: 'The content of a contract is primarily determined by subjective interpretation, i.e., by the real and common intention of the parties (article 18(1) CO). Only if an actual overlap of intentions remains unproven, the declarations of the parties are to be interpreted for the determination of the presumed intention of the parties on the basis of the principle of trust as they could and had to be understood according to their wording and context as well as the overall circumstances.'
195. Decision of the Swiss Federal Supreme Court dated 17 December 1999, DSC 126 III 25, para. 3.c: 'If it [the lower instance court] has ascertained the real intention of the appellant, this is a finding of fact which is binding on the Swiss Federal Supreme Court before which an appeal for

215 Unlike the parties' actual intention, which focuses on the parties' subjective intentions, the principle of trust dictates an objective approach. By applying the principle of trust, the court seeks to establish the meaning that the parties could and should have given, pursuant to the rules of good faith, to their reciprocal expressions of intent, taking into account all the circumstances which preceded or accompanied its conclusion.[196] The principle of trust makes it possible to impute to a party the objective meaning of his statement or behaviour, even if it does not correspond to his actual intention.[197]

216 Above all, a court will look at the wording of a contract. Words are to be understood in accordance with their common usage (*allgemeiner Sprachgebrauch, sens courant, linguaggio commune*):

> In the interpretation according to the wording, the meaning of the word ascribed to it by common usage is of decisive importance. In the absence of other indications, it must be assumed that the parties used a word in accordance with the common usage at the time of the conclusion of the contract, i.e., in the sense of everyday or colloquial language at that time. Accordingly, the common sense of the word must be taken into account, which can also be derived from common dictionaries and encyclopaedias.[198]

217 Yet, there are some limitations to relying on the wording if the parties refer to technical or specialist terms in a contract. A literal interpretation is only appropriate if all involved parties can be expected to understand the meaning of such terms:

> Accordingly, case law does not attribute decisive importance to the fact that the parties have used precise legal terms. In particular, such wording may not be relied upon without further examination if the committing party is a foreign person or the expression of intent was made by him in a foreign language. However, a strict interpretation according to the wording may be appropriate for persons experienced in business and skilled in the use of technical terms.[199]

218 Although clear wording is not necessarily decisive in itself and a purely literal interpretation is prohibited, a court will require serious reasons to depart from unambiguous wording.[200]

---

reform is lodged; if it has interpreted the appellant's conduct according to the principle of trust, admitting consent by conclusive act, this is a question of law which may be reviewed.'

196. Decision of the Swiss Federal Supreme Court dated 7 July 2014, no. 4A_124/2014, para. 3.4.1.
197. Decision of the Swiss Federal Supreme Court dated 6 April 2010, DSC 136 III 186, para. 3.2.1; Decision of the Swiss Federal Supreme Court dated 26 August 2021, no. 4A_223/2021, para. 3.1: 'Accordingly, the party must let its declaration stand as it could and had to be understood by the addressee in good faith according to its wording and context as well as the entire circumstances.'
198. Decision of the Swiss Federal Supreme Court dated 24 October 2002, no. 5C.87/2002, para. 2.3.1.
199. Decision of the Swiss Federal Supreme Court dated 23 September 2003, DSC 129 III 702, para. 2.4.1.
200. Decision of the Swiss Federal Supreme Court dated 6 April 2010, DSC 136 III 186, para. 3.2.1: 'The meaning of an apparently clear text is not necessarily decisive, so that purely literal interpretation is prohibited. Even if the content of a contractual term appears clear at first sight,

219 If a wording is not sufficiently clear or if there are reasons to depart from a clear wording, the interpretation of a contract must rely on other aspects of a contract than its pure wording.[201] Namely, the negotiation history of a contract as well as the circumstances surrounding its conclusion must be considered.[202] The context of a specific provision must be taken into account, as a contract must be interpreted as a whole and not a set of isolated provisions.[203] Further, a contract must be understood in light of the parties' respective interests[204] and the purpose of the contract in question (as often expressed in the preamble of a contract).[205]

220 In contrast, the subsequent conduct of the parties, i.e., after conclusion of contract, is not relevant for the interpretation according to the principle of trust.[206]

C Specific Rules of Contract Interpretation

221 Over time, certain rules of contract interpretation have developed in case law and doctrine.[207] These rules exist in parallel without one having per se priority over the others.

222 *Ex tunc interpretation*: A court must interpret the contract from the parties' perspective at the time of conclusion of the contract.[208] Post-contractual events must not be taken into consideration when interpreting a contract under the principle of trust.

it may result from other terms of the contract, the purpose pursued by the parties or other circumstances that the text of the term does not accurately convey the meaning of the agreement concluded. There is, however, no reason to depart from the literal meaning of the text adopted by the interested parties where there is no serious reason to believe that it does not correspond to their wishes.'

201. Coincidentally, there reasons for departing from the wording may be found in these other aspects of a contract.
202. Decision of the Swiss Federal Supreme Court dated 27 April 2020, no. 4A_535/2019, para. 4.2.2.
203. Decision of the Swiss Federal Supreme Court dated 2 October 2012, DSC 138 III 659, para. 4.2.1.
204. Decision of the Swiss Federal Supreme Court dated 27 June 1996, DSC 122 III 426, para. 5.b: 'From the interests to be taken into account as an element of interpretation it clearly follows that for the buyers it was not the quality of the building land at the time of the conclusion of the contract or the transfer of risk that was essential, but the receipt of the building permit to be applied for in due time. Accordingly, for them the guarantee had to refer to the time of the building decision, and the defendant, as a *bona fide* seller, could not assume anything else in good faith.'
205. Swiss Federal Supreme Court dated 27 April 2020, no. 4A_535/2019, para. 4.3: 'Furthermore, the circumstances under which these declarations were made are to be taken into account, in particular the purpose of the contractual rule pursued by the declarant as the recipient of the declaration could and had to understand it in good faith. As a rule, it must be assumed that the recipient of the declaration could assume that the declarant was aiming for a reasonable, appropriate rule.'
206. Decision of the Swiss Federal Supreme Court dated 19 May 2016, no. 4A_615/2015, para. 5.1.
207. The interpretation of general terms and conditions follow special rules that will be explained herein below in paras 257 et seqq.
208. Decision of the Swiss Federal Supreme Court dated 8 July 2003, DSC 129 III 675, para. 2.3.

223 *Holistic interpretation*: An individual provision of a contract must not be considered in isolation but must always be interpreted in the context of the whole contract.[209]

224 *Statute-compliant interpretation*: In case of doubt, the interpretation which corresponds most with the (non-mandatory) provisions of the law (namely, the Code of Obligations) must be followed.[210]

225 *In dubio contra stipulatorem*: If the interpretation of a contract does not result in a clear meaning, the meaning which is less favourable to the party that has drafted the contract in question shall prevail.[211]

226 *Assumption of reasonableness*: When interpreting a contract there is a general presumption that parties did not intend to enter into an unreasonable contract.[212]

227 *In favorem negotii*: Preference is to be given to the interpretation which does not render the contract invalid or unreasonable.[213]

228 Finally, parties are free to agree on specific rules of interpretation in their contract. Such pre-agreed rules of interpretation are binding on a court.[214] This typically concerns agreed definitions of certain terms used in a contract.

II LIMITATIONS ON THE CONTENT OF A CONTRACT

229 Swiss contract law is governed by the principle that parties are free to decide on the content of their contractual relationships (freedom of contract). This principle is enshrined in Article 19(1) CO: 'The terms of a contract may be freely determined within the limits of the law.'

230 While the parties' contractual freedom is paramount and far-reaching under Swiss contract law, it is not limitless. Some limits are based on mandatory provisions of Swiss law. Public order and good morals equally set forth certain outer limits of contractual freedom. Finally, contractual terms must not result in an excessive restriction of one's legal personality and must not be impossible to fulfil.

209. Decision of the Swiss Federal Supreme Court dated 21 November 1996, DSC 123 III 165, para. 3.a: 'The decisive factor is how the recipient was to understand it [expression of intent] in good faith. In doing so, the overall context must always be kept in mind, i.e., the individual provisions of a contract or the statements of a contracting party must not be detached from their context, but must be judged from their concrete meaning.'
210. Decision of the Swiss Federal Supreme Court dated 11 February 1987, DSC 133 II 49, para. 1.b: '[one] also take into account which interpretation corresponds to the non-mandatory law, which normally protects the interests of the parties sufficiently, and therefore a party wishing to depart from it must express this with sufficient clarity, unless such intention is clear from the circumstances'.
211. Decision of the Swiss Federal Supreme Court dated 19 October 2006, no. 5C.61/2006, para. 3.3.
212. Swiss Federal Supreme Court dated 27 February 2014, DSC 140 III 134, para. 3.2: 'In doing so, the court must take into account what is appropriate because it cannot be assumed that the parties intended an unreasonable solution.'
213. Decision of the Zurich High Court dated 13 September 2016, no. LB160025, para. II.4.
214. *See* Gauch/Schluep/Schmid, Schweizerisches Obligationenrecht, Zurich 2020, N 1236 et seqq.

231 The legal consequences of not adhering to these limits are set forth in Article 20 CO. A contract is considered void if its terms are impossible, unlawful or immoral (Article 20(1) CO). If the defect pertains only to certain terms, those terms alone are void unless there is cause to assume that the parties would not have concluded the contract without these terms (Article 20(2) CO).

A Limits Imposed by Law

232 A contractual term is unlawful in the sense of Article 20(1) CO if it violates a mandatory provision of Swiss private or public law. Whether such a violation exists must be determined in accordance with the law in force at the point in time of conclusion of a contract.[215] The violation may result from its content or the (direct or indirect) purpose of the contract (e.g., contractual obligation to commit a murder).

233 Terms that deviate from statutory provisions are not per se unlawful. Only where a statutory provision is considered to be mandatory, any deviation automatically results in the unlawfulness of the contractual term (Article 19(2) CO). Whether a statutory provision is mandatory must be determined by ways of interpretation of the respective provision. The mandatory nature may be deduced from the explicit wording of a provision[216] or its rationale and purpose.[217] While the CO contains various mandatory provisions on employment and rent agreements, the parties' contractual freedom is much less limited in regard to commercial contract types, such as sales contracts.

234 Parties are free to deviate from non-mandatory provisions as long as the other limits imposed by Article 19(2) CO (good morals, public order and protection of legal personality) are respected.

B Limits Imposed by Public Order and Good Morals

235 Public order is considered to be the consolidation of values inherent to the general legal order. In doctrine, it is controversial whether the criteria of 'public order' contains

215. Decision of the Swiss Federal Supreme Court dated 21 December 1976, DSC 102 II 401.
216. For example, Article 100(1) CO: 'Any agreement purporting to exclude liability for unlawful intent or gross negligence in advance is void.'
217. Decision of the Swiss Federal Supreme Court dated 27 November 2007, DSC 134 III 52, para. 1.1: 'According to article 20(1) CO, a contract that has an unlawful content is void. According to the case law of the Federal Supreme Court, a contract is unlawful in the sense of this provision if its subject matter, the conclusion with the agreed content or its common indirect purpose violates objective law. This can be private law or public law norms, namely those of criminal law. A prerequisite for voidness, however, is that this legal consequence is expressly provided for in the law in question or results from the meaning and purpose of the infringed provision.' Also *see* hereinabove paras 35 et seqq.

any limitation to the parties' contractual freedom that is not already covered by the criteria of unlawfulness.[218]

236 Contracts which are immoral in the sense of Article 20(1) CO are contracts which violate the prevailing morals, i.e., the general sense of decency or the ethical principles and standards of value immanent in the overall legal system.[219] Immorality is not to be assumed lightly. An example of immorality is contracts obliging one party to furnish sexual services.

C Limits Imposed by the Protection of Legal Personality

237 The protection of legal personality is enshrined in Article 27 of the Swiss Civil Code:

> 1 No person may, wholly or in part, renounce his or her legal capacity or his or her capacity to act.
> 2 No person may surrender his or her freedom or restrict the use of it to a degree which violates the law or public morals.

238 A contract may violate the principle of protection of legal personality either by the object of the contractual commitment (e.g., obligation pertaining to the highest personal rights of a human being, such as physical integrity) or by the excessive nature of the contractual commitment. A contractual commitment is considered to be excessive if it exposes the obligated party to the arbitrariness of another, if it eliminates his economic freedom or if it restricts it to such an extent that the foundations of his economic existence are jeopardised.[220] Thus, only extreme circumstances justify a court to intervene in the parties' contract.

D Impossible Content

239 If already at the time the contract is concluded it is certain that at least one of the promised performances is objectively impossible - i.e., cannot be provided by any person - the contract has an impossible content. For example, it is objectively impossible to sell the 'philosopher's stone', as such stone does not exist.

240 In contrast, a contract whose obligations have become impossible only after conclusion is not considered impossible in the sense of Article 19(2) CO. Rather, this scenario is addressed by Articles 97 and 119 CO.[221]

218. *See* Schwenzer/Fountoulakis, Schweizerisches Obligationenrecht - Allgemeiner Teil, Bern 2020, N 32.03.
219. Decision of the Swiss Federal Supreme Court dated 26 September 1989, DSC 115 II 232, para. 4.a.
220. Decision of the Swiss Federal Supreme Court dated 21 June 1988, DSC 114 II 159, para. 2.a.
221. *See* below para. 332.

III SUPPLEMENTING A CONTRACT: TERMS IMPLIED BY LAW OR THE COURT

241 A contract may be supplemented if the parties have failed to address a specific issue in the contract. In this context, one speaks of a lacuna (gap in the contract).[222] A lacuna presupposes that a contract has been concluded. Accordingly, the lacuna cannot concern an objectively essential term.

242 If a lacuna exists, the contract must be supplemented. Primarily, the completion of a contract is left to the parties. This resorts from the first sentence of Article 2(2) CO. If the parties fail to find an agreement, completion of the contract falls to the court.

243 When supplementing a contract, a court primarily turns to the non-mandatory provisions of the Code of Obligations. These terms are implied by law. For example, if a sales contract is silent on the issue of passing of risks, a court will apply the rule of Article 185 CO to that issue. Article 185 CO is treated as if agreed on by the parties.

244 If the provisions of the Code of Obligations are silent on the specific issue in question and there is no customary law addressing the specific issue (Article 1(2) CC), the court must complete the contract by establishing the parties' hypothetical will. It must examine what the parties would have agreed on in good faith if they had been aware of the lacuna.[223]

245 In doctrine, it is argued that if a court comes to the conclusion that while there is a non-mandatory provision that could fill a lacuna, but such provision does not correctly reflect the parties' hypothetical will, the court should give preference to the parties' hypothetical will.[224] Yet, this is highly controversial. Scholars disagreeing with this solution argue that the court – contrary to the parties – is bound by the non-mandatory provisions of the Code of Obligations.[225]

222. Decision of the Swiss Federal Supreme Court dated 21 November 1989, DSC 115 II 484, para. 4.a: 'A contractual lacuna exists if the parties have not or not completely settled a legal issue concerning the content of the contract. Whether the contract needs to be supplemented in this sense must first be determined by empirical interpretation and, if this is inconclusive, by normative interpretation.'
223. Decision of the Swiss Federal Supreme Court dated 21 November 1989, DSC 115 II 484, para. 4.b: 'If an incomplete contract is to be completed, the judge – in the absence of non-mandatory legal provisions – must determine what the parties would have agreed in good faith if they had considered the unaddressed point. In determining this hypothetical will of the parties, the judge must be guided by the thoughts and actions of reasonable and *bona fide* parties and by the nature and purpose of the contract.'
224. Huguenin, Obligationenrecht, Zurich 2019, N 316.
225. Gauch/Schluep/Schmid, Schweizerisches Obligationenrecht, Zurich 2020, N 1255.

IV AMENDING THE CONTENT OF A CONTRACT DUE TO CHANGED CIRCUMSTANCES (*CLAUSULA REBUS SIC STANTIBUS*)

246 Generally, changed circumstances do not liberate a party from its contractual obligations. The principle of *pacta sunt servanda* is of paramount importance in Swiss contract law.

247 Nonetheless, a party may demand under certain circumstances an amendment to a contract under the principle of *clausula rebus sic stantibus*. Pursuant to this principle, a party is entitled to an amendment of the contractual terms if circumstances have unforeseeably changed and have led to an extraordinary disbalance between the obligations of the parties. The disbalance must be of such a nature that one cannot reasonably expect the disadvantaged party to still fulfil the contract.

248 Courts adopt a strict approach when assessing whether the conditions for application of *clausula rebus sic stantibus* are met:

> However, according to the practice of the Swiss Federal Supreme Court, the *clausula rebus sic stantibus* only very rarely leads to a judicial dissolution or adjustment of the contract. Such a solution is only affirmed if the relationship between performance and consideration is so disturbed as a result of an extraordinary and unforeseeable change in circumstances that the creditor's insistence on his contractual claim constitutes a downright usurious exploitation of the disproportion and thus a manifest abuse of rights.[226]

249 If the conditions of *clausula rebus sic stantibus* are met, the judge may intervene in the contract to remedy the disbalance. The judge may do so either by amending the terms of the contract or by dissolving the contract in full.[227] When amending the contract, the judge must follow the parties' hypothetical intentions.[228]

V GENERAL TERMS AND CONDITIONS

250 General terms and conditions (GTCs) are a set of terms that have been preformulated for use in a multitude of contractual relationships with different contracting parties. They may have been drafted by one of the parties or by a third party (e.g., a lease contract drafted by the association of homeowners). A party using GTCs aims to standardise a large number of contracts both with regard to the conclusion of the contract and its execution. Often, the party using GTCs is in a superior bargaining position to its counterparties who are left with the choice to either agree to the GTCs or not conclude the contract at all.

---

226. Decision of the Swiss Federal Supreme Court dated 21 March 1996, DSC 122 III 97, para. 3.a.
227. Decision of the Swiss Federal Supreme Court dated 24 April 2001, DSC 127 III 300, para. 6.b.
228. *See* hereinabove para. 227.

251 Specific clauses will not, however, be considered to form part of GTCs if they have been individually negotiated between the parties. In order to be considered individually negotiated, the terms must have been the subject of serious negotiations.[229]

A Incorporation of General Terms and Conditions

252 GTCs are only binding upon the parties if they have been incorporated into the contract. Incorporation may occur by directly including GTCs in a contract or by referring to the GTCs in the main contract (e.g., by including a clause stating that the general terms and conditions as per the website of the seller apply).

253 An incorporation of GTCs requires that the party agreeing to the GTCs is able to reasonably determine their content before concluding the contract. The party must therefore have had reasonable access to the GTCs. Such access is ensured if the GTCs are handed over to the agreeing party before conclusion of the contract (also a link to GTCs available online is generally sufficient). Making the GTCs available only after conclusion of the contract (e.g., by attaching them to the order confirmation) constitutes an offer to amend the concluded contract which requires (explicit or implicit) acceptance from the counterparty for the GTCs to become part of the contractual terms.

254 Incorporation of GTCs does, however, not require that the agreeing party has actually read and reviewed the GTCs. If the agreeing party has accepted the GTCs without having read or understood their content, it is a case of a so-called global adoption (*Globalübernahme, intégration globale, ripresa globale*). GTCs are deemed to have been globally adopted if, according to general experience, a weak or inexperienced party does not read them, does not take note of them or does not understand their implications.[230] While globally adopted GTCs are generally considered to form part of the contract, they are subject to the unusualness rule (*Ungewöhnlichkeitsregel, règle de l'insolite, regola dell'insolito*).[231]

255 Particular problems arise where both parties attempt to base the contract on their respective GTCs (so-called battle of the forms). According to a previously prevailing view, in such situations, the GTCs of the party that sent the GTCs last should be binding (referred to as the 'theory of the last word' or 'last shot rule'). The more recent doctrine, however, largely rejects this theory. It argues that a court should review both parties' GTCs and apply those rules that are identical in substance. Where the GTCs provide for differing rules on a specific matter, there is a (partial) disagreement, so that neither party is able to rely on its GTCs ('knock-out rule'). The lacuna in the contract created by the partial disagreement is to be supplemented by the court according to Article 2(2)

229. *See* Ehle/Moss, Changes to the Swiss law on general terms and conditions: what do construction practitioners need to know?, Construction Law International, June 2013, pp. 19 et seq.
230. Decision of the Swiss Federal Supreme Court dated 15 December 2003, no. 4C.282/2003, para. 3.1.
231. *See* below para. 259.

CO which usually leads to the application of the non-mandatory provisions of the Code of Obligations.[232]

B Interpretation of General Terms and Conditions

256 In case law, special rules as to the interpretation of GTCs have evolved. In particular:

257 *Priority of individually negotiated provisions*: Individually negotiated provisions in a contract have priority over conflicting provisions in GTCs.[233] Thus, provisions in GTCs are deemed the fall-back solution if the individually negotiated part of a contract remains silent on an issue.

258 *Ambiguity rule*: If the interpretation of a provision in GTCs does not yield a definite result, the ambiguity rule applies. The rule is deduced from the general principle *in dubio contra stipulatorem*. Accordingly, the interpretation favouring the non-drafting party has priority.[234]

C Illegal or Unenforceable Content of General Terms of Conditions

259 Although correctly incorporated into a contract, GTCs (or individual provisions of GTCs) may be deemed unlawful due to their content. The legal basis for such intervention in the contractual content is the 'unusualness rule' (*Ungewöhnlichkeitsregel, règle de l'insolite, regola dell'insolito*), which applies only to globally adopted GTCs,[235] or Article 8 of the Federal Act on Unfair Competition, which applies only to *b2c*-contracts.

260 According to the unusualness rule, unusual or surprising GTC clauses which are not specifically brought to the attention of a weaker or less sophisticated party are not enforceable.[236] Both a subjective and objective test apply when determining whether or

232. *See* hereinabove paras 240 et seqq.
233. Decision of the Swiss Federal Supreme Court dated 14 April 2016, no. 4A_512/2005, para. 3.1: 'However, if the contracting parties make an expression of intent that deviates from the GTC, this can reasonably only be interpreted by them in such a way that this concrete declaration takes precedence over the abstract GTC.'
234. Decision of the Swiss Federal Supreme Court dated 12 July 2015, no. 5C.271/2004: para. 2: 'In the case of GTCs, the ambiguity rule applies if the other means of interpretation fail. According to this rule, ambiguous terms in GTCs are, in case of doubt, to be interpreted to the detriment of the party who drafted them.'
235. *See* above para. 253.
236. Decision of the Swiss Federal Supreme Court dated 12 July 2015, no. 5C.271/2004: para. 2: 'The validity of pre-formulated contractual provisions is finally limited by the unusualness rule, according to which all unusual clauses are excluded from the globally declared consent to general terms and conditions, the existence of which has not been separately pointed out to the weaker or less business-savvy party.' Also *see*, Decision of the Swiss Federal Supreme Court dated 28 October 2008, DSC 135 III 1, para. 2.1: 'The validity of pre-formulated general terms and conditions is limited by the unusualness rule. According to this rule, all unusual clauses are

not a clause is unusual or surprising. Subjectively, it must be inconsistent with what the agreeing party could reasonably expect. Objectively, its content must be alien to the type of contract in question.[237]

261 Under Article 8 of the Federal Act on Unfair Competition, a provision in GTCs is considered unlawful and unenforceable if it creates a considerable and unjustifiable imbalance between contractual rights and obligations to the disadvantage of consumers. This provision provides courts with a wide discretion to interfere with overly one-sided GTCs in consumer contracts.

VI CONDITIONAL OBLIGATIONS

262 An obligation is conditional if, according to the parties' intention, its enforceability depends on a fact whose (non-) occurrence is objectively uncertain. The debtor's obligation is still uncertain in principle and not merely with regard to the time of performance.[238]

263 The Code of Obligations distinguishes between two types of conditions: the condition precedent and the condition subsequent. The former makes a contract's binding nature dependent on the occurrence of an event that is not certain to happen (Article 151 CO). The latter makes a contract's termination dependent on the occurrence of an event that is not certain to happen; the contract lapses as soon as that condition is fulfilled (Article 154 CO).

excluded from the globally declared consent to general terms and conditions, the existence of which has not been separately pointed out to the weaker or less business experienced party. According to the principle of trust, the author of general terms and conditions must assume that an inexperienced contractual partner will not agree to unusual clauses. The unusualness is assessed from the point of view of the consenting party at the time of the conclusion of the contract. The assessment is made in relation to the individual case. The clause in question must lead to a substantial change in the character of the contract or fall outside the legal framework of the type of contract to a considerable extent. The more a clause impairs the legal position of the contractual partner, the more it is to be qualified as unusual.'

237. Decision of the Swiss Federal Supreme Court dated 11 December 2000, DSC 5C.220/2000, para. 2.a: 'Unusualness is assessed from the point of view of the consenting party at the time the contract is concluded. The assessment is made on a case-by-case basis; even a clause that is customary in the industry can be unusual for someone from outside the industry. In accordance with the principle of trust, the personal ideas of the policyholder are decisive to the extent that they are recognizable to the insurer; it is not sufficient that the policyholder is inexperienced in the industry. In addition to the subjective requirement, the clause in question must also have an objectively judged content that is foreign to the business, i.e., it must lead to a significant change in the character of the contract and fall outside the legal framework of the type of contract to a considerable extent. The more a clause impairs the legal position of the policyholder, the more it may be described as unusual.'

238. Decision of the Swiss Federal Supreme Court dated 5 December 1995, DSC 122 III 10, para. 4.b.

A Permissibility of Conditions

264 Legal transactions can generally be made dependent on the occurrence of a condition.

265 However, if a condition is attached with the intention of encouraging an unlawful or immoral act or omission, the conditional claim is void (Article 157 CO). This provision complements Articles 19 and 20 CO which render a contract void due to the illegal obligations contained in it. Article 157 CO addresses the situation where the obligations itself is not illegal, but the condition attached to it. It is the condition that encourages illegal behaviour and as such makes the contract's purpose illegal.

266 The notion of 'unlawful or immoral act' is to be interpreted in the same way as for Articles 19 and 20 CO.[239] Despite the misleading wording of Article 157 CO, pursuant to which only the conditional claim becomes void, the same legal consequences as under Articles 19 and 20 CO apply. Thus, an unlawful or immoral condition renders the entire contract void, unless Article 20(2) applies.[240]

267 Further, exercising a formative right (e.g., notice of termination) may generally not be made contingent upon the occurrence of a condition.[241] In such a case, the exercising of the right is deemed without effect. Exceptionally, a condition is permissible if the uncertainty created by the condition is deemed acceptable for the other party. This is the case if the occurrence of the condition depends on the receiving parties' will (e.g., termination of contract, unless the receiving party accepts a particular amendment of the contract).

B Legal Situation Before Occurrence of Condition

268 The legal situation before occurrence of a condition differs depending on the type of the condition in question – precedent or subsequent.

269 Before realisation of a condition precedent the legal transaction is in a limbo state. Only upon occurrence of the condition, the contract enters into effect and the legal obligations contained in the contract arise (Article 151(2) CO). However, the Code of Obligations contains some provisions governing the parties' duties during the limbo

239. *See* above paras 231 et seqq.
240. *See* above para. 230.
241. Decision of the Swiss Federal Supreme Court dated 30 October 2001, DSC 128 III 70, para. 2: 'By exercising such formative right, a legal relationship is terminated without the consent of the other party being required. The unilateral creative power of the beneficiary corresponds to a commitment on the part of the party opposing the declaration to accept this creation and the intrusion into its own legal sphere that it entails and to accept it as valid against itself. Since the beneficiary is granted unilateral creative power by the formative right, safeguards must be provided in the interest of the other party so that the encroachment on the latter's legal sphere is manageable and limited to the necessary extent. From this need for protection of the other party, its interest in a clear situation, follows the principle that the exercise of formative rights is irrevocable and may not be made subject to conditions.'

state, i.e., for the interim between conclusion of the contract and the realisation of the condition (Articles 152 et seq. CO). Notably, the debtor must refrain from any act which might prevent the due performance of his conditional obligation.

270 With a condition subsequent, the legal transaction enters into effect immediately. Until occurrence of the condition, the contract has the same effects as if it were concluded without any conditions. However, until non-occurrence of the condition subsequent is certain, the parties must abstain from any acts that would prevent them from fulfilling their duty of restitution that arises if the condition subsequent occurs (Article 152(3) CO, *ad analogiam*).[242]

C Legal Situation after Occurrence of Condition

271 With occurrence of the condition the limbo state ends. Upon realization of the condition precedent, the legal obligations contained in the contract arise (Article 151(2) CO). Unless the parties have agreed otherwise, the obligations arise at the point in time of occurrence of the condition (*ex nunc*) and there is no retroactive effect (Article 151(3) CO).[243]

272 If a condition subsequent occurs, the contract in question lapses (Article 154(1) CO). This effect arises *ipso iure*, i.e., regardless of the parties' knowledge of the condition subsequent's occurrence and without further ado. Same as for conditions precedent, the occurrence of a condition subsequent does not have retroactive effect, unless (explicitly or impliedly) agreed otherwise (Article 154(2) CO). This means that for the time until occurrence of the condition subsequent, the contract in question is considered valid and binding. After occurrence of the condition subsequent, any benefits obtained under contract must be returned. The claims for return are considered contractual in nature - and not based on unjust enrichment (Articles 62 et seqq. CO).

D Legal Situation If Occurrence of Condition Becomes Impossible or Is Prevented in Bad Faith

273 If the occurrence of the condition precedent has become impossible after conclusion of the contract, the legal transaction in question is without effect. Generally, no obligations arise. If goods have already been transferred despite the condition precedent, they must be returned (Article 153 CO).

242. Schwenzer/Fountoulakis, Schweizerisches Obligationenrecht - Allgemeiner Teil, Bern 2020, N 12.06.
243. But *see* Article 153 CO regarding the benefits obtained from goods transferred before occurrence of the condition.

274 If a condition subsequent becomes impossible, the legal transaction remains unaffected. The restraints put on the parties by Article 152(3) CO simply cease to exist.[244]

275 Where one of the parties has prevented the occurrence of a condition (or made its occurrence impossible) by acting in bad faith, the condition is deemed occurred for purposes of the contract in question (Article 156 CO). It is not necessary for the infringing party to act with the specific intention of preventing the occurrence of the condition; it suffices that it violates the rules of good faith and due to this violation (link of causality) the condition does not occur.[245] The rule of Article 156 CO also applies if the condition in question consists of a party making a specific expression of intent (so-called potestative condition, *Potestativbedingung, condition potestative, condizione potestativa*).[246]

---

244. *See* above para. 256.
245. Decision of the Swiss Federal Supreme Court dated 1 March 1983, DSC 109 II 20, para. 2.b.: 'The opinion has sometimes been expressed in doctrine that the rule in article 156 CO would only be effective if the person concerned had acted intentionally with the aim of preventing the condition precedent from coming into effect or of provoking the occurrence of the condition subsequent. This opinion cannot be followed. The legal text does not contain such a requirement. Although it provides that the party must have "prevented the occurrence (of the condition) in disregard of the rules of good faith", the past participle "prevented" ("*verhindert*") refers to causality, not intention; as for the conduct "in disregard of the rules of good faith", it does not presuppose intention either. In support of his argument, the appellant invokes the marginal note of the French text "*empêchement frauduleux*". This element alone is not decisive, because the non-technical term "fraud" is used both to designate intentional deception and, sometimes, to designate offences that can also be committed through negligence.'
246. Decision of the Swiss Federal Supreme Court dated 13 June 1991, DSC 117 II 273, para. 5.c: 'The freedom of action of the conditionally obligated party is, however, limited by the principle of good faith. According to this, a condition is also deemed to have occurred if its occurrence has been prevented contrary to good faith by a contracting party – namely the party to whose disadvantage the occurrence of the condition would be (article 156 CO). Contrary to a view expressed in the literature, the provision also applies in the area of potestative conditions. Whether conduct in this sense is contrary to good faith is usually determined by an interpretation of the legal transaction in question based on the principle of trust. In this context, the overall conduct must be assessed, taking into account all the circumstances of the individual case; the conduct appears to be in breach of trust, in particular, if it is directed against the nature of the legal transaction. According to case law, it is not necessary that the conduct preventing the occurrence of the condition is intentional; it is sufficient if it violates the principle of trust; however, it must always be considered unfair.' Also *see* decision of the Swiss Federal Supreme Court dated 16 July 2007, DSC 133 III 527, para. 3.3: 'In order to determine whether a certain conduct violates the rules of good faith, it must be assessed taking into account all the circumstances of the individual case, in particular the motives and the purpose pursued; one must be careful not to interpret Art. 156 CO too broadly, because by agreeing to a condition, the parties have introduced an element of uncertainty into their relationship which they must assume; they are not obliged to favour the occurrence of the condition, and good faith does not require that they sacrifice their own interests for this purpose.'

CHAPTER 4

Performance of Contractual Obligations

276 Once it is established that a contract has been concluded (Chapter 2) and therefrom ensuing obligations have been determined (Chapter 3), one must assess how the obligations are to be performed. By proper performance, the obligation will cease to exist (Article 114 CO).

277 The Swiss Code of Obligations contains specific provisions on how (i.e., by whom, when and where) an obligation is to be performed (section I). In addition, it sets forth certain particularities that apply to money obligations (section II). Further, the scenarios of multiple creditors or debtors (section III) and the role of third parties (section IV) will be addressed. Finally, performance might be hindered in that it proves impossible or the creditor fails to carry out the necessary preparations for the debtor to perform the obligation (section V).

I MODALITIES OF PERFORMANCE

278 The Swiss Code of Obligations contains general rules on who needs to perform a specific obligation when and where to the benefit of whom. These rules are generally not mandatory and may be deviated from by the parties.

A Person Performing the Obligation

279 Pursuant to Article 68 CO, the debtor is generally not obliged to perform the obligation personally. He is free to delegate performance to a third party. A duty to personally perform an obligation may arise from the parties' agreement or the circumstances.

280 A personal duty of performance arises from the circumstances where the individual (physical, professional, mental, moral) characteristics of the debtor are of such importance that the obligation could not be equally performed by a third person. For a company, the performance-relevant characteristics of the company (experience, know-how, employees' level of training, patents and licenses) must be taken into account.

281 For certain types of contracts, the Code of Obligations contains a presumption that circumstances warranting a duty of personal performance exist. Unless the parties have agreed to the contrary, the debtor incurs a duty to personally perform the obligation when agreeing to such a contract. Examples of such presumption are the employee's obligation to render his services (Article 321 CO), the contractor's obligation to carry out the work under a contract for work (Article 364 CO) or the mandatee's duty to carry out his services as per the mandate agreement (Article 398 CO).

282 Importantly, even if a duty of personal performance exists, the debtor is entitled to rely on the support of third parties.[247] He is considered performing personally, as long as the material emphasis lies on his contribution, not the assistance of the third parties.

B Recipient of Performance

283 Generally, an obligation must be performed to the benefit of the creditor. Under certain circumstances, the debtor must or may perform to the benefit of a third party.

284 The contract may stipulate that the debtor has the right or the duty to perform to the benefit of a third party.[248] Such duty may also arise from the law, although this is rarely the case.[249]

285 Even if not expressly stipulated in the contract, a creditor is entitled to request the debtor to perform to the benefit of a third party (e.g., issue payment to the third party's bank account). Such right is provided by Articles 466 et seqq. CO (payment instruction). The debtor must comply with the payment instruction, provided that in doing so his own position is in no way prejudiced.[250]

C Object of Performance

286 The contract determines the object of performance. Performance is directed by the content of the obligation as per the contract.

287 At times, the contract is, however, silent on certain aspects pertaining to the content of an obligation. For such cases, Articles 71 et seqq. CO set forth certain

247. But *see* below para. 415 regarding the debtor's vicarious liability for any act of such third party.
248. *See, e.g.*, Article 112 CO.
249. *See, e.g.*, Article 99 Federal Act on Debt Enforcement and Bankruptcy (if the obligation in question forms the object of an attachment or seizure). For further examples *see* Gauch/Schluep/Emmenegger, Schweizerisches Obligationenrecht, Zurich 2020, N 2083.
250. Article 468(2) CO.

assumptions.[251] First, if the object is defined only in generic terms (so-called generic obligation, *Gattungsschuld, dette d'une chose de genre, debito riguardante uno cosa generica*),[252] the debtor may choose what specific object is given, but must not offer an object of less-than-average quality.[253] Second, if a contract permits an obligation to be discharged by one of several alternative types of performance, the debtor may choose which performance to make.[254] Third, if an obligation involves the payment of interest but the rate is not set by contract, law or custom, interest is payable at a rate of 5 % per annum.[255]

288 The debtor must perform the obligation in full. The creditor is not obliged to accept several partial performances unless agreed otherwise (explicitly or implicitly) in the contract.[256] Statutory law stipulates some exceptions to this general rule among others in the areas of succession and debt enforcement law.[257] Further, the Swiss Federal Supreme Court requires a creditor to accept a partial performance where the principle of good faith dictates so.[258]

289 While the Code of Obligations provides the debtor with no right to discharge a contractual obligation by providing a service other than the one owed under the contract, the creditor may authorise the debtor to render such alternative service (so-called performance surrogate). Such authorisation can take the form of a modification of the contractual terms or a one-sided declaration that the creditor would accept the alternative service in place of the owed service.

D Place of Performance

290 The place of performance determines where the debtor must fulfil the act of performance. Performance provided at the wrong place does not discharge the obligation and the debtor may be deemed in default.

---

251. The assumption is taken to correspond to the parties' will, unless the opposite is proven.
252. For example, obligation to deliver twenty apples. *See* Decision of the Swiss Federal Supreme Court dated 5 December 1995, DSC 121 III 453, para. 4.a: 'In the case of a generic purchase, on the other hand, only an item of a certain type is owed, which is why a delivered item in this type of purchase only corresponds to the purchased item if it has the agreed generic characteristics (article 71(1) CO). Therefore, the question arises as to which concept of *genus* is decisive. The Swiss Federal Supreme Court initially assumed an abstract, objective concept of *genus*, which corresponds to the essence of the object, then restricted this to the extent that it took into account the market perception and the intended use agreed in the individual case and finally switched to a relative generic concept, which is based on the concrete description of the object of purchase by the parties.'
253. Article 71 CO.
254. Article 72 CO.
255. Article 73 CO.
256. Article 69 CO, which applies also to non-monetary obligations.
257. *See* Schroeter, commentary on Article 69, in: Basler Kommentar, OR I, N 8.
258. Decision of the Swiss Federal Supreme Court dated 29 March 1949, DSC 75 II 137, para. 4.d: 'Furthermore, a deviation may be required by the nature of the matter, for example if a service has to be divided due to its extraordinary scope. Finally, good faith sometimes dictates the acceptance of a partial performance, for example, if this only shows a minor difference to the total performance and this difference is insignificant for the creditor.'

291 The place of performance depends upon the parties' express or implied agreement. If no such agreement exists, the Code of Obligations contains several fallback rules for determining the place of performance.

292 The most relevant rule as to the place of performance is to be found in Article 74 CO. This provision distinguishes between three types of obligations:

- obligations to make a payment must be fulfilled at the place where the creditor is domiciled at the time of performance;
- obligation to deliver a specific (non-generic) good must be fulfilled at the place where the good was located at the time of conclusion of contract; and
- all other obligations must be fulfilled at the place where the debtor was domiciled when entering into the contract.

E Time and Order of Performance

293 In regard to the time of performance, the Code of Obligations distinguishes between the point in time as of when the debtor may discharge the obligation and the point in time as of when the creditor may call in the obligation. If the former point in time has arrived, the debtor is entitled to execute performance and the creditor is obliged to accept performance. The latter point in time constitutes the due date. Upon the due date, the creditor is entitled to request performance.

294 Article 75 CO sets forth the general rule regarding both points in time: 'Where no time of performance is stated in the contract or evident from the nature of the legal relationship, the obligation may be discharged or called in immediately.' For some contracts, the Code of Obligations deviates from this general rule. For example, in a sales contract, a seller may only call in the purchase price after having transferred the goods to the buyer.[259]

295 The parties are free to deviate from these rules in their contract. When parties agree on a specific date or duration concerning the performance of a contractual obligation, the Code of Obligations stipulates some rules as to how such terms must be interpreted.[260] In particular, Article 81 CO provides that although the parties have defined a specific due date, the debtor is generally entitled to perform at an earlier point in time, unless agreed otherwise.[261]

296 As to the order of performance, the Code of Obligations generally sets forth that the parties must fulfil their obligations at the same time. A party may not demand performance until he has discharged or offered to discharge his own obligation (Article

259. Article 213(1) CO. Also *see* Article 318 CO regarding repayment of a loan. Importantly, parties are free to deviate from these non-mandatory rules of the Code of Obligations.
260. Articles 76–78 CO.
261. Article 81 CO.

82 CO).[262] Of course, the parties are free to deviate from this rule and agree otherwise. Often, the nature and circumstances of the contract lead to the conclusion that the parties have implicitly deviated from the rule of Article 82 CO. Further, the special part of the Code of Obligations foresees advance performance by a party for certain contract types.[263]

II PARTICULARITIES OF PERFORMING MONETARY OBLIGATIONS

297 Monetary obligations require the debtor to pay a certain sum of money to the creditor. This kind of obligation brings with it several issues which the Code of Obligations addresses.

A Currency of Payment

298 Pursuant to Article 84(1) CO, monetary debts must be discharged in legal tender of the currency in which the debt was incurred. As a result, the debtor must pay in the currency in which the contract denominates the debt.

299 However, Article 84(2) CO provides the debtor with the right to discharge a monetary debt in another currency if the agreed currency is not the national currency of the place of payment.[264] In such case, the debtor may pay in the national currency of the place of payment at the rate of exchange that applies on the day the debt falls due. The parties may, however, exclude the application of Article 84(2) CO by stipulating that payment may only be made in a specific currency.

300 While the debtor might be entitled to perform in another currency than contractually agreed, the creditor may not request performance in that other national currency. The creditor is limited to demanding payment in the contractual currency. If a creditor sues for payment in the wrong currency, a court must reject such a claim.[265]

262. Also *see*, herein below para. 356.
263. *See*, *e.g.*, Article 213(1) CO.
264. Article 74(2) CO defines the place of payment as the domicile of the creditor at the time of performance, *see* hereinabove para. 280.
265. Decision of the Swiss Federal Supreme Court dated 1 October 2015, no. 4A_391/2015, para. 3: 'In the case of foreign currency debts [i.e., monetary debt in a currency other than the national currency of the place of performance], the creditor is indeed required to accept payment in Swiss francs; however, the entitlement to performance in the national currency (article 84(2) CO) applies only to the debtor, not to the creditor. His claim is exclusively for payment in foreign currency, and according to article 84(1) CO he can only demand performance in the agreed foreign currency. Accordingly, the court may only award payment in the foreign currency owed.'

B Duty to Pay Interests

301 A duty to pay interest may arise by agreement (e.g., loan interest) or by law. The latter's most prominent examples are the duty to pay default interest[266] and the duty to pay interest on damages.

302 Where the parties agreed on a duty to pay interest but have failed to stipulate the interest rate and no interest rate may be deduced from custom, the Code of Obligations sets forth an interest rate of 5% per annum.[267] The same rate applies to default interests.[268]

303 The parties' freedom to define the interest rate is not limitless. Public law may impose restrictions.[269] For example, for consumer credits, the maximum interest rate is set at 10%.[270] The prohibition of profiteering[271] and immorality[272] sets further boundaries. Although there is no specific numerical limit to be found in case law, courts generally accept interest rates of 12.5% and lower.[273]

C Allocation of Payments

304 If the debtor has more than one monetary obligation towards a creditor (e.g., payment of interests and of main debt), the question arises which obligation a debtor performs with a specific payment. The Code of Obligations addresses this in Articles 85–87 CO. These rules are non-mandatory, and the parties may deviate from them.

305 Generally, the debtor may indicate which debt he wishes to discharge with a specific payment.[274] However, he may not allocate a payment to his main debt if he is in default with interest payments. First, the interest payments must be discharged in full, before a payment may be allocated to the main debt.[275] Further, if the creditor has received securities for certain debts (e.g., a guarantee from a third party), the debtor must first pay the unsecured debts.[276]

306 If the debtor makes no indication as to which debt he wishes to discharge with a specific payment, the creditor may make such indication in his stead. He must

266. Article 104(1) CO.
267. Article 73(1) CO.
268. Article 104(1) CO: 'A debtor in default on payment of a pecuniary debt must pay default interest of 5% per annum even where a lower rate of interest was stipulated by contract.'
269. Article 73(2) CO.
270. Article 14 of the Federal Act on Consumer Credits in combination with Ordinance of the Federal Department of Justice and Police on Maximum Interest Rate for Consumer Credits dated 22 November 2021.
271. Article 157 of the Criminal Code.
272. Article 20(1) CO.
273. *See* Schroeter, commentary on Article 84 CO, in: Basler Kommentar, OR I, N 18.
274. Article 86(1) CO.
275. Article 85(1) CO.
276. Article 85(2) CO.

communicate such indication to the debtor when confirming receipt of the money.[277] The debtor may then object to the creditor's indication, whereupon the allocation is determined in accordance with Article 87 CO.

307 In the absence of any indication, allocation is made in accordance with Article 87 CO. Said provision instals an order of allocation: Payment is allocated to whichever debt is due or, if several are due, to the debt that first gave rise to enforcement proceedings against the debtor or, in the absence of such proceedings, to the debt that fell due first.[278] If several debts fall due at the same time, the payment is allocated to them proportionately.[279]

III MULTIPLE CREDITORS AND/OR DEBTORS

A Multiple Debtors

308 With a multitude of debtors, a distinction must be made whether the creditor may only request partial performance from each debtor (each debtor only being liable for his share) or whether he may request full performance of the entire obligation from any one of the debtors (joint and several liability; *Solidarschuld, solidarité passive, debito solidale*).

309 As a general rule, debtors are only jointly and severally liable if they state so or if prescribed by law.[280,281] Joint and several liability may therefore be expressly or tacitly agreed on or may result from the circumstances.[282] It may be established either by joint conclusion of a contract or by the subsequent accession of new debtors to an already existing obligation. Further, the law prescribes joint and several liability in numerous instances.[283]

310 With regard to the legal consequences of joint and severable liability, the Code of Obligations distinguishes the external relationship between the debtors and the creditor (Articles 144–147 CO) from the internal relationship between the debtors (Articles 148–149 CO). These provisions are non-mandatory.

---

277. Contrary to the wording of Article 86(2) CO, the indication must not necessarily be made in the receipt, but may be communicated separately (Schroeter, commentary on Article 84 CO, in: Basler Kommentar, OR I, N 15).
278. Article 87(1) CO.
279. Article 87(2) CO.
280. *See, e.g.*, Article 403(1) CO.
281. Article 143 CO.
282. Decision of the Swiss Federal Supreme Court dated 14 February 2011, DSC 4A_599/2010, para. 3.2: 'In the case of several debtors, joint and several liability is not presumed. Joint and several liability requires that the joint and several debtors make a declaration to this effect to the creditor (article 143(1) CO). The will to commit oneself jointly and severally can be expressed by conclusive acts, when it results from the context and the particular content of the contract. These circumstances are interpreted according to the principle of trust. The conclusion of a contract by several parties is not sufficient to create a joint and several obligation between the debtors.'
283. *See, e.g.*, Articles 50, 181 and 308 CO.

311 The creditor is entitled at his discretion to demand performance of the entire obligation (or, at his discretion, only part of it) from each jointly and severally liable debtor.[284] If one joint and several debtor satisfies the creditor by payment or set-off, the others are also discharged to that extent.[285] However, where one joint and several debtor is released from liability without the satisfaction of the creditor, such release does not benefit the others save to the extent justified by the circumstances or the nature of the obligation.[286]

312 The internal relationship between the debtors is governed by the general rule that each of them assumes an equal share of the payment made to the creditor unless agreed otherwise.[287] The debtor who has made full payment to the creditor is entitled to recover the amount that he has paid in excess of his share from the other debtors.[288]

B Multiple Creditors

313 At times, an obligation must be performed to the benefit of several creditors. There are three types of multiple creditors.

314 Pro rata creditors (*Teilgläubigerschaft, créanciers partiels, creditori parziari*) are entitled to the same claim, but in such a way that each of them is only entitled to claim a share of the total payment from the debtor. Each creditor must act individually against the debtor. Pro rata creditorship is the fallback rule for contractual obligations.[289]

315 If there is a community of creditors (*Gläubigergemeinschaft, créanciers collectifs, creditori collettivi*), the creditors are entitled to the entire claim undivided in such a way that all creditors can only assert the claim jointly.[290] Conversely, the debtor cannot discharge his obligation by paying an individual creditor, but only by paying all creditors jointly. A community of creditors only arises if there is a joint ownership relationship between the creditors (e.g., community of heirs[291]).

316 Multiple creditors become joint and several creditors (*Solidargläubigerschaft, créanciers solidaires, credito solidale*) in the cases prescribed by law[292] and where the debtor states that he wishes to grant each of them the right to receive full performance of the debt.[293] The debtor may choose which creditor to satisfy. Performance to one creditor discharges the debtor against all creditors.

284. Article 144(1) CO.
285. Article 147(1) CO.
286. Article 147(2) CO.
287. Article 148(1) CO.
288. Articles 148(2–3) and 149 CO. However, *see* Article 145(2) CO regarding a debtor's liability towards the other debtors for failure to raise an objection against the obligation.
289. Decision of the Swiss Federal Supreme Court dated 3 March 2014, DSC 140 III 150, para. 2.2.3.
290. Decision of the Swiss Federal Supreme Court dated 3 March 2014, DSC 140 III 150, para. 2.2.2.
291. Article 602(2) of the Swiss Civil Code.
292. *See, e.g.*, Article 399(3) CO.
293. Article 150 CO.

317 The Code of Obligations is silent on the relationship between the creditors. The internal relationship and in particular the question of possible recourse among the joint and several creditors is therefore governed exclusively by the agreement in question. In general, the legal relationship between the joint and several creditors is likely to result in an entitlement to equal shares analogous to Article 148(1) CO.

IV ROLE OF THIRD PARTIES IN THE PERFORMANCE OF CONTRACTUAL OBLIGATIONS

318 Third parties can play a role in contractual relationships in several ways. They may support a party in performing its contractual obligations, or even perform such obligations in the debtor's stead (section A). Further, they may be liable for non-performance of an obligation by a contract party (section B). Finally, they may also be the beneficiary (section C) or at least the recipient of the contractual performance (section D).

A Third Parties Performing Contractual Obligations

319 Generally, a party is not required to perform an obligation personally.[294] It may delegate performance to a third party. The third party essentially operates as a subcontractor of the obliged contractual party. As such, the third party does not become a party to the original contract.

320 However, it is possible that a third party fulfils a contractual obligation in its own name. This is addressed by Article 110 CO, which provides that a third party who satisfies the creditor is by operation of law subrogated to his right if the debtor notifies the creditor that the third party is to take the creditor's place. The most prominent example of this is a third party paying a monetary debt instead of the contractually obliged party.

B Guarantee of Performance by a Third Party

321 In some instances, it is clear from the outset that the contracting party will not carry out performance of the obligation itself, but rather guarantee proper performance by a specified third party. In this scenario, the obliged party (the guarantor) guarantees a third party's performance in the contract. Often, there exists a separate contract between the beneficiary of the guarantee and the third party whose performance is secured by the guarantee.

322 Article 111 CO sets forth that in such case, the guarantor is liable for damages if the third party fails to adequately perform the specified obligation. However, the

294. *See* hereinabove para. 267.

guarantor must not himself perform the obligation forming the object of the guarantee. The remedy, unless agreed otherwise, is limited to damages.

323 The guarantee in the sense of Article 111 CO is closely related to the surety in the sense of Article 492 CO. In many cases, it is not clear whether the undertaking to compensate for a third party's default is to be qualified as a guarantee or rather a surety. While the Swiss Federal Supreme Court has developed certain criteria for distinguishing between the two, their application by the courts is not uniform.[295] The qualification is, however, of practical importance, as the conclusion of a surety must observe certain form requirements, without which the undertaking is invalid and thus unenforceable.

C Contracts in Favour of a Third Party

324 Article 112 CO addresses the scenario in which the debtor promises the creditor to perform to the benefit of an identified third party. The Code of Obligations differentiates between a real and an unreal contract in favour of a third party. The former entitles the third party to sue for performance,[296] while the latter merely empowers the third party to receive performance, but only the contracting party may sue for performance.[297]

325 Whether a contract qualifies as a real or unreal contract in favour of a third party is determined in accordance with the parties' agreement and customary practice. At times, statutory law sets forth that a certain contract qualifies as a real contract in favour of a third party.[298]

D Unilateral Payment Instruction

326 Provided that the debtor's situation does not deteriorate as a result thereof, the creditor is entitled, even after the contract has been concluded, to demand performance to a third party by means of a unilateral instruction to the debtor (payment instruction; *Anweisung, assignation, assegno*).[299] A payment instruction to a third party's bank account does not typically deteriorate the debtor's position.

295. For a detailed analysis, *see* Emmenegger, Garantie, Schuldbeitritt und Bürgschaft – vom bundesgerichtlichen Umgang mit gesetzgeberischen Inkohärenzen, ZBJV 2009, pp. 561 et seqq.
296. Article 112(2) CO. The contracting party may also sue for performance, but only performance to the third party.
297. Article 112(1) CO.
298. *See, e.g.*, Article 113 CO.
299. Article 468(2) CO.

V HINDRANCES TO PERFORMANCE

327 There are generally two hindrances to performance that exclude the debtor's default: the impossibility of performance (section A) and creditor default (section B).

A Impossibility of Performance (Force Majeure)

328 The Swiss Code of Obligations does not explicitly regulate force majeure, nevertheless, this principle is recognised in case law and is subsumed under the doctrine of impossibility of performance.

329 Impossibility of performance excludes that the debtor is deemed in default. Impossibility exists if performance can no longer be effected at all (objective impossibility) or can no longer be effected by the particular debtor (subjective impossibility).[300] Importantly, payment of a sum of money is always deemed possible due to the general Swiss law principle of 'one has to have money' (*Geld hat man zu haben*). Further, impossibility is not assumed when performance has merely become more cumbersome for the debtor, but in extreme cases, the doctrine of *clausula rebus sic stantibus* may apply.[301]

330 Pursuant to Article 119 CO, an obligation is deemed extinguished where its performance is made impossible by circumstances not attributable to the obligor.[302] According to the case law of the Swiss Federal Supreme Court and prevailing doctrine, Article 119 CO applies to both objective and subjective impossibility.[303] If, in contrast, performance was objectively impossible from the start of the contractual relationship, the contract is considered void *ab initio*.[304]

331 The relevant circumstances are among others determined by Articles 97, 101 and 103 CO. Therefore, Article 119 CO does not apply if the impossibility is due to the

300. Decision of the Swiss Federal Supreme Court dated 15 January 2009, DSC 135 III 212, para. 3.1: 'A distinction must be made between objective and subjective impossibility. The former is given if no one is able to fulfil the claim; the latter is given if the fulfilment is possible in itself, but the debtor is unable to do so. Performance is subjectively impossible if, in good faith, the debtor can no longer reasonably be expected to perform. However, it is not sufficient that performance is merely considerably more difficult; rather, the obstacle to performance must prove to be virtually insurmountable for the debtor.'
301. *See* paras 232 et seqq. hereinabove.
302. In turn, the released debtor will have to give back anything received under the contract and lose any outstanding claims under the contract in question, unless the particular risk had already previously passed to the creditor (Article 119(2-3) CO).
303. Decision of the Swiss Federal Supreme Court dated 2 October 2012, no. 4A_ 189/2012: para. 5.2: 'The claim ceases to exist when performance has become impossible, regardless of whether it is a subjective or objective impossibility. However, a distinction must be made with regard to the effects: According to article 119 CO, the claim is considered extinguished only to the extent that the debtor is not responsible for the circumstances that led to the impossibility. Otherwise, the debt is not extinguished, but is transformed into a liability for damages according to article 97 CO.'
304. Article 20 CO. *See* hereinabove para. 231.

debtor's own fault,[305] the action of an associate of the debtor,[306] or an accident or force majeure event if at the time of occurrence of the accident or the force majeure event the debtor was already in default.[307]

332 In contrast, if the debtor was not in default at the time of occurrence of the force majeure event rendering performance impossible, he is generally considered released from his obligation under Article 119 CO.

333 Importantly, Article 119 CO does not form a mandatory legal provision. Thus, parties are free to deviate from it. The parties are free to contractually assign certain risks to each other.[308] If such risk occurs the circumstances of an impossibility are considered attributable to a party and thus the legal consequences of Article 119 CO do not apply. For certain contracts, the Code of Obligations foresees such risk attribution in its non-mandatory provisions.[309]

334 Equally, the parties may include a so-called force majeure clause in their contract defining which events constitute force majeure and what consequences are attached to a force majeure event. The meaning and content of such clauses are to be determined by interpreting the relevant contractual clauses in the context of the entire contractual relationship.

B Creditor Default

335 Often, the debtor is only able to perform properly if the creditor undertakes certain preparation and cooperates. For example, a builder can only construct a house if he is given access to the relevant plot of land.

336 These preparatory acts of cooperation are, however, in principle not contractual obligations, but merely non-actionable duties of the creditor (so-called incumbency; *Obliegenheit, incombance, incombenza*). Accordingly, a creditor's failure to perform such acts does not constitute a breach of contract, but he is considered to be in creditor default (*Gläubigerverzug, demeure du créancier, mora del creditore*).

337 Pursuant to Article 91 CO, the creditor is in default if he refuses without good cause to accept performance properly offered to him or to carry out such preparations as he is obliged to make and without which the debtor cannot render performance.

305. Article 97 CO.
306. Article 101 CO.
307. Article 103(1) CO. However, the debtor may free himself of any liability by proving that his default occurred through no fault of his own or that the object of performance would have suffered the accidental damage to the detriment of the creditor even if performance had taken place promptly (Article 103(2) CO).
308. Article 119(3) CO.
309. *See, e.g.*, Article 185(1) CO defining at which point in time the risk of damage to the goods passes from the seller to the buyer in a sales contract.

Creditor default has two main consequences attached to it: (i) it prevents the debtor from being deemed in default; and (ii) it gives the debtor the right to either sell or deposit the goods in question[310] or to withdraw from the contract.[311]

310. Articles 92 et seqq. CO.
311. Article 95 CO.

CHAPTER 5

Failure to Perform a Contractual Obligation (Breach of Contract)

I THE CONCEPT OF 'BREACH OF CONTRACT' IN SWISS CONTRACT LAW

338 In contrast to other legal systems, there is no general and uniform notion of 'breach of contract' in Swiss contract law. Rather, failure to perform a contractual obligation may take one of three forms under the Swiss Code of Obligations: (i) non-performance (section II); (ii) delayed performance (section III); or (iii) inadequate performance (section IV).

339 Dependent on the specific kind of performance failure, the Code of Obligations offers the creditor a range of remedies to select from (section V). Not only the remedy's availability but also the consequences attached to it may differ according to the type of performance failure.

340 There are generally two ways to defend against a 'breach of contract'-claim. *First*, the debtor may assert that there is no performance failure (i.e., that the conditions of non-performance, delayed performance or inadequate performance are not met in the case at stake). For example, it may demonstrate a valid hindrance to performance[312] or invoke a delay-specific defence.[313] *Second*, in some instances, the debtor will be able to successfully put forth a defence against the remedy chosen by the creditor, such as the defence of prescription (section VI).

341 Failure of performance and its legal consequences are covered by Articles 97–109 CO. These provisions are not mandatory, except for Articles 100 and 101(3) CO

312. *See* hereinabove paras 328 et seqq.
313. *See* herein below paras 356 et seqq.

(limitation of liability).[314] Thus, the parties are given large discretion to contractually modify the Code of Obligation's regime on failure of performance. They may extend or reduce a creditor's remedies in case of performance failure.

342 For certain contract types, the special part of the Code of Obligations contains additional (largely non-mandatory) provisions on failure of performance.[315] In principle, it is to be assumed that the rules of the special part take priority and apply exclusively.[316] However, there are exceptions to this general rule, for example, in the law of sales.[317]

II FIRST TYPE OF BREACH OF CONTRACT: NON-PERFORMANCE

343 Non-performance must be distinguished from default in performance. The latter relates to a debtor failing to perform, although performance would still be possible. The former refers to impossibility of performance. Impossibility exists if performance can no longer be effected at all (objective impossibility) or can no longer be effected by the particular debtor (subjective impossibility). Only in such cases, non-performance is considered permanent.

344 Three scenarios of impossibility must be distinguished:[318]

- Performance was objectively impossible from the start. In this case, the contract is considered void *ab initio*. The debtor might be liable based on *culpa in contrahendo* if he should have been aware of the impossibility.[319]
- The impossibility is not attributable to the debtor. If the impossibility is not attributable to the debtor, impossibility is not considered to constitute a failure of performance. Rather, such impossibility results in the debtor being released from the obligation in question.[320]

314. *See* herein below paras 419–421.
315. *See, e.g.*, Articles 197 et seqq. CO (sales contract; *see* below paras 573 et seqq.) and Articles 367 et seqq. CO (contract of work; *see* below paras 672 et seqq.).
316. Decision of the Swiss Federal Supreme Court dated 27 October 2014, no. 4A_387/2014, para. 4.2: 'The provisions of the contract for work concerning liability for defects contain a conclusive special provision; the customer may not invoke article 97 CO instead if it has not exercised the rights under the contract for work.'
317. Decision of the Swiss Federal Supreme Court dated 19 February 2007, DSC 133 III 335, para. 2.4.1: 'However, it grants the buyer the right to derive from a defect of the item not only warranty claims pursuant to articles 197 et seq. CO, but alternatively also claim for damages according to the general rule of liability for inadequate performance according to article 97(1) CO, whereby it restricts the alternative insofar as the buyer in both cases must comply with the duties of inspection and notification according to article 201 CO and observe the prescription period according to articles 210 and 219(3) CO respectively.'
318. *See* hereinabove paras 328 et seqq.
319. *See* hereinabove paras 192–194.
320. Article 119 CO. *See* hereinabove para. 330.

- The impossibility is attributable to the debtor. Only in this case, impossibility is considered a failure of performance in the sense of Articles 97 et seqq. CO.[321]

345 If impossibility is attributable to the debtor, the creditor is entitled to compensation for the damage caused by the non-performance.[322] Importantly, the debtor bears the burden of proving that impossibility is not attributable to him.[323]

346 The remedy of specific performance is not available if performance is proven to be impossible. The claim for damages replaces the original claim for specific performance. Equally, the Swiss Federal Supreme Court has denied the remedy of rescission for cases of impossibility.[324] However, this issue is discussed controversially in doctrine.[325]

III SECOND TYPE OF BREACH OF CONTRACT: DEFAULT IN PERFORMANCE

347 Delayed performance consists of improper performance in terms of time. Although an obligation is due[326] and performance is possible, the debtor has not yet performed the obligation in question. If additional requirements are met, the debtor is in default of his obligation. While occurrence of the debtor's default is independent of fault, its consequences differ depending on whether the debtor is responsible for the delay or not.

321. There is a minority in doctrine arguing that an obligation, which was from the start subjectively impossible for the debtor to perform, constitutes a case of debtor default (Articles 102 et seqq. CO; *see, e.g.*, Gauch/Schluep/Emmenegger, Schweizerisches Obligationenrecht, Zurich 2020, N 2575 et seqq.). The Swiss Federal Supreme Court did not follow this approach in older cases (when the minority opinion had not yet been expressed in doctrine), but did not yet have an opportunity to address this minority doctrine either (*see, e.g.*, decision of the Swiss Federal Supreme Court dated 10 July 1956, DSC 82 II 332, para. 5).
322. Article 97(1) CO. Regarding the remedy of damages *see* herein below paras 397 et seqq.
323. Wiegand, commentary on Article 119 CO, in: Basler Kommentar, OR I, N 20.
324. Decision of the Swiss Federal Supreme Court dated 9 March 2006, no. 1P.802/2005, para. 7.2: 'However, this rule concerning the debtor's contractual default only makes sense and is therefore only applied if the debtor's later performance is still possible. Conceptually, default can only exist if and as long as the owed performance is possible and can be made up for. If performance has subsequently become impossible, i.e., after the conclusion of the sales contract, article 107 CO does not apply, since neither the grace period for subsequent performance provided for in para. 1 nor the creditor's right of choice provided for in para. 2 could still effect performance. Even if in practice it may be difficult for the creditor of the non-performed service to recognize the impossibility of the service owed to him and to take the appropriate action, the debtor who knew of the impossibility of the service owed by him cannot claim that the creditor did not use the remedies provided for a debtor's default – which did not exist in the specific case – and did not make the corresponding declarations.'
325. Gauch/Schluep/Emmenegger, Schweizerisches Obligationenrecht, Zurich 2020, N 2587.
326. *See* hereinabove para. 296.

A Conditions of Debtor's Default

348 Debtor default is subject to four conditions:

- the obligation is due;
- the debtor fails to perform despite the possibility to do so;
- the creditor has issued a formal reminder (or is dispensed from doing so); and
- the debtor has no valid defence.

349 *First*, only a due obligation may trigger debtor's default. An obligation's due date depends on the parties' (implicit) agreement. Lacking any agreement between the parties, an obligation becomes due immediately upon arising.[327] That said, a creditor may postpone the due date of an obligation (even after it has already passed) by unilaterally providing the debtor with additional time or agreeing to a payment plan (so-called deferral; *Stundung, prorogation du délai, proroga*).[328]

350 *Second*, despite the obligation being due, the debtor has failed to perform although performance is still possible. If performance turns out to be impossible, the debtor is not considered in default. Rather, the consequences of non-performance and impossibility apply.[329]

351 If performance is generally possible, but hindered by the creditor, the creditor might be deemed in default.[330] Creditor default prevents the debtor from being deemed in default.[331]

352 *Third*, mere failure to perform a due obligation does, in principle, not automatically result in debtor's default. Rather, the debtor is only in default after receiving a formal reminder (*Mahnung, interpellation, interpellazione*) from the creditor.[332] A formal reminder is a declaration by the creditor addressed to the debtor, by which the creditor unambiguously – explicitly or implicitly – demands immediate performance of a due obligation.[333]

327. Article 75 CO. *See* hereinabove paras 294–295.
328. Decision of the Zurich High Court dated 31 August 2020, no. RT 200041, para. 6.1: 'Deferral means the postponement of the due date of a debt. The deferral is an expression of intent by the creditor, the issuance of which constitutes a fact, which must be proved by the debtor.'
329. *See* hereinabove paras 342–345.
330. *See* hereinabove paras 337 et seqq.
331. Decision of the Zurich Commercial Court dated 9 May 2019, no. HG160051, para. 4.2.5.
332. Article 102(1) CO.
333. Decision of the Swiss Federal Supreme Court dated 16 May 2003, DSC 129 III 535, para. 3.2.2: 'The formal reminder is a declaration of the creditor addressed to the debtor expressing that he demands performance without default. With the reminder, the performance to be rendered must be described so precisely that the debtor recognizes what the creditor wants to demand. If the claim is for money, the amount must usually be specified. However, it is not necessary to specify the amount in the reminder if, for example, reference is made to a previously delivered invoice indicating the amount of money. The doctrine is rightly of the opinion that a figure is not necessary if it is not possible at the time the claim is due because its exact amount has not yet been determined.'

353 However, where a deadline for performance of the obligation has been set by agreement (*Verfalltag, terme comminatoire, termine comminatorio*)[334] or results from a duly exercised right of termination, no formal reminder is required.[335] The debtor is automatically in default upon the expiry of the deadline. Equally, where the debtor declares in a definite and final manner his refusal to perform, a formal reminder is not needed.[336]

354 *Fourth*, the debtor lacks any defence against the default. Importantly, the debtor may not excuse a default by invoking a lack of fault or responsibility.[337] The debtor's default occurs regardless of whether he is at fault.[338]

355 Apart from general defences (such as prescription or set-off),[339] there are two specific defences that apply to debtor's default. They are suspensory defences (*dilatorische Einrede, exception dilatoire, eccezione sospensiva*) in the sense that they suspend any debtor's default for the time of their existence. Importantly, the debtor must invoke the defence (at least implicitly) for it to take effect.

356 Defence of non-performance (Article 82 CO; *Einrede des nichterfüllten Vertrags, exception d'inexécution, eccezione di macato adempimento del contratto*): A debtor may refuse performance for as long as the creditor has failed to counter-perform his own obligation unless the contract or the law[340] stipulates advance performance by the debtor.[341] Although Article 82 CO only addresses synallagmatic contracts, the Swiss Federal Supreme Court has extended the scope of the rule to non-synallagmatic

334. For example, a specific payment date set forth in the contract.
335. Article 102(2) CO.
336. Decision of the Swiss Federal Supreme Court dated 15 May 1984, DSC 110 II 141, para. 1.b: 'According to the case law, if the debtor announces before the due date that he will not perform (*see* article 102(2) CO), and if a reminder appears to be unnecessary from the outset, the contract can be terminated or dissolved by the creditor by analogous application of articles 107 CO et seqq. However, as in the case of article 108(1) CO, a reminder with a deadline can only be avoided if it would be pointless; this is the case if the debtor's refusal to perform appears to be clear and definite. However, the debtor's request for a grace period, his statement that he cannot perform at the moment, or his doubts as to the validity of the contract are not sufficient in themselves.'
337. However, a lack of fault and responsibility is relevant for determining the remedies available to the creditor; *see* below paras 362 et seqq.
338. Decision of the Swiss Federal Supreme Court dated 9 June 2009, no. 4A_40/2009, para. 4.3: 'Moreover, it is not true that default would require fault on the part of the debtor, as the appellants argue. The debtor of a monetary debt has to pay default interest by law, unless otherwise agreed, as soon as he is in default with the payment of the debt (article 104(1) CO). This provision is based on the fiction that the debtor in default may continue to dispose of the amount of money until performance and that the creditor thereby suffers a corresponding loss of assets. Neither proof of damage by the creditor nor fault on the part of the debtor is required, which is why the debtor must pay default interest even if he was not aware of his payment obligation or its amount at the time the default occurred.'
339. *See* herein below paras 439 et seqq.
340. *See* hereinabove para. 296.
341. Article 82 CO: 'A party to a bilateral contract may not demand performance until he has discharged or offered to discharge his own obligation, unless the terms or nature of the contract allow him to do so at a later date.'

contracts by deducing a so-called obligatory right of retention (*obligatorisches Retentionsrecht, droit de rétention fondé sur le CO, diritto di ritenzione fondato sul diritto delle obbligazioni*) from an analogous application of Article 82 CO.[342] Yet, the creditor's and debtor's obligations in question must not be disproportionate in quality or quantity, as otherwise invoking the defence might be considered to constitute an abuse of rights (Article 2(2) CC).[343]

357 Defence of insolvency (Article 83 CO, *Einrede der Zahlungsunfähigkeit, exception d'insolvabilité, eccezione dell' insolvenza*): A debtor is entitled to withhold performance if the creditor has become insolvent after conclusion of the contract and refuses to provide security for the creditor's consideration. Insolvency in the sense of Article 83 CO does not require the opening of bankruptcy proceedings but is already established if the debtor no longer has the necessary means to satisfy his creditors for the foreseeable future.[344] In contrast to Article 82 CO, the debtor may invoke this defence despite any obligation to advance performance.

B Legal Consequences of Debtor's Default

358 While the creditor is still entitled to demand specific performance,[345] the debtor's default provides the creditor with further remedies. A distinction must be drawn between remedies of the creditor that arise automatically with the debtor's default and such that require further actions by the creditor.

1 General Legal Consequences

359 A debtor's default in performing an obligation results in specific legal consequences addressed by Articles 103–106 CO. While Article 103 CO sets forth the basic legal consequences of debtor's default, Articles 104–106 CO address legal consequences that only apply to monetary obligations. These provisions are not of a mandatory nature meaning that parties are free to modify this regime in their contract.

342. Decision of the Swiss Federal Supreme Court dated 29 October 1968, DSC 94 II 263, para. 3.a: 'The gratuitous mandate agreement is not a synallagmatic contract. The expenses and expenditures of the mandatee are not to be considered as consideration of what he has to deliver to the mandator on the basis of conducting the business in the sense of article 400 CO. Article 82 CO is therefore not directly applicable. However, it is in accordance with equity and the law actually in force that the mandator cannot enforce his claim for delivery without reimbursing the expenses and expenditures of the mandatee and that, conversely, the mandatee cannot demand the fulfillment of his claims without performing his obligation. This connection is established in Swiss law – corresponding to § 273 BGB – by the obligatory right of retention, by virtue of which a contracting party can refuse its performance until it is granted the counter-performance from the same legal relationship.'

343. Huguenin, Obligationenrecht, Zurich 2019, N 932.

344. Decision of the Swiss Federal Supreme Court dated 30 January 1979, DSC 105 II 28, para. 1.

345. *See* herein below paras 393 et seqq.

a Liability for Damages due to Delay

360 The defaulting debtor is liable for damages due to late performance (Article 103(1) CO). The creditor must be put in the position he would be in if the contract had been timely performed. However, he may discharge himself from such liability by proving that his default occurred through no fault of his own.[346] The defaulting debtor bears the burden of proof in this regard.[347]

361 Recoverable damages[348] include, for example, loss of profit due to late delivery of a machine, compensation that had to be paid to a third party (e.g., penalty for late delivery),[349] and currency losses due to late payment.[350] For monetary obligations any statutory default interest[351] must be deducted from the damage caused by delay; only the damage in excess of the default interest is owed under Article 103(1) CO.[352]

b Liability for Accidental Damage

362 The defaulting debtor bears the negative consequences of events that are neither due to his nor the creditor's fault (accidental damage).[353] If performance becomes impossible while the debtor is in default, the debtor becomes liable for damages (Articles 97 et seqq. CO) even if the impossibility is not attributable to him.[354]

363 A debtor may escape liability for accidental damage by proving that the default is not due to the debtor's fault. Equally, the debtor may discharge himself from any liability for accidental damage by proving that the creditor would have suffered the accidental damage even if performance had taken place promptly.[355]

346. Article 103(2) CO.
347. Decision of the Swiss Federal Supreme Court dated 19 June 1990, DSC 116 II 441, para. 2.b: 'If the debtor is in default, he is liable, among other things, for the damage caused by the delay (article 103(1) CO), however not strictly, but due to fault, whereby the burden of proof of exculpation lies with him (article 103(2) CO).'
348. For further details on the remedy of damages *see* herein below paras 397 et seqq.
349. Decision of the Swiss Federal Supreme Court dated 19 June 1990, DSC 116 II 441, para. 3: 'The claimant claims a contractual penalty in the amount of FF 300,000. - or CHF 78,600. - as damages for delay, which it owes from its resale contract with the company C. due to non-compliance with the agreed fixed date.'
350. Decision of the Swiss Federal Supreme Court dated 7 May 1997, DSC 123 III 243, para. 3.a: 'As a rule, concrete proof of loss is required for this. Thus, if a creditor claims to have suffered currency losses as a result of the debtor's delayed performance, he must provide evidence that he would have promptly converted the amount in question into another currency if he had performed on time. However, according to the case law of the Federal Supreme Court, in such cases it must be presumed, based on general life experience and the ordinary course of events, that the creditor would have converted the money into the legal currency of its place of residence or business.'
351. *See* herein below paras 366 et seqq.
352. Article 106(1) CO.
353. Article 103(1) CO.
354. *See* hereinabove para. 333.
355. Article 103(2) CO.

c Default Interest

364 Pursuant to Article 104 CO, a defaulting debtor is obliged to pay default interest if the obligation in question is for payment of money.

365 The default interest amounts to 5% per annum.[356] The default interest rate set by the Code of Obligations is not mandatory; parties are free to agree on higher or lower interest rates: where the parties have agreed on payment of interest as part of their contract (e.g., loan interest), the rules of Article 104(1–2) CO apply: where the contractual interest rate is higher than 5%, this rate also applies to the default interest; where it is lower than 5%, the creditor may nonetheless rely on the 5% per annum as envisaged by Article 104(1) CO.

366 The Swiss Federal Supreme Court has summarised the situation as follows:

> If interest higher than 5% has been stipulated directly or indirectly in the contract, it may be demanded even during the default pursuant to article 104(2) CO. In contrast to the default interest rate according to Article 104(3) CO, the default interest rate according to para. 2 is, like the statutory interest rate of para. 1, a rigid interest rate which does not take into account the fluctuations of the market interest rates. In contrast to the interest rate according to para. 3, it is related to the past. The legislator has thus accepted – as with the statutory interest rate of para. 1 – that the default interest rate owed may be higher than the market interest rate applicable during the default. This expresses the penalty element inherent in the default interest. The legal determination of the amount of the default interest resulting from article 104 CO cannot be shaken by the proof that the creditor would not have received any or less benefit during the period of default, nor can it be reduced by the court. If the damage suffered by the creditor due to the delay exceeds the amount of the statutory default interest, the debtor is also obliged to compensate this damage according to article 106 CO, unless he proves that he is not at fault.[357]

367 In general, default interest starts running from the first date of the debtor's default, i.e., one working day after receipt of the formal reminder by the debtor or one day after the expiry of the deadline for performance,[358] respectively. Article 105(1) CO provides an exception to this rule: a debtor in default on the payment of interest, annuities or gifts is liable for default interest only as of the day on which enforcement proceedings are initiated or legal action is brought.

368 While default interest is due regardless of the occurrence of any actual damage, the creditor is free to prove that he incurred damage exceeding the default interest. In such a case, he is entitled to claim the surpassing part as damages under Article 106 (1) CO.[359]

356. Article 104 para. 1 CO. An exception applies in business dealings where the normal bank discount rate at the place of payment is higher than 5% per annum (Article 104 para. 3 CO).
357. Decision of the Swiss Federal Supreme Court dated 2 March 2004, DSC 130 III 312, para. 7.1.
358. *See* hereinabove paras 354–355.
359. *See* hereinabove para. 363.

2 *Special Remedies at the Creditor's Choice*

369 Under Article 107(2) CO, the debtor's default entitles the creditor to further remedies at his choice. These remedies are provided in addition to the ones in Articles 103–106 CO.[360] While the wording of Article 107(2) CO suggests that these remedies are only available with synallagmatic contracts, the majority of doctrine confirms that the remedies should also be available in other constellations, namely when the debtor is in default of a material obligation in a non-synallagmatic contract.[361]

370 Articles 107–109 CO provide the creditor with a sequence of choices that might lead to him rescinding the contract or demanding negative or positive damages for non-performance – and not just for delayed performance as under Article 103(1) CO.[362] However, such options only become available after the creditor has set the debtor a grace period for performing the obligation in question.

a *Grace Period*

371 Pursuant to Article 107(2) CO, the creditor must set the debtor an additional period for performing the obligation in question (grace period, *Nachfrist*, *délai de grâce*, *termine supplementare*). The setting of the grace period may be combined with the formal reminder of Article 102(1) CO.[363] Only if the debtor fails to perform within such grace period, the remedies of Articles 107–109 CO become available to the creditor.

372 The grace period must be of appropriate length permitting the debtor to actually perform the obligation. The appropriate length depends on a case-by-case assessment

360. Decision of the Swiss Federal Supreme Court dated 19 June 1990, DSC 116 II 441, para. 2.a: 'The special provisions for synallagmatic contracts contained in articles 107 et seqq. CO does not change this. It merely supplements the general order. The creditor is only required to proceed in accordance with these provisions with regard to legal consequences that go beyond the general consequences of default, namely if he prefers damages for non-performance under article 97 CO to specific performance or wants to rescind the contract and have the negative interest compensated. The debtor, on the other hand, is liable for the damage caused by delay with the occurrence of the default, irrespective of a grace period or the existence of a fixed term transaction.'
361. *See, e.g.*, Huguenin, Obligationenrecht, Zurich 2019, N 949; Gauch/Schluep/Emmenegger, Schweizerisches Obligationenrecht, Zurich 2020, N 2733, with further references.
362. In contrast, Articles 103 and 106 CO only entitle the creditor to claim damages caused by the delayed performance.
363. Decision of the Swiss Federal Supreme Court dated 17 May 1977, DSC 103 II 102, para. 1.a: 'Certainly, the setting of a grace period according to article 107(1) CO usually requires that the performance is due and that the debtor is in default. However, this does not prevent the creditor from combining the setting of a grace period with the reminder. This is obvious because the setting of a grace period is also a reminder and the creditor wants to urge the debtor to perform in one case as well as in the other, i.e., he pursues the same purpose. The two legal actions [formal reminder and grace period] can not only coincide in time, but even precede the due date, if its date is already fixed.'

for which also the creditor's interest in prompt performance may be considered.[364] If a debtor considers the grace period set by the creditor to be too short, the debtor must immediately protest and request an extension of the grace period. Otherwise, the grace period is deemed sufficiently long.[365]

373 Like the formal payment reminder, there are also exceptions to the requirement of setting a grace period. A grace period may be dispensed with if any of the following conditions are met (Article 108 CO):

- it is evident from the conduct of the debtor that a grace period would serve no purpose;
- performance has become pointless to the creditor as a result of the debtor's default; or
- the contract makes it clear that the parties intended that performance take place at or before a precise point in time (*Fixgeschäft, terme fixe, contratto a termine fisco*), which must not be inferred from the mere setting of a deadline in a contract, but requires amplifying of the deadline's importance by including wording such as 'at the latest until' or 'no later than'.[366]

b The Creditor's First Choice

374 If the debtor fails to perform within the grace period or if the creditor is dispensed from setting such period, the creditor may choose whether to insist on performance or to forego performance (Article 107(1) CO).

375 If the creditor insists on performance, he keeps the right to demand specific performance and enjoys the remedies of Articles 103–106 CO. He is not bound by such choice, but may set yet another grace period, after which he may alter his choice.[367]

---

364. Decision of the Swiss Federal Supreme Court dated 1 March 2017, no. 4A_201/2016, para. 5.2: 'The appropriate length of time depends on the circumstances of the particular case (article 4 CC). The creditor's interest in prompt performance may justify a very short deadline.'; decision of the Swiss Federal Supreme Court dated 17 May 1977, DSC 103 II 102, para. 1.b: 'This is not decided in general, but depends on the circumstances of the individual case, namely on the nature of the performance and the interest of the creditor in the prompt performance. The greater this interest and the easier the performance, the shorter the time limit may be, and *vice versa.*'
365. Decision of the Swiss Federal Supreme Court dated 24 September 1990, DSC 116 II 436, para. 2.a: 'When the time limit is objectively too short, the debtor does not have the right to simply ignore it. He must protest and ask his counterparty for an extension. If he fails to do so, he is deemed to have accepted the deadline set. Furthermore, the conversion of a too-short deadline into a reasonable one only makes sense if the debtor performs within the period deemed reasonable or, in any case, makes a serious offer to do so within a period that can be considered reasonable.'
366. Decision of the Swiss Federal Supreme Court dated 10 February 1970, DSC 96 II 47, para. 2.
367. Decision of the Swiss Federal Supreme Court dated 24 October 1950, DSC 76 II 303, para. 1: 'This is all the more self-evident since, according to established case law and doctrine, the creditor does not need to decide immediately even after expiry of the grace period, but can set a grace period again, even several times, with the consequence that after fruitless expiry of each

376 If the creditor wishes to forego performance, he must make an immediate declaration to this effect (Article 107(2) CO). 'Immediate' refers to the time between the expiry of the grace period and the creditor's declaration to the debtor. The purpose of the requirement of immediacy is to protect the debtor against the creditor delaying the decision in order to speculate on the development of surrounding circumstances, such as fluctuations in the market. While the creditor must act swiftly, the law still grants the creditor some time for reflection. The exact duration of such reflection time must be determined on a case-by-case basis taking into consideration the complexity of the situation, the importance of the contract for the parties and their interests.[368]

377 In cases of Article 108 CO, the necessity of an immediate declaration also applies. However, the Swiss Federal Supreme Court makes an exception for certain cases under Article 108(1) CO, where the debtor's insistence on an immediate declaration would be abusive.[369]

378 The declaration to forego performance must be directed at the debtor and must be clear in its content. The debtor must know whether performance is still expected from him. Since the declaration constitutes the exercise of a formative right, no conditions may be attached to it.[370] Yet, the declaration must not meet any form requirement.

379 If the creditor fails to properly declare foregoing performance, it is assumed that the creditor chooses to insist on performance. The creditor must thus set a new grace period in order to access the additional remedies of Articles 107–109 CO. Yet, the special part of the Code of Obligations assumes for certain types of contract that the lack of any declaration implies that the creditor chooses foregoing performance.[371] In these instances, the creditor must make a timely declaration in order to maintain his right to demand specific performance.

---

grace period he is again entitled to the choices under article 107(2) CO. Thus, after expiry of the grace period on 10 June 1948, the claimant again had the right to choose one of the three options listed in article 107(2) CO.'

368. *See, e.g.*, Decisions of the Swiss Federal Supreme Court dated 20 April 1918, DSC 44 II 172 (denying immediacy for a declaration made fourteen days after expiry of grace period), and dated 24 October 1950, DSC 76 II 300 (denying immediacy for a declaration made sixteen days after expiry of grace period).
369. Decision of the Swiss Federal Supreme Court dated 4 September 2017, DSC 143 III 495, para. 4.3.2: 'Due to the circumstances of the individual case, in some cases an exception to the general rule was applied, while in the others the principle was applied. Only the debtor who clearly, definitively and unconditionally refuses his own performance and then invokes the creditor's lack of an immediate declaration of renunciation behaves inconsistently and contrary to good faith. By his attitude, the debtor *de facto* deprives the creditor of the possibility to hold on to specific performance with a prospect of success, whereby the creditor practically can no longer choose between the fulfilment of the primary obligation to perform and the waiver thereof (e.g., cancellation of the order by the debtor because the manufacturer cannot deliver). On the other hand, in DSC 54 II 30 with reference to DSC 48 II [220 para. 2 p.] 224 et seq., it was correctly stated that there was no comparable breach of trust, since in the case under review the debtor did not refuse delivery outright, but (only, albeit wrongfully) under the conditions set by the other party (advance performance). In such a case, there is a need for the creditor to declare clearly and without delay whether he adheres to the performance or waives it; in this case, the debtor does not act in bad faith if he invokes the lack of a corresponding declaration.'
370. *See* hereinabove para. 267.
371. *See, e.g.*, Article 190 CO (commercial sales contract).

c The Creditor's Second Choice

380 If the creditor foregoes performance, he may choose to either uphold or rescind the contract (Article 107(2) CO).

381 Upholding the contract leads to a modification of the debtor's obligation. The debtor's obligation to perform the defaulted obligation transforms into an obligation to pay damages for non-performance (positive damages, i.e., the creditor is put in the financial situation as if the debtor had properly performed the contract).[372] In turn, the creditor remains obliged to perform his obligations under the contract.

382 By rescinding the contract both parties are released from their obligations under the contract.[373] At the same time, the creditor may claim negative damages.[374] However, for continuing contracts,[375] the Swiss Federal Supreme Court decided to exclude the remedy of rescission and instead provides the creditor with a termination right by which the creditor may set an end to the contract with immediate, but not retroactive effect (*ex nunc*).[376]

IV THIRD TYPE OF BREACH OF CONTRACT: INADEQUATE PERFORMANCE

383 Inadequate performance is addressed by Article 97 CO. It refers to the case that the debtor has fully performed his main obligation under a contract, but either the performance is defective in terms of quality (defective performance; *Schlechterfüllung, exécution imparfaite, esecuzione imperfetta*) or the debtor has violated an ancillary duty under the contract (*Nebenpflichten, obligation accessoire, obbligazione accessoria*). To put it simply, any violation of a contractual duty amounts to inadequate performance.[377]

384 Generally, performance of an obligation must comply with certain quality requirements. A creditor must not accept any type of performance. For example, a sales contract requires transfer of a good conforming to the quality standard owed under the

372. The debtor may escape payment of damages by proving absence of fault (*see* below paras 413 et seqq.).
373. For details on remedy of rescission, *see* below paras 423 et seqq.
374. *See* herein below para. 428.
375. *See* hereinabove para. 66.
376. *See* below para. 427.
377. Decision of the Swiss Federal Supreme Court dated 8 February 2010, no. 4A_306/2009, para. 6.1: 'Any breach of a contractual duty therefore constitutes inadequate performance within the meaning of this provision [Article 97 CO].'

contract.[378] Equally, a mandate agreement obliges the mandatee to render his services in a diligent fashion.[379]

385 While the Code of Obligations sets forth certain general quality standards, the parties are free to further specify or deviate from such standards. Often, the required standard of quality is a matter of contract interpretation.

386 Defective performance entitles a creditor to damages under Article 97 CO.[380] Further, if the defective performance is so grave that it amounts to a material breach of contract, the remedy of rescission might become available if further conditions are met.[381] As long as performance remains possible, the creditor may, however, also choose to insist on specific performance and claim only damages for delay.[382] There are particular provisions for specific performance of cease and desist obligations[383] as well as for the various contract types in the special part of the Code of Obligations.[384]

387 Even if a debtor properly performs his main obligation under a contract, he might breach the contract by violating an ancillary duty. Such duties may arise from statute,[385] be agreed by contract or (to a limited extent) be implied by the general principle of good faith.[386] By their nature, they are secondary to the main obligations arising under a contract.[387] Their exact nature, designation, as well as content, are heavily debated in doctrine. The Swiss Federal Supreme Court sums it up as follows:

> A form of inadequate performance is, in particular, the breach of ancillary duties under the contract. These include duties of conduct which have the purpose of

378. *See* Article 197(1) CO: '... breach of warranty of quality and for any defects that would materially or legally negate or substantially reduce the value of the object or its fitness for the designated purpose.'
379. *See* Article 398(2) CO: 'The mandatee is liable to the mandator for the diligent and faithful performance of the business entrusted to him.'
380. *See* below paras 397 et seqq.
381. *See* below para. 428.
382. Huguenin, Obligationenrecht, Zurich 2019, N 810.
383. If there is an interest in continued compliance with the obligation to cease and desist despite an occurred infringement (e.g., reinstatement of a non-compete clause), the creditor – in addition to the claims for damages (Article 98(2) CO), for rectification and substitute performance (Article 98(3) CO) – has a the general claim for (further) injunctive relief (i.e., specific performance of the cease and desist obligation, such as a non-compete obligation).
384. Article 368(2) CO: 'In the case of minor defects in the work or only slight deviations from the contractual terms, the customer may ... require the contractor to rectify the work at his own expense ... .'
385. For example, Article 188 CO.
386. Decision of the Swiss Federal Supreme Court dated 7 December 2010, no. 4A_494/2010, para. 4.1: 'The main statutory duties of a certain type of contract are often supplemented by ancillary duties regulated by statute or contractual agreement. In addition, unwritten ancillary duties may arise from the general clause of good faith (article 2(1) CC), such as the general duty to protect the contractual partner's legal interests, which is unrelated to the main performance owed under the contract.'
387. For example, under a sales contract the main obligations are transfer of ownership and payment of the purchase price. But, maybe the parties also agreed on a duty of confidentiality regarding the amount of the purchase price. Such duty would qualify as an ancillary duty.

> supplementing the main performance and ensuring its proper fulfilment or achieving the purpose of the contract, such as duties of protection, care, advice, omission, information and clarification. The legal basis of such duties lies in the conclusion of the contract, whereby these duties become directly part of the contract even without an expression of the parties' will in this respect due to the duty arising from article 2 CC to show comprehensive consideration for the interests of the contractual partner and to behave loyally. In this case, the ancillary duties result from an interpretation or supplementation of the contract, whereby the judge must be guided by the thinking and actions of reasonable and honest contracting parties as well as by the nature and purpose of the contract. In principle, it is to be assumed that ancillary duties always form part of the scope of performance and do not extend the primary duty of performance in the sense of a substantive change of the obligation, but can only describe the debtor's actions in more detail with regard to the purpose of performance.[388]

388 The generally available remedy for breach of an ancillary duty is damages under Article 97 CO. However, there are some ancillary duties for which a creditor may demand specific performance.[389] Whether a creditor may separately (i.e., independent from the main obligation) claim specific performance depends on the ancillary duty's content. It is a matter of interpretation whether the parties intended for such remedy to be available.[390] In contrast, rescission will not be an available remedy for breach of an ancillary duty, unless the ancillary duty would be of paramount importance.[391]

V THE CREDITOR'S REMEDIES

389 As demonstrated in the previous chapters, failure to adequately or timely perform contractual obligations gives rise to different remedies depending on the failure in question. In this chapter, further details on the available remedies are provided.[392]

390 Two aspects must be remembered: (i) the special part of the Code of Obligations sets forth special remedies for certain types of contract; and (ii) the remedy regime of the Swiss Code of Obligations is largely non-mandatory meaning that the parties are free to extend or reduce a creditor's remedies.[393]

388. Decision of the Swiss Federal Supreme Court dated 8 February 2010, no. 4A_306/2009, para. 6.1.
389. In this respect, Swiss doctrine distinguishes between primary ancillary duties (*Nebenleistungspflichten*) and secondary ancillary duties (*Nebenpflichten i.e.S./Verhaltenspflichten*). *See, e.g.*, Huguenin, Obligationenrecht, Zurich 2019, N 102–103.
390. Wiegand, commentary on Article 97 CO, in: Basler Kommentar OR I, N 32. For example, reporting duties are often deemed of such nature permitting a claim for specific performance (*see, e.g.*, Article 400 CO). Equally, non-compete clauses give rise to specific performance.
391. *See* below para. 426.
392. The term 'remedies' encompasses both judicial and extra-judicial ('self-help') remedies.
393. *See* hereinabove paras 342–343.

A Specific Performance

391 Specific performance is the primary remedy in Swiss contract law. It follows from the core principle *pacta sunt servanda* that a creditor may insist on performance and thus request a court to order a debtor to perform the obligation in question.[394]

392 Specific performance may be requested as soon as the obligation is due.[395] Even if the debtor successfully invokes the defence of non-performance (Article 82 CO),[396] a claim for specific performance would not be dismissed. Rather, a tribunal would then order the debtor to perform his obligation concurrently, 'step by step' (*Leistung Zug um Zug, exécution simultanée des prestations, esecuzione simultanea delle prestazioni*)[397] meaning that any enforcement action based on such judgment could only take place once the creditor has performed or offered to perform his own obligation:

> In the case of a synallagmatic contract, a person who wishes to request the other to perform must either have already performed or offer to perform, unless the content or nature of the contract requires him to perform at a later date (article 82 CO). As stated for the last time in DSC 107 II 223, para. 2.b, this provision gives the debtor a suspensory defence with the effect that he may withhold the required performance until counter-performance has been rendered or offered. The creditor may sue for unconditional performance; it is up to the debtor to raise the defence. If the defence is justified, i.e., if the creditor has neither performed nor offered performance, the judge protects the action in the sense that he orders the debtor to perform concurrently, i.e., a suspensive obligation. If the debtor has wrongly raised the defence under article 82 CO, be it that the creditor has fulfilled or at least offered performance in a proper manner, be it that the counterclaim does not exist at all, he is unconditionally ordered to perform.[398]

393 There are, however, instances of performance failure by the debtor that render the remedy of specific performance unavailable:

- In case of non-performance (impossibility), specific performance is not available.[399]
- In case of delayed performance, the creditor waives the remedy of specific performance if he chooses to forego performance (Article 107 CO).[400] However, if he chooses to insist on performance the remedy remains available.

394. The enforcement of such order is governed by Articles 335 et seqq. of the Swiss Civil Procedure Code (for non-monetary obligations) and by the Swiss Federal Act on Debt Enforcement and Bankruptcy (for monetary obligations).
395. *See* hereinabove paras 294–295.
396. *See* hereinabove para. 357.
397. For example, if the creditor sues for transfer of shares under a share purchase agreement without yet himself having paid the purchase price, the court would order the debtor to transfer the shares 'step by step' against payment of the purchase price (*see, e.g.*, decision of the Zurich Commercial Court dated 8 January 2021, no. HG200116).
398. Decision of the Swiss Federal Supreme Court dated 5 November 1985, DSC 111 II 463, para. 3.
399. *See* hereinabove para. 347.
400. *See* hereinabove paras 375–377.

- In case of inadequate performance, the remedy of specific performance is generally available, as far as performance still remains possible.[401] But, the special part of the Code of Obligations at times deviates from this. Further, if the creditor claims damages, the remedy of specific performance is deemed to merge into the claim for damages and thus to evaporate.[402] In practice, there are very few cases where inadequate performance occurs, but specific performance will still be sought.

394 Finally, if the creditor insists on a specific performance, but does not trust that the debtor will eventually succeed with such performance, he may resort to Article 98 CO. This provision enables him to request the court for permission to perform the obligation himself or entrust a third party with the performance at the obligor's expense (performance by substitution; *Ersatzvornahme, exécution par substitution, esecuzione sostitutiva*).

B Damages

395 The remedy of damages is always available when there is a failure of performance. Although it is dogmatically not the primary remedy, it is in practice the remedy most often called upon by a creditor.

396 There are two types of damages that a creditor may seek:

(i) positive damages (*positives Vertragsinteresse, intérêt positive, interesse positivo*) with which the creditor is to be put in the position he would be in if the debtor had properly performed; and
(ii) negative damages (*negatives Vertragsinteresse, intérêt négatif, interesse negativo*) with which the creditor is to be put in the position he would be in if he had never met the debtor and thus not concluded the contract.

397 This distinction is important as it affects the remedy's conditions.

1 Conditions of Remedy

398 Article 97 CO (for inadequate and non-performance) and Article 109 CO (for debtor default) form the main statutory basis of the damages remedy. They set forth the following conditions: There must be a performance failure (section a) that causes (section c) a damage (section b) and for which the debtor is deemed at fault (section d).

401. *See* hereinabove paras 388 and 390.
402. Decision of the Swiss Federal Supreme Court dated 13 June 1991, DSC 117 II 273, para. 4.c: 'Like the creditor's claim for damages under articles 97 et seqq. CO, the claim under article 377 CO also originates from the original contractual claim directed towards performance and is deemed to be a continuation thereof.'

a Failure to Adequately or Timely Perform

399 The remedy of positive damages is available in the following constellations of performance failure:

- non-performance if the impossibility of performance is attributable to the debtor;[403]
- delayed performance if the creditor foregoes performance, but chooses to uphold the contract nonetheless (Article 109 CO);[404] and
- inadequate performance.[405]

400 Negative damages may be claimed in the case of:

- delayed performance if the creditor foregoes performance and chooses to rescind the contract;[406]
- violation of rules of good faith in contract negotiations (*culpa in contrahendo*);[407] and
- liability for evoked trust.[408]

b Damage

401 A damage consists of the involuntary reduction of one's net assets. To determine a damage, courts apply the so-called theory of difference (*Differenztheorie, théorie de la difference, teoria della differenza*).[409] A damage corresponds to the difference between the actual amount of the creditor's net assets after the debtor's performance failure and the creditor's hypothetical amount of net assets if the contract had been properly performed (positive damages) or had not been concluded at all (negative damages).

403. *See* hereinabove para. 346.
404. *See* hereinabove paras 381–382. In addition, a defaulting debtor may be held liable for damages under Article 103(1) CO (*see* hereinabove para. 361), but such damages only encompass those that relate to the lateness of performance. Further, the creditor may claim payment of default interest (*see* hereinabove paras 365 et seqq.).
405. *See* hereinabove paras 365 et seqq.
406. *See* hereinabove para. 338.
407. *See* hereinabove para. 193.
408. *See* hereinabove paras 196 et seqq.
409. Decision of the Swiss Federal Supreme Court dated 20 May 2019, DSC 145 III 225, para. 4.1.1: 'According to settled case law, damage is deemed to be the involuntary reduction of the net assets. The damage corresponds – according to the theory of difference prevailing in Switzerland – to the difference between the current state of the assets and the (hypothetical) state that the assets would have had without the damaging event. It may consist of an increase in liabilities, a decrease in assets or lost profits. The prohibition of enrichment, recognised as a general principle in liability law, precludes awarding the injured party compensation that exceeds the loss suffered as a result of the harmful event.' Also *see* decision of the Swiss Federal Supreme Court dated 20 May 2019, no. 4A_394/2018, para. 4, regarding relevant point in time for determining the difference (generally the point in time when judgment is rendered, but with some exceptions).

Such a difference may result from a decrease in assets or an increase in liabilities (*damnum emergens*) as well as a non-increase in assets or a non-decrease in liabilities (*lucrum cessans*).[410]

402 Typical damage positions of a claim for positive damages are:

- Value of proper performance of the obligation in question. In case of non-performance, the damage consists in the entire value of performance, whereas for inadequate performance the damage consists in the reduced value as compared to proper performance.
- Costs incurred due to performance failure, such as costs of repair, costs of bridging measures, costs of an expert or costs of a cover transaction. Yet, the costs of attorneys are only recoverable as far as they are not covered by any compensation attainable under the applicable procedural law.[411]
- Loss of profit:[412] For a loss of profit claim, the creditor must prove that he would have made a profit in the claimed amount if the debtor had performed his obligation. Due to the hypothetical nature of loss of profit claims such proof is challenging, but Swiss law recognises a lowering of the standard of proof for such situations and even authorises a tribunal to estimate the hypothetical profits under Article 42(2) CO.[413]

403 Typical damage positions of a claim for negative damages include:

- Unnecessarily incurred costs and expenses related to the negotiation and conclusion of the contract (e.g., transport costs, lawyer's fees for negotiating the contract).
- Loss of profit, such as missed opportunity to enter into a possibly advantageous similar contract with a third party.
- Losses resulting from the liability of the aggrieved party towards third parties.

410. Decision of the Swiss Federal Supreme Court dated 1 November 2005, DSC 132 III 186, para. 8.1: 'According to the established case law of the Federal Supreme Court, damage is the involuntary reduction of the net assets. It may consist of a reduction in assets, an increase in liabilities or lost profits and corresponds to the difference between the current state of assets and the state that the assets would have had without the damaging event.'
411. Decision of the Swiss Federal Supreme Court dated 18 July 2000, DSC 126 III 388, para. 10.b: 'The fees of the experts appointed by the customer to ascertain the defects and the lawyer's fees incurred before legal proceedings, provided that they are not covered by the costs awarded under cantonal procedural law and that the lawyer's involvement was justified, form part of the loss for which compensation may be claimed.'
412. For a detailed analysis of Swiss court decisions on loss of profit, *see* Haberbeck, An analysis of Swiss court decisions concerning loss of profit claims, Berne 2017.
413. Decision of the Swiss Federal Supreme Court dated 9 June 2017, DSC 143 III 297, para. 8.2.5.2: 'According to the practice of the Federal Supreme Court, there is an easing of the burden of proof in cases where the profit cannot be strictly proven in terms of figures. In this case, the judge may consider the profit to be proven on the basis of an estimate in analogous application of Article 42(2) CO, whereby this facilitation of proof refers to both the existence and the amount of the profit.'

404 In contrast, loss of an opportunity (*perte d'une chance*) is not a recoverable element of damage,[414] although this is conversely debated in doctrine. Equally, a deprivation of use that is due to performance failure is not recoverable.[415] Further, punitive damages are alien to Swiss law and thus not awarded by courts.

405 Recoverability of damage is further restricted by the general principle of non-overcompensation (*Bereicherungsverbot, interdiction de l'enrichissement, divieto di arricchimemento*) pursuant to which the upper limit of the claim for damages is always the actual loss suffered.[416] Under this principle, the aggrieved party must account for any benefit that stands in direct relation to the damaging act and must thus accept a corresponding reduction of the recoverable damages (*Vorteilsanrechnung, imptuation des avantages, imputare i benefici*).[417]

406 The aggrieved party does not only carry the burden of proof for the existence of any alleged damage but also for the quantum of such damage.[418] The required standard of proof is rather high under Swiss law, as the aggrieved party must demonstrate and quantify the concrete damage that it suffered.[419] But in some circumstances the Code of Obligations allows for an easing of the burden of proof:

> Article 42(2) CO contains a provision of evidence under federal law which is intended to facilitate the aggrieved party's proof of damage. The provision grants

414. Decision of the Swiss Federal Supreme Court dated 13 June 2007, DSC 133 III 462, para. 4.4.3: 'Admittedly, one way of getting round this difficulty is to describe the loss of the opportunity itself as compensable damage. However, it is not easy to equate an opportunity with an asset. It is not enough to say that an opportunity has an economic value for this to be the case. The opportunity is not part of current assets if it has been lost. But it does not appear in hypothetical assets either, because it would have been transformed into an increase in wealth, or it would not have been realised for unknown reasons. By its very nature, opportunity is provisional and tends towards realisation: it will either turn into a gain or nothing at all. Given its dynamic or evolving nature, opportunity is not destined to remain in the estate. However, the theory of difference, applicable in Swiss law to the calculation of damages, is based on the state of the assets at two specific points in time; it therefore does not allow the lost opportunity to be appraised economically. ... . It follows from the foregoing that the acceptance in Swiss law of the theory of the loss of an opportunity developed in particular by French case-law is, to say the least, problematic.'
415. Decision of the Swiss Federal Supreme Court dated 18 July 2000, DSC 126 III 388, para. 11.a: 'Even if the desire to compensate for the deprivation of the use of an asset is understandable, particularly when the asset has intrinsic economic value, this approach cannot be followed. As some authors have rightly pointed out, the loss of use of an asset is only a possible source of damage, not the damage itself. By compensating this loss, the concept of damage resulting from a failure would lose any concrete link with a reduction in net assets.'
416. Decision of the Swiss Federal Supreme Court dated 14 September 2004, DSC 131 III 12, para. 7.1.
417. Decision of the Swiss Federal Supreme Court dated 25 March 1959, DSC 85 IV 101, para. 2.b: 'It is a recognized principle in Swiss law on damages that a benefit must be offset, as otherwise the aggrieved party would be enriched. The only prerequisite for the offsetting of benefits is that the damage and the benefit were caused by acts that are intrinsically related to each other.'
418. Article 99(3) in combination with Article 42(1) CO.
419. Decision of the Swiss Federal Supreme Court dated 15 November 1994, DSC 120 II 296, para. 3.b: 'In principle, the buyer must establish the concrete elements of his damage (article 42(1) CO applicable by reference to article 99(3) CO); he will thus have to show, for example, that he had to acquire the goods elsewhere on less favourable terms, or that he was deprived of the profit that resale would have brought him, or that he had to compensate his own buyer in turn.'

the court an extended discretion in cases where strict proof of the damage is impossible, by allowing it to consider the damage as proven on the basis of a mere estimate. According to case law, article 42(2) CO is not only applicable in cases where it is impossible to prove the amount of the damage in figures, but also in cases where it cannot be strictly proven that any damage has occurred at all.

However, contrary to what the claimant seems to assume, this is not intended to open up the possibility for the aggrieved party to make claims for damages in any amount without providing further details. Article 42(2) CO merely aims at easing the burden of proof and not at relieving the aggrieved party of the burden of proof in general. In its case law, the Federal Supreme Court expressly states that the aggrieved party must allege and prove, as far as possible and reasonable, all circumstances that speak for the occurrence of a damage and allow or facilitate its estimation.[420]

c Link of Causality

407 There must be a link of causality (*Kausalität, causalité, causalità*) between the failure of performance in question and the alleged damage.

408 Above all, there must be a factual link of causality (*natürliche Kausalität, causalité naturelle, causalità naturale*) meaning that there is a logical relationship between the performance failure and the damage. Without the former, the latter would not have occurred. A debtor may demonstrate the lack of any factual link of causality by proving that the damage would have occurred even if he had properly performed his obligations (lawful alternative behaviour; *rechtmässiges Alternativverhalten, comportement de substitution licite, comportamento di sostituzione lecito*). Yet, Swiss courts request strict proof in this regard.[421]

409 In addition, there must also be a legal link of causality (*adequate Kausalität, causalité adéquate, causalità adeguata*). A legal link of causality presupposes that the performance failure was sufficiently likely, in the ordinary course of events and according to the general life experience, to cause a damage of the same kind as the one that has occurred.[422] In essence, this boils down to a question of foreseeability. This

420. Decision of the Swiss Federal Supreme Court dated 4 June 1996, DSC 122 III 219, para. 3.a. Also *see* decision of the Swiss Federal Supreme Court dated 16 April 2018, no. 4A_586/2017, para. 2.3: 'If the aggrieved party does not provide all the information necessary for the estimation of the damage, one of the conditions of article 42(2) CO is not met and the easing of the burden of proof does not apply.'

421. Decision of the Swiss Federal Supreme Court dated 4 October 2004, DSC 131 III 115, para. 3.3: 'Particularly in view of the fact that the exculpatory evidence regarding lawful alternative behaviour must be provided strictly, this evidence must be considered to have failed if it emerges in the specific case that the damage could possibly have occurred even if the required care had been exercised. The remaining possibility that the occurrence of the damage would still have been avoided excludes the exemption from liability.'

422. Decision of the Swiss Federal Supreme Court dated 29 June 2016, DSC 142 III 433, para. 4.5: 'An event shall be deemed to be an adequate cause of a result if, according to the usual course of events and general experience of life, it is in itself likely to bring about a result of the kind that has occurred, i.e., the occurrence of the result generally appears to be favoured by the event.'

additional requirement enables a court to exclude damage that is too remote from the debtor's performance failure.

410 If the performance failure consists of an omission, causality is assessed on a hypothetical level (hypothetical causality; *hypothetische Kausalität, causalité hypothétique, causalità ipotetica*). Thus, it must be assessed whether, in the ordinary course of events and according to the general life experience, the damage would have occurred if the debtor had not omitted to act.

d *Fault*

411 In general, damages are only available if the debtor is at fault (*Verschulden, faute, colpa*).

412 The concept of fault is composed of a subjective and an objective element. Subjectively, the debtor must be capable of judgment, which is presumed (Article 18 CC). Objectively, the circumstances must be such that the debtor can be blamed for the breach of contract, it being irrelevant whether he acted by intention or negligence (Article 99(1) CO).[423]

413 Under Article 97 CO, a debtor's fault is presumed. The burden of proof is thus reversed.[424] The debtor must prove that he was not at fault.

414 The debtor must prove that he has exercised all necessary diligence in performing the obligation in question. In practice, a debtor can avoid liability by proving that the performance failure was caused by accident, force majeure or by a third party's fault that cannot be attributed to him.[425]

415 If the debtor uses auxiliaries to perform his obligations,[426] he is generally liable for any actions of his auxiliaries (Article 101 CO).[427] The debtor's ability to avoid liability is limited, as he may not merely rely on himself not having committed any fault. Any fault by its auxiliaries is attributable to the debtor. Only where the actions of the auxiliaries are of such nature that if the debtor had committed them himself, he could not be blamed, he may escape liability.[428]

423. However, *see* below paras 419–421 regarding exclusion of liability relieving a debtor from any liability as long as it has not acted intentionally or by gross negligence.
424. Article 97 CO: '... unless he [the debtor] can prove that he was not at fault.'
425. Wiegand, commentary on Article 97 CO, in: Basler Kommentar OR I, N 42.
426. *See* hereinabove paras 280 and 283 regarding a debtor's freedom to perform with the support of third parties.
427. However, the parties may agree on an exclusion of this liability (Article 101(2) CO).
428. Decision of the Swiss Federal Supreme Court dated 25 June 1968, DSC 94 I 248, para. 2.b: 'Incidentally, article 101 CO does not intend to replace liability for fault with strict liability; its basic idea is rather that whoever uses an auxiliary person to exercise rights or fulfil duties instead of acting himself must allow his actions and omissions to be imputed to him as if he had acted himself. It is always examined whether the principal could be accused of a breach of his duties if he himself had acted in the same way as the auxiliary person. Anyone who has the

416 In some cases, the law establishes strict liability on the debtor meaning that liability arises regardless of the debtor's fault. The most prominent example is the liability of the defaulting debtor for accidental loss (Article 103(1) CO).

e *Addendum: Limitation of Liability*

417 The principle of freedom of contract enables the parties to exclude a debtor's liability for performance failure. However, such freedom is limited by Article 100(1) CO which deems any exclusion of liability for unlawful intent or gross negligence void. The special part of the Code of Obligations contains further restrictions for certain contract types.[429] Thus, an exclusion of liability clause contained in a contract must be reduced in its effect so that a debtor is liable for damages, but only if he acted with unlawful intent or in gross negligence.[430]

418 While the term wrongful intent needs little explanation, gross negligence is not as intuitive. The Swiss Federal Supreme Court has provided the following explanation:

> The legal question, however, is whether this results in gross negligence. This is to be affirmed if basic duties of care were disregarded, which would have been obvious to any reasonable person under the given circumstances.[431]

419 Importantly, an exclusion of liability leads to a reversal of the burden of proof. It is not the debtor who must prove that he was not at fault. Rather, the creditor must prove that the debtor acted with unlawful intent or in gross negligence.[432]

2 ***Content of Remedy***

420 The remedy of damages (*Schadenersatz, indemnité, indennità*) entails the debtor's duty to compensate the creditor for the damage suffered.

---

advantage of being able to fulfil or exercise his or her duties and rights through auxiliary persons should also bear the disadvantages of doing so.'

429. *See, e.g.*, Article 199 CO (sales contract).

430. Wiegand, commentary on Article 100 CO, in: Basler Kommentar OR I, N 4. However, this is not undisputed in doctrine (*see* Schwenzer/Fountoulakis, Schweizerisches Obligationenrecht – Allgemeiner Teil, Bern 2020, N 24.08, who argue that the entire limitation of liability clause is void and thus the debtor is liable for any kind of fault).

431. Decision of the Swiss Federal Supreme Court dated 2 June 1981, DSC 107 II 161, para. 7.c.

432. *See* decision of the Swiss Federal Supreme Court dated 2 June 1981, DSC 107 II 161, para. 7.c: 'Although the claimant should be required to prove that the defendant was at fault within the framework of article 100(1) CO, the lower court could certainly assume negligence on the part of the defendant in view of the care required when handling oil heating systems.' However, parts of doctrine disagree with this approach (*see, e.g.*, Schwenzer/Fountoulakis, Schweizerisches Obligationenrecht – Allgemeiner Teil, Bern 2020, N 24.04).

421 The compensation is to be calculated in accordance with the principles of tort liability in Articles 42-61 CO.[433] Accordingly, the determination of the compensation amount must be divided into two phases.

422 First, the actual damage must be assessed (*Schadensberechnung, évaluation du prejudice, valuazione dell danno*). The creditor bears the burden of establishing the existence and amount of the damage suffered.[434]

423 In a second step, the court must determine the owed compensation (*Schadenersatzbemessung, fixation de l'indemnité, determinazione dell' indemnità*). While generally full compensation of the established damage is owed, a court has the power to reduce compensation if the conditions of Article 43 or 44 CO are met. Namely, a reduction may take place if the creditor was also at fault or if the creditor has violated his duty[435] of mitigation.[436]

424 In addition to the compensation amount, the creditor may claim compensatory interest (*Schadenszins, intérêt compensatoire, interessi del danno*) in an amount of 5% p.a.[437] from the time when the damage occurred until payment of the compensation.[438] The purpose of this compensatory interest is to place the creditor in the same position as if he had been immediately compensated on the day of the occurrence of the damage.

C Rescission

1 Conditions of Remedy

425 By statute, rescission becomes available in cases of debtor default. In case of default, the creditor may choose to forego performance and declare rescission of the contract (Article 107(2) CO).[439] Further, the special part of the Code of Obligations foresees rescission in other scenarios.[440]

---

433. Article 99(3) CO.
434. Regarding penalties and liquidated damages, *see* below paras 432 et seqq.
435. Technically, mitigation is only an incumbency.
436. Decision of the Swiss Federal Supreme Court dated 20 December 2005, DSC 132 III 359, para. 4.3: 'This overlooks the fact that according to case law and doctrine, the aggrieved party can only be required to take reasonable measures to avert or mitigate the damage.'
437. But the creditor may prove a higher damage caused by the belated compensation, *see* Decision of the Swiss Federal Supreme Court dated 14 September 2004, DSC 131 III 12, para. 9.4.
438. Decision of the Swiss Federal Supreme Court dated 14 September 2004, DSC 131 III 12, para. 9.1: 'According to settled case law, the damage includes the interest from the time when the damaging event had a financial impact. It runs until the date of payment of the damages. The purpose of this compensatory interest is to place the claimant in the same position as if he had been satisfied for his claim on the day of the tortious act or for its economic effects when it occurred. In contrast to default interest, it requires neither a reminder from the creditor nor default on the part of the debtor, but fulfils the same purpose. It is intended to compensate for the disadvantage caused by the fact that a capital cannot be used.'
439. *See* hereinabove paras 381 et seqq.
440. *See, e.g.,* Article 375(1) CO (rescission due to exceeding cost estimate).

426 Yet, it is largely admitted in doctrine that the remedy of rescission should also be available in certain cases of inadequate performance despite the lack of an explicit statutory basis to that effect.[441] The remedy of rescission is available if the inadequate performance amounts to a material breach of contract that is of such nature that the aggrieved party cannot reasonably be expected to continue the contractual relationship.

427 Finally, in case of non-performance, the Swiss Federal Supreme Court permits rescission if the impossibility occurs after conclusion of the contract (so-called subsequent impossibility), the impossibility is attributable to the debtor and any performed part of the obligation is of no use to the creditor.[442]

2 Content of Remedy

428 By rescinding the contract both parties are released from their obligations under the contract. The rescission transforms the contract into a liquidation relationship (*Abwicklungsverhältnis, rapport de liquidation, rapporto di liquidazione*).[443] Under this liquidation relationship, the parties have a contractual claim to be returned any performance already made under the rescinded contract. In addition, the creditor has a claim for damages arising from the rescission (negative damages, i.e., the creditor is put in the financial position as if the contract had never been concluded).[444] Thus, the remedy of rescission may be combined with a claim for negative damages.[445]

429 However, for continuing contracts[446] transformation into a liquidation relationship often proves difficult. The parties might have been engaged in such a contract for a considerable period of time regularly exchanging performances. Restitution of all the performances made would be cumbersome and often unpracticable. Based on these considerations, the Swiss Federal Supreme Court decided to exclude the remedy of rescission for continuing contracts and instead provides the creditor with a termination right by which the creditor may set an end to the contract with immediate but not

441. *See, e.g.*, Huguenin, Obligationenrecht, Zurich 2019, N 903a et seqq.; Schwenzer/ Fountoulakis, Schweizerisches Obligationenrecht – Allgemeiner Teil, Bern 2020, N 68.09 et seq.
442. Decision of the Swiss Federal Supreme Court dated 21 July 2015, no. 4A_101/2015, para. 4.5: 'In the event of subsequent impossibility of performance attributable to the debtor, the creditor should be treated no worse than the creditor of a debtor who is in default. This is why modern legal scholars believe that a gap should be filled in article 97(1) CO in relation to subsequent impossibility of performance and that the creditor, for whom the part of the performed obligation is of no use, should be given the right to rescind the contract *ex tunc*, by analogy with articles 107(2) and 109 CO. These doctrinal opinions are convincing and should be followed.'
443. Decision of the Swiss Federal Supreme Court dated 6 March 2000, DSC 126 III 119, para. 2.c.
444. The debtor may escape payment of damages by proving lack of fault (*see* hereinabove paras 413 et seqq.).
445. Article 109(2) CO.
446. *See* hereinabove para. 66.

retroactive effect (*ex nunc*).[447] Thus, the parties are released from their obligations for the future but are not granted claims of restitution for performances already made.

D Penalty

430 The parties may agree that the debtor must pay a penalty (*Konventionalstrafe, clause pénale, pena convenzionale*) if it fails to perform an obligation or violates a contract in any other form (Article 160 CO).

431 Technically, a penalty is an obligation with a condition precedent,[448] i.e., failure to adhere to the duty in question. If the condition is met, payment of the penalty is owed regardless of whether the creditor has actually suffered any damage.[449]

432 A penalty must be distinguished from a liquidated damages clause (*pauschalierter Schadenersatz, indemnisation forfaitaire, risarcimento forfettario*), under which the parties agreed to a lump-sum compensation. The latter still requires the creditor to prove the existence of a damage but not the quantum. It is a question of interpretation whether the parties intended for a clause to provide for a penalty or liquidated damages.[450]

433 Contrary to other legal systems, penalties are generally permissible under Swiss contract law. There is only an exception for penalty clauses aimed at reinforcing an unlawful or immoral undertaking.[451]

434 Despite this general permissibility, a court has the power to reduce a penalty if it considers the penalty to be excessive.[452] This power of the court is a deviation from the principle of contractual freedom.[453] As such, the court shall only exercise its discretion

447. Decision of the Swiss Federal Supreme Court dated 27 February 1997, DSC 123 III 124, para. 3.b. However, some scholars make an exception if the non-performed part of the debtor's obligation were of high importance to the creditor or if the creditor has made significant advance performances (*see* Gauch/Schluep/Emmenegger, Schweizerisches Obligationenrecht, Zurich 2020, N 2815).
448. Regarding conditions precedent, *see* hereinabove para. 263.
449. Article 161 CO.
450. Decision of the Lucerne High Court dated 24 January 2012, no. 1B 11 54, para. 4.2: 'According to the general rule (article 18(1) CO), it is the actual intention of the parties that decides whether a contractual penalty or liquidated damages is applicable in the individual case, not the possibly incorrect designation. A contractual penalty is to be assumed if the parties are primarily concerned with giving the entitled party a means of exerting pressure. The fact that the specific agreement covers various breaches of contract, all of which are sanctioned in the same way, is also an indication of a contractual penalty. Furthermore, the contractual penalty is appropriate if the damage would be difficult to determine or if a negative performance (= omission) or if ideal interests are to be enforced. If, on the other hand, it is open to the debtor to prove that the creditor has not suffered damage amounting to the sum in question, liquidated damages are more likely to be accepted.'
451. Article 163(2) CO.
452. Article 163(3) CO. This also applies analogously if the clause provides for liquidated damages (decision of the Swiss Federal Supreme Court dated 19 April 2016, no. 4A_601/2015, para. 2.3).
453. Article 163(1) CO: 'The parties are free to determine the amount of the contractual penalty.'

to reduce a penalty very restrictively. This has been confirmed by the Swiss Federal Supreme Court on multiple occasions:

> Under article 163(3) CO, the court must reduce penalties that it considers excessive. This is a mandatory rule of public policy that the court must apply even if the debtor has not expressly requested a reduction.
>
> He will, however, observe a certain reserve, as the parties are free to set the amount of the penalty (article 163(1) CO) and contracts must in principle be respected; a judge's intervention is only necessary if the amount set is so high that it exceeds any reasonable measure, to the point of no longer being compatible with the law and equity.
>
> A reduction in the penalty is justified in particular where there is a gross disproportion between the amount agreed and the creditor's interest in maintaining his claim in full, measured in concrete terms at the time when the contractual breach occurred. In assessing whether the contractual penalty is excessive, it is important not to reason in the abstract, but to take into account all the specific circumstances of the case. … .
>
> The judge's discretion (article 163(3) CO; article 4 CC) relates both to the excessive nature of the penalty and to the question of the extent of the reduction.
>
> If the court agrees that the penalty is excessive, it must in principle only reduce it so that it is no longer excessive. In other words, he must not set the penalty at the amount he considers to be correct.[454]

435 Like the remedy of damages, a debtor may escape payment of a penalty by proving that he was not at fault.[455]

436 In addition to the penalty, the creditor may claim compensation for any damage exceeding the amount of the penalty.[456] However, the creditor must prove that the debtor was at fault. In contrast, specific performance is usually not available in addition to a penalty. The (non-mandatory) rule of Article 160 CO stipulates that a creditor must choose between a penalty or specific performance unless the penalty concerns compliance with an agreed time or place of performance.

VI THE DEBTOR'S DEFENCES AGAINST REMEDIES

437 If a creditor asserts a claim for performance failure, the debtor has several options to defend. He may purport that there was no obligation at all (hereinabove section 2)

454. Decision of the Swiss Federal Supreme Court dated 5 March 2007, DSC 133 III 201, para. 5.2. Also *see* decision of the Swiss Federal Supreme Court dated 22 June 1988, DSC 114 II 264, para. 1.b: 'However, this does not mean that a contractual penalty is excessive simply because it exceeds the amount that the entitled party could claim as damages from the breach of contract. The indication for the excessiveness is not the damage incurred, but the maximum possible damage. The contractual penalty is the subject of an independent obligation that is to be distinguished from liability for damage; this is already evident from the fact that according to article 161(1) CO it is owed even if the creditor has not suffered any damage.'
455. Article 163(2): '… or, unless otherwise agreed, where performance has been prevented by circumstances beyond the debtor's control'.
456. Article 161(2) CO.

or that there was no obligation with the content as asserted by the creditor (hereinabove section 3). Further, he may deny that there was any performance failure or that the conditions of the remedy in question are met (this Chapter 5).

438 But even if the conditions for the remedy in question are met, the debtor may raise the defence of prescription (section A) or a set-off defence (section B).

A Prescription

439 Claims become time-barred after a certain period of time, so-called prescription (also referred to as statute of limitations; *Verjährung, préscription, prescrizione*). In contrast to other legal systems, prescription is a concept of substantive law under the Code of Obligations. It is governed by Articles 127–142 CO, but certain contract types are subject to particular rules on prescription contained in the special part of the Code of Obligations.

440 Once a claim is prescribed, the creditor has no longer the power to procedurally force the debtor to perform. If the debtor raises the defence of prescription, a court must deny the claim. It may, however, disregard the defence if the debtor's reliance on that defence amounts to an abuse of rights.[457]

441 In any case, a court may not consider prescription *sua sponte.*[458] In this respect, prescription must be distinguished from forfeiture (*Verwirkung, péremption, perenzione*) which entails the extinguishment of a substantive claim and not just of the procedural right to force performance. A court must consider forfeiture *sua sponte*, i.e., even if not raised by the debtor.

442 Prescription may serve as a defence in two ways: *One*, the debtor may refuse performance of an obligation by invoking prescription, thus also barring any claim for performance failure in respect of that obligation; *two*, any claim for damages arising from a performance failure is also subject to prescription.

443 The prescription period generally starts running on the day an obligation falls due.[459] In case of damages due to performance failure, the prescription period starts running on the day of the performance failure, even if the damage occurs later.[460]

444 The length of the prescription period depends on the claim in question. Generally, contractual claims prescribe after ten years.[461] There are some exceptions to this.

457. Decision of the Swiss Federal Supreme Court dated 16 June 2017, DSC 143 III 348, para. 5.5.1: 'The debtor commits an abuse of rights (article 2(2) CC) by availing himself of prescription not only when he tricks the creditor into not acting in good time, but also when, without malicious intent, he behaves in such a way as to induce the creditor to refrain from taking legal action during the prescription period and when, according to a reasonable assessment based on objective criteria, this delay appears understandable.'
458. Article 142 CO.
459. Article 130(1) CO. Regarding calculation of the duration, *see* Article 132 CO.
460. Decision of the Swiss Federal Supreme Court dated 16 December 2013, DSC 140 II 7, para. 3.3.
461. Article 127 CO.

Above all, periodic payments, employees' salaries, and attorney fees are subject to a five-year prescription period.[462] Further, the special part of the Code of Obligations foresees shorter limitation periods for certain contract types.[463]

445 A running prescription period may be suspended (Article 134 CO) or interrupted (Articles 135–138 CO). If a prescription period is suspended, the remainder of the period resumes running at the end of the day on which the cause of suspension ceases to apply. In contrast, if prescription is interrupted, a new prescription period begins running from the start.[464] The most common ground for interruption is the initiation of court or enforcement proceedings as well as (implicit) acknowledgement of the claim by the debtor.[465]

446 The parties' ability to modify the regime of prescription set forth in Articles 127–142 CO is limited. Namely, a shortening of the prescription period is not permitted.[466] However, this limitation does not apply to prescription periods contained in the special part of the Code of Obligations. Further, a party may waive invoking the prescription defence, but only after the prescription period has started running.[467]

B Set-Off

447 If the debtor has a counter-claim against the creditor, he may reduce or extinguish the creditor's claim by declaring a set-off (*Verrechnung, compensation, compensazione*). Set-off is governed by Articles 120–126 CO.

448 A set-off is not automatic but requires the offsetting party to make an expression of intent to that effect.[468] A set-off may be declared if five conditions are met:

(i) Reciprocity of claims: The claims used for the set-off must bind the same parties. There are, however, a few exceptions to this rule, namely in case of assignment.[469]
(ii) Identity of claims: The claims used for the set-off must be identical in nature. Thus, two monetary claims may be set off against each other, but not a monetary claim against a claim for transfer of ownership of an object. If monetary claims are denominated in different currencies, they may still be set off against each other by converting them into the same currency, unless such conversion has been contractually excluded.
(iii) The offsetting claim is due and actionable: The offsetting claim of the debtor must be due. An exception to this rule applies in case of bankruptcy.[470] In

462. Article 128 CO.
463. *See, e.g.*, Article 210 CO (action for breach of warranty in sales contract).
464. Article 137(1) CO.
465. Article 135 CO.
466. Article 129 CO.
467. Article 141 CO.
468. Article 124(1) CO.
469. Article 169(2) CO.
470. Article 123 CO.

addition, the offsetting claims must not be prescribed. However, a prescribed claim may still be used for a set-off if it had not yet been prescribed at the time it became eligible for set-off.[471]

(iv) The set-off claim is executable: The creditor's claim does not have to be due, but it must be executable.[472] Unless agreed otherwise, a claim is executable immediately upon arising.[473]

(v) No exclusion of the right to set-off: The debtor must not have waived the set-off defence, e.g., by agreeing to a prohibition of set-off in the contract in question.[474] Further, set-off must not be excluded by statute.[475]

449 If the conditions are met and a set-off is declared, the creditor's and debtor's claims extinguish to the extent of the lower claim without the need for any order from a court. The claims are deemed extinguished from the time when they first became susceptible to set-off.[476]

450 Like prescription, also a set-off may serve as a defence in two ways: *One*, the debtor may extinguish an obligation by declaring set-off, thus also barring any claim for performance failure in respect of that obligation; *two*, any claim for damages arising from a performance failure may be countered with set-off and thus be defended against by that defence.

451 Importantly, a declaration of set-off contains an acknowledgement of debt. By declaring a set-off, the debtor acknowledges the creditor's claim. As the set-off declaration constitutes the exercise of a formative right, it may not be made contingent upon a condition (such as the existence of the creditor's claim).[477] Yet, in the context of court or arbitration proceedings, a respondent may mount a two-fold defence by first arguing that there is no claim and, second, declaring a set-off in case there was any claim.[478] This is deemed permissible despite the set-off being made contingent upon a condition (i.e., the court or arbitral tribunal finds that there is a claim).[479]

---

471. Article 120(3) CO.
472. The wording of Article 120(1) CO is misleading in this respect (*see* Huguenin, Obligationenrecht, Zurich 2019, N 760).
473. *See* hereinabove paras 294–295.
474. Article 126 CO. However, exclusion of set-off is deemed void for some contract types (*see, e.g.*, Article 323b(2) CO for employment contracts).
475. *See* Article 125 CO and Articles 213–214 of the Federal Act on Debt Enforcement and Bankruptcy.
476. Article 124(2) CO.
477. *See* hereinabove para. 267.
478. *See* decision of the Swiss Federal Supreme Court dated 3 August 2016, no. 5A_748/2015, para. 3.4.1: 'The procedural objection of set-off (*objection de compensation*) is to be distinguished from the declaration of set-off (*déclaration de compensation*) pursuant to article 124(1) CO. The declaration of set-off triggers – according to substantive law – the effect of set-off; the objection of set-off in the proceedings makes – according to the rules of procedural law – the question of set-off the subject matter of the proceedings. The declaration of set-off and the procedural assertion can coincide, but also diverge.'
479. Schwenzer/Fountoulakis, Schweizerisches Obligationenrecht – Allgemeiner Teil, Bern 2020, N 78.03.

CHAPTER 6

Termination of Contracts

452 There are several ways to put an end to a contract. The consequences of such an end vary. The ending of a contract must be distinguished from the extinguishment of a single obligation that may arise out of a contract. The extinguishment is governed by Articles 114–142 CO and generally does not put an end to the contractual relationship as a whole.

453 There are five ways by which parties may put an end to a contract. First, the parties may agree on its dissolution (section I). Second, a party may rescind the contract (section II). Third, a party may terminate a contract by unilaterally issuing a notice of termination (section III). Further, an end may result from the principle of *clausula rebus sic stantibus* (section IV) or by statute (section V)

I TERMINATION BY AGREEMENT

454 By means of a dissolution agreement, the parties can agree, for example, that a contract is to be terminated *ex tunc* by mutual agreement. Article 115 CO is applied analogously to such contract meaning that there is no form requirement that the parties must comply with.[480] The agreement can also be structured in such a way that the contract is terminated *ex nunc* or at another point in time.

455 The legal consequences of such dissolution must be determined by interpreting the terms of the dissolution contract.

480. Decision of the Swiss Federal Supreme Court dated 17 December 1969, DSC 95 II 419, para. 2.d: 'From this point of view, the settlement proves to be simply a cancellation of the agreement of 15 December 1966. This cancellation could be made informally according to article 115 CO, because according to established doctrine, this provision is not only applicable to the extinguishment of claims, but also to the dissolution of legal transactions.'

II TERMINATION BY RESCISSION

456 Rescission is exercised unilaterally, i.e., by means of an expression of intent which must be received. Its exercise leads to the contractual relationship being converted into a contractual liquidation relationship.[481]

457 Rescission is a remedy available in case of debtor default if the conditions of Articles 107–109 CO are met.[482] Further, creditor default may also lead to rescission.[483] The special part of the Code of Obligations sets forth other scenarios in which rescission is available.[484] Additionally, the parties are free to stipulate other conditions under which rescission becomes available.

III TERMINATION BY NOTICE

458 A continuing contract[485] may be terminated by issuing a notice of termination (*Kündigung, résiliation, disdetta*). Like rescission, termination by notice is exercised by means of an expression of intent which must be received by the other party. It puts an end to the contractual relationship with effect *ex nunc,* i.e., with effect for the future from the time when termination occurs but not with retroactive effect.

459 The general part of the Code of Obligations does not contain any provisions on the termination of contracts by notice. Nevertheless, termination by notice is regulated in the special part of the Code of Obligations for certain contracts.[486]

460 There are two types of termination by notice: ordinary termination by notice (*ordentliche Kündigung, résiliation ordinaire, disdetta ordinaria*), by which termination is declared with a statutory or contractual notice period, and extraordinary termination by notice (*ausserordentliche Kündigung, résiliation extraordinaire, disdetta straordinaria*) by which termination is based on a special ground and declared without adherence to any notice period.

A Ordinary Termination by Notice

461 The right to ordinary termination by notice may arise from contract or statute. The special part of the Code of Obligations foresees a right to ordinary termination by notice for most nominate continuing contracts.[487] Yet, these provisions are usually non-mandatory and may be deviated from by agreement. In the case of innominate

481. *See* hereinabove para. 429.
482. *See* hereinabove paras 426–428.
483. Article 95 CO.
484. *See, e.g.,* Article 205 CO (redhibition of sales contract for breach of warranty).
485. Term defined hereinabove in para. 66.
486. *See, e.g.,* Article 404 (termination of mandate agreement).
487. *See, e.g.,* Article 545(1)(6) CO (simple partnership).

contracts, a right to ordinary termination with an appropriate notice period may be inferred if there is no contractual termination provision and a *lacuna*[488] may be assumed.[489]

462 If such right exists, a party may terminate the contract without giving reasons. In most cases, a notice period must be observed and/or the contract may only be terminated on certain dates (e.g., per end of a quarter).[490] The calculation of the notice period is governed by Articles 76–78 CO.

463 For purposes of calculating a notice period, it is important to consider that a termination notice only takes effect once received by the other party (so-called theory of receipt; *Empfangstheorie, théorie de la reception, teoria dell'atto ricettizio*). Receipt is assumed if the expression of intent enters the sphere of influence of the recipient in such a way that under normal circumstances it can be expected to be taken note of; whether and when the addressee actually becomes aware of the statement is not relevant.[491] If a party illegitimately avoids receipt, the expression of intent is deemed received.[492] Parties are free to deviate from the theory of receipt in their contract.

488. *See* hereinabove paras 241 et seqq.
489. Decision of the Swiss Federal Supreme Court dated 13 October 1981, DSC 107 II 411, para. 7: 'It may also be assumed that prudent contracting parties in a comparable situation would have included a notice period in their contract that would allow them to prepare for the end of the contract in good time. In the present case, however, it is the task of the judge to determine, in application of articles 2(2) CO, which notice period is appropriate to the concrete circumstances.'
490. *See, e.g.*, Articles 266a et seqq. CO (lease agreement for residential property).
491. Decision of the Swiss Federal Supreme Court dated 19 May 2014, DSC 140 III 244, para. 5.1: 'In DSC 137 III 208, handed down in connection with the extraordinary notice period based on article 261(2)(a) CO, the Federal Supreme Court examined in detail the question of receipt of the notice of termination of a lease, the starting point for calculating this time limit under the substantive law laid down in the Code of Obligations. It confirmed that when a time limit under substantive law runs from the communication of an expression of intent, the theory of absolute receipt must be applied: the starting point of the time limit corresponds to the moment when the expression of intent has reached the sphere of influence (*Machtbereich*) of the addressee or his representative, so that by normally organising his affairs he is in a position to take cognisance of it. Thus, in particular, when the postal officer has not been able to deliver the registered letter to its addressee or to a third party authorised to take delivery of it and he leaves a notice of collection in the addressee's letterbox or post office box, the letter is received as soon as the addressee is in a position to take cognisance of it at the post office according to the notice of collection. Otherwise, as a general rule, on the day following that day. The Federal Court noted that this was a view endorsed by the majority of legal scholars.' Also *see* decision of the Swiss Federal Supreme Court dated 22 January 1992, DSC 118 II 42, para. 3.b: 'According to these principles, an expression of intent in letter form is received by the addressee as soon as it enters his or her sphere of control. In the case of a message that is delivered by private or unregistered post, this is the case if it is placed in the addressee's letterbox at a time when it can be expected to be emptied.' Regarding receipt of email, *see* Schwenzer/Fountoulakis, Schweizerisches Obligationenrecht – Allgemeiner Teil, Bern 2020, N 27.23: 'The business recipient has a retrieval obligation, so that notices are received when they are stored in the respective server, insofar as at this point in time, the recipient can be expected to take note of the message.'
492. Decision of the Swiss Federal Supreme Court dated 28 February 1933, DSC 59 III 66, p. 67: 'The lower court rightly assumed that the retention order had lapsed if the creditor had not filed an action within ten days of service of the document, and that the document must also have been deemed served if the creditor had unjustifiably refused to accept it.'

464 If a party terminates a contract by notice but indicates the wrong notice period or miscalculates the date of effective termination, the termination by notice is not considered void. Rather, the termination by notice with incorrect notice period or dates is converted into a notice with correct periods and dates.[493] Thus, the contract in question binds the parties until the termination's effective date that results from the correct application of the notice period.

B Extraordinary Termination by Notice

465 An extraordinary termination presupposes a sufficient ground for termination (*Kündigungsgrund, motif de résiliation, motivo per una disdetta*).[494] The grounds permitting extraordinary termination may result either from statute,[495] the parties' agreement or case law.

466 Swiss case law permits extraordinary termination in one particular scenario. A party may always terminate a continuing contract by notice for good cause (also referred to as important reasons for termination; *wichtige Gründe, justes motifs, motivi gravi*), i.e., if the contract's continuation would be intolerable to the terminating party.[496] This is a fundamental and mandatory principle of Swiss contract law. The termination right exists even if not explicitly agreed on by the parties and even if the parties stipulate the opposite (or attempt to reduce its scope).[497]

467 The question of which events give rise to a good cause for termination often leads to disputes. The Swiss Federal Supreme Court has summed up the required standard as follows:

> According to case law, good cause for the termination of a continuing contractual relationship exists if being bound by the contract has become intolerable for the party due to changed circumstances, i.e., not only from an economic point of view, but also from other aspects affecting the personality. The court decides at its discretion whether good cause exists in an individual case (article 4 CC). This is an equitable decision based on an objective weighing of interests, taking into account the circumstances of the case under consideration.[498]

---

493. There are, however, exceptions to this principle. For example, in the context of lease agreements of residential property, the Swiss Federal Supreme Court is very reluctant to admit such conversion (*see, e.g.*, decision of the Swiss Federal Supreme Court dated 1 May 2009, DSC 135 III 441, para. 3).
494. An exception forms Article 404 CO, which permits immediate termination of a mandate agreement despite absence of any ground (*see* below paras 739 et seqq.).
495. *See, e.g.*, Articles 266g, 418r and 527 CO.
496. Decision of the Swiss Federal Supreme Court dated 9 April 2010, no. 4A_87/2010, para. 4.1.2: 'In order to determine whether good cause exists, it is decisive whether the continuation of the contractual relationship until the possibility of an ordinary termination or an extraordinary termination provided for in the contract is intolerable for one of the contracting parties.' Also *see*, decision of the Swiss Federal Supreme Court dated 8 September 2011, no. 4A_148/2011, para. 4.3.1.
497. Decision of the Swiss Federal Supreme Court dated 8 September 2011, no. 4A_148/2011, para. 4.3.1.
498. Decision of the Swiss Federal Supreme Court dated 12 May 2006, no. 4C.67/2006, para. 2.1.

468 In practice a two-fold test has emerged:[499] First, from an objective point of view the court must answer the question of whether a reasonable person in the shoes of the terminating party could, based on the circumstances of the individual case, not be reasonably expected to tolerate continuation of the contract until the next ordinary termination date. The courts set a high threshold for this test. Namely, a simple violation of a contractual duty is not sufficient. There must be either a particularly serious breach of contract or a repetition of breaches that occur despite warnings.[500]

469 Second, there is also a subjective test to be conducted. Continuation must also be intolerable to the terminating party in question. Usually, where the objective test is passed, the subjective test will not cause any issues. However, a subjectively good cause is to be denied if the party who wants to terminate the continuing obligation: (i) fails to timely notify the other party of its intention to terminate; or (ii) continues to perform the contract regardless of the events that have occurred.[501] By such behaviour, a party demonstrates that the continuation of the contract is not subjectively intolerable.[502]

470 Timely notification of termination depends on the individual circumstances. Case law permits waiting periods of two days[503] up to a week and in some instances even several weeks depending on the complexity and importance of the situation.[504] Namely, if the situation requires further investigations, a longer period seems justified. If the terminating party waits longer than permitted, the right to extraordinary termination is considered forfeited.

471 At times, parties agree in their contract that certain reasons are considered 'important reasons' constituting good cause for termination. Equally, they may agree on deadlines to be observed or the further modalities of termination. Such agreements

499. *See* Vetter/Gutzwiller, Voraussetzungen und Rechtsfolgen der ausserordentlichen Beendigung von Dauerschuldverhältnisses, Aktuelle Juristische Praxis 2010, p. 705; Venturi-Zen-Ruffinen, La résiliation pour justes motifs des contrats de durée, Zurich 2007, N 405.
500. Decision of the Swiss Federal Supreme Court dated 5 April 2012, DSC 138 III 304, para. 7: 'In the case of particularly serious breaches of contract, good cause is generally to be affirmed. However, even less serious breaches of contract can make it intolerable for the other party to continue the contract if they have occurred repeatedly despite warnings or reprimands, so that further warnings cannot be expected to deter the contractual partner from further breaches of contract.'
501. Decision of the Swiss Federal Supreme Court dated 25 September 1973, DSC 99 II 308, para. 5.a.
502. Decision of the Swiss Federal Supreme Court dated 29 December 2011, DSC 138 I 113, para. 6.3.1 (concerning a employment contract): 'If there is good cause, the extraordinary termination shall be declared immediately. Otherwise, it shall be assumed that compliance with the ordinary notice period is subjectively tolerable for the terminating party and the right to immediate termination of the contract shall be forfeited.'
503. *See* decision of the Swiss Federal Supreme Court dated 21 July 2021, no. 4A_57/2021, para. 3.2.2 (concerning an employment contract).
504. For an overview, *see* Venturi-Zen-Ruffinen, La résiliation pour justes motifs des contrats de durée, Zurich 2007, N 1190 et seqq.

are generally permissible,[505] as long as they do not restrict the right to terminate for good cause, but rather lower the threshold for extraordinary termination.[506]

472 Similarly, long-term contracts often contain a clause permitting immediate termination if a party 'materially' breaches the agreement (sometimes linked with failure to cure such breach within a specified period). When terminating based on such contractual ground, the Swiss Federal Supreme Court has clarified that a 'material breach' presupposes only violation of a main obligation under a contract, but not that such breach makes the continuation intolerable for the aggrieved party – unless agreed otherwise by the parties.[507] In such cases, termination is based on a contractual ground, rather than the ground of 'important reasons'.

473 An extraordinary termination declared without sufficient grounds does generally not produce any effect unless provided otherwise by statute.[508] Importantly, an invalid extraordinary termination is not converted into an ordinary termination.[509] Thus, if a declared extraordinary termination is invalid, the contract in question remains in effect and the parties must perform their obligations.[510]

505. An exception must be made for contract types for which the Code of Obligations stipulates a mandatory right of termination for good cause (e.g., employment or lease contracts).
506. Wolfer, Die vertragliche Regelung der Vertragsauflösung 'aus wichtigem Grund', Aktuelle Juristische Praxis 2014, p. 624; Vetter/Gutzwiller, Voraussetzungen und Rechtsfolgen der ausserordentlichen Beendigung von Dauerschuldverhältnisses, Aktuelle Juristische Praxis 2010, p. 706; Venturi-Zen-Ruffinen, La résiliation pour justes motifs des contrats de durée, Zurich 2007, N 1229.
507. Decision of the Swiss Federal Supreme Court dated 8 September 2011, no. 4A_148/2011, para. 4.4.1: 'The general termination clause of a material breach of contract ("any other material breach of this Agreement"; clause 8.1.3 of the Agreement) corresponds to a widely used, typical contract clause. The doctrine is of the opinion that in the case of such a serious breach of contract, especially if it is permanent, an important reason can generally be seen which makes a continuation of the contract unbearable for the other party. This does not mean, however, that the examination of whether there is a material breach of contract coincides with the examination of whether there is an important reason that makes a continuation of the contractual relationship unbearable. Thus, it cannot be said that the question of whether a breach of contract is material can only be determined by an interpretation in which an unbearableness test is applied, as the appellant claims. Rather, the question of whether a breach of contract in a case where no grounds for early termination of the contract have been agreed constitutes a material ground for early termination must be distinguished from the question of whether a breach of contract that has occurred qualifies as a material breach of contract which – if the parties have permissibly agreed such a breach as a ground for termination, as is the case here – entitles them to terminate the contract without any further unbearableness test.'
508. *See, e.g.*, Article 337c CO (extraordinary termination without grounds sets an end to employment contract, but gives rise to a claim for compensation).
509. Decision of the Swiss Federal Supreme Court dated 5 April 2012, DSC 138 III 304, para. 11: 'First of all, according to the case law of the Federal Supreme Court, an invalid extraordinary termination cannot be converted into an ordinary termination unless the termination was merely erroneously designated as an extraordinary termination (article 18 CO), which, however, is not asserted here.' In doctrine, some scholars propose such conversion outside of rent lease agreements, *see, e.g.*, Vetter/Gutzwiller, Voraussetzungen und Rechtsfolgen der ausserordentlichen Beendigung von Dauerschuldverhältnisses, Aktuelle Juristische Praxis 2010, p. 709.
510. Decision of the Swiss Federal Supreme Court dated 6 March 2007, DSC 133 III 360, para. 8.1.2.

474 In contrast, if an extraordinary termination is valid, it puts an immediate end to the contractual relationship with effect *ex nunc*. If the ground for termination was a breach of contract, the terminating party might be entitled to also claim damages.[511]

IV TERMINATION BY *CLAUSULA REBUS SIC STANTIBUS*

475 Pursuant to the principle of *clausula rebus sic stantibus*, a party is entitled to an amendment of the contractual terms if circumstances have unforeseeably changed and have led to an extraordinary disbalance between the obligations of the parties.[512] Generally, the disbalance is remedied by an amendment of the contract's terms. But, if the disbalance cannot be remedied otherwise, the court may dissolve the contract prematurely.[513]

V TERMINATION BY STATUTE

476 Finally, statutory law provides for automatic termination by death, incapacity or bankruptcy of a party for a number of contracts, the vast majority of which are also continuing contracts.[514]

511. *See* hereinabove paras 396 et seqq.
512. *See* hereinabove paras 246 et seqq.
513. Decision of the Swiss Federal Supreme Court dated 24 April 2001, DSC 127 III 300, para. 6.b.
514. *See, e.g.*, Article 405 CO (mandate agreement).

CHAPTER 7

Specific Legal Acts Relevant to Contractual Obligations

I ACKNOWLEDGMENT OF DEBT

477 An acknowledgement of debt (*Schuldanerkennung/Schuldbekenntnis, reconnaissance de dette, riconoscimento del debito*) is a declaration by the debtor to the creditor that a certain debt exists and that the debtor intends to fulfil it.[515] Article 17 CO clarifies in this respect that such acknowledgement of debt is valid even if it does not refer to the specific cause of the debt (so-called abstract acknowledgement of debt).

478 An acknowledgement of debt is not subject to any form requirement. It may be given explicitly or implicitly. The (allegedly) recognising party's expression of intent must be interpreted according to the usual rules.[516] Importantly, silence does generally not amount to an acknowledgement of debt.[517] However, where the contract stipulates that an invoice is deemed acknowledged if not objected to within a certain time limit, silence may amount to an acknowledgement of debt.[518]

479 Although an acknowledgement of debt may serve as a cause of action for the creditor, the debtor may still prove that the debt does not exist or is not actionable. The main legal effect of the acknowledgement of debt is therefore a reversal of the burden

515. Decision of the Swiss Federal Supreme Court dated 14 April 2009, no. 4A_17/2009, para. 3.2.
516. *See* hereinabove paras 207 et seqq.
517. Decision of the Swiss Federal Supreme Court dated 10 August 2010, no. 4A_231/2010, para. 2.4.1.
518. Decision of the Swiss Federal Supreme Court dated 4 August 2006, no. 4C.175/2006, para. 2.1 (concerning account statements of banks): 'With the fiction of approval, the parties agree that passive behaviour on the part of the bank's customer is to be regarded as acceptance of the account statement within the meaning of article 6 CO. The agreed approval by silence is to be understood as approval according to the principle of trust only insofar as a positive reaction is possible and the bank does not know or must know according to the circumstances that the bank's customer lacks the will for approval.'

of proof.[519] The debtor is only deprived of defences and objection against the debt if he has waived them when acknowledging the debt, which is only to be assumed restrictively.[520] The use of words such as 'irrevocably' or 'unconditionally' in an acknowledgement of debt may, however, indicate such waiver.[521]

II WAIVER OF CLAIMS

480 Parties to a contract may freely agree on the extinction of a claim. By agreeing to its extinction, the creditor waives his claim.

481 Such waiver is not subject to any form requirement.[522] It may be given explicitly or implicitly. This is a question of interpretation of the parties' expressions of intent. But a waiver of claims must not be assumed lightly.[523] The burden of proof for such intention lies on the debtor.[524]

---

519. Decision of the Swiss Federal Supreme Court dated 20 September 2013, no. 4A_152/2013, para. 2.3: 'The acknowledgement of debt reverses the burden of proof. The debtor who disputes the debt must establish the cause of the obligation (in the case of an abstract acknowledgement), respectively show that the cause of the obligation is invalid, for example because the legal relationship on which the acknowledgement is based is non-existent, null and void (articles 19 and 20 CO), has been simulated (article 18(1) CO) or invalidated (article 31 CO).' Decision of the Swiss Federal Supreme Court dated 14 April 2009, no. 4A_17/2009, para. 3.2: 'More generally, the debtor may invoke all objections and defences directed against the acknowledged debt.'
520. Decision of the Swiss Federal Supreme Court dated 21 June 2007, no. 4C.69/2007, para. 6.3: 'In principle, an acknowledgement of debt has no influence on the substantive status of the debtor's obligation. The debtor who has acknowledged a claim is therefore entitled to all defences and objections from the underlying contract vis-à-vis the creditor. Only in exceptional cases is there an additional agreement connected with the acknowledgement of the debt that the debtor waives certain defences with regard to the acknowledged debt. Such a waiver of defences is not to be assumed lightly and must be unambiguous, as it is of great consequence for the debtor. The burden of proof for such a limitation of defences is on the creditor.'
521. Decision of the Zurich Commercial Court dated 5 April 2000, published in Blätter für Zürcherische Rechtsprechung (ZR) 2001, pp. 166 et seqq., para. V.3: 'If a bank gives a promise to pay which is described as irrevocable ("irrevocably") and unconditional ("unconditionally") and which is to be made without protest or notification, i.e., uses clauses which already express an unrestricted intention to pay and which, as far as the first two are concerned, are known from (non-accessory) bank guarantees, the bank must accept the argument that it has given an acknowledgment of debt freed of defences and objections.'
522. Article 115 CO.
523. Decision of the Swiss Federal Supreme Court dated 7 July 2003, no. 4C.363/2001, para. 3: 'An implied offer [to agree on the extinction of the claim] is to be assumed if the creditor's conduct, according to general experience of life and the view of the market, gives reason to conclude that there is an intention to waive. According to case law, however, such an intention may not be inferred lightly. Thus, neither the mere letting of a claim become prescribed nor the occasional non-exercise of a right nor the non-enforcement of a claim for a longer period of time without additional special circumstances added to the merely passive behaviour of the creditor is sufficient.'
524. Decision of the Swiss Federal Supreme Court dated 8 December 2010, no. 4A_544/2010, para. 2.3: 'The appellant maintains that this rent debt no longer existed, because it had been extinguished by a waiver of debt (article 115 CO). A waiver of debt is an informal bilateral contract between the creditor and the debtor. As the position of article 115 CO in the Code shows, it is a ground for extinguishing the obligation. It follows from article 8 CC that the

III ASSIGNMENT OF CLAIMS

482 Assignment (*Abtretung/Zession, cession, cessione*) is the contractual transfer of an individual claim arising from a contractual obligation by the original creditor (assignor) to a third party (assignee) who becomes the new creditor. The debtor is not involved in this legal transaction.[525] Assignment is governed by Articles 164–174 CO.

A Conditions of Assignment

483 The act of assignment must be made in writing in order to be valid.[526] This refers to simple written form in the sense of Article 13 CO.[527] Accordingly, all the essential points must be covered by the act in the required form, in particular, an identifiable claim and the will to transfer it to the assignee.[528] In contrast to the act of assignment, the contract in which the assignor undertakes to transfer the claim is generally not subject to any form requirements, unless the underlying transaction is itself subject to a form requirement (e.g., promise of a gift[529]).[530]

484 Generally, all claims[531] may be assigned unless provided otherwise by statutory or contractual provisions.[532] The creditor and debtor may exclude the assignability of a claim in advance or subsequently (*pactum de non cedendo*). Further, for certain contract types, the Code of Obligations restricts assignability of claims.[533] Finally, the nature of the claim may bar assignment if the performance to the assignee cannot take place without altering the claim's content or if the purpose of the claim would be frustrated or jeopardised by the assignment.[534]

485 Future claims may be assigned provided that the content of the claim as well as the debtor are sufficiently specified.[535] The assignment of an indefinite number of existing or future claims arising from a business or commercial activity of the assignor is permissible (so-called global assignment; *Globalzession, cession globale, cessione*

---

creditor must prove the facts on which his claim is based, while the debtor must prove the facts that lead to the extinction or loss of the right.'

525. In this regard, the assignment of a claim must be distinguished from the transfer of an entire contract. The latter requires consent of all involved parties.
526. Article 165(1) CO.
527. *See* hereinabove para. 147.
528. Decision of the Swiss Federal Supreme Court dated 25 May 1979, DSC 105 II 83, para. 2.
529. Article 243(1) CO.
530. Article 165(2) CO.
531. In this context, it is important to distinguish claims from formative rights. The latter may, in general, not be assigned.
532. Article 164(1) CO.
533. *See, e.g.*, Articles 325 and 333(4) CO (employment contracts).
534. Decision of the Swiss Federal Supreme Court dated 17 July 1989, DSC 115 II 264, para. 3.b.
535. Decision of the Swiss Federal Supreme Court dated 20 October 2008, DSC 135 V 2, para. 6.1.2: 'Furthermore, civil case law and doctrine also allow future claims to be assigned within the limits of article 27(2) CC and article 20 CO. However, the content of the future claim as well as the person of the debtor and the legal basis of the claim must be sufficiently identified or at least identifiable.'

globale) if the claims and debtors are identifiable.[536] A global assignment must, however, be limited in terms of time and subject matter, otherwise, it violates Article 27(2) CC and would therefore be void.[537]

B Consequences of Assignment

486 Upon valid assignment, the assignee becomes the new creditor of the claim. The assignment includes the transfer of all preferential and accessory rights except those that are inseparably linked to the person of the assignor.[538] In addition, the assignee may request the assignor to furnish him with the legal documents pertaining to the debt together with all available evidence thereof and to furnish him with all information necessary to assert the claim.[539]

487 For the debtor, the assignment means that he must now perform his obligation vis-à-vis the assignee in order to validly discharge his obligation. Yet, this only applies if the debtor has been notified of the assignment.[540]

488 The assignor is no longer the creditor of the assigned claim and can thus no longer request performance of the obligation. The relationship between the assignor and the assignee is governed by Articles 171–173 CO which provide for a (non-mandatory) warranty regime.

IV ASSUMPTION OF DEBT

489 By an assumption of debt (*Schuldübernahme, reprise de dette, assunzione di debito*) a third party (the substituting party) substitutes himself for the debtor permitting the creditor to request performance from the substituting party. It is governed by Articles 175–183 CO.

490 Three types of assumptions of debt must be distinguished:

---

536. Decision of the Swiss Federal Supreme Court dated 20 October 2008, DSC 135 V 2, para. 6.1.2: 'With regard to the global assignment, this requirement must be met at the time the claim arises or is asserted and not already at the time the formally valid declaration of assignment is made. On the other hand, the declaration of assignment itself must contain all elements that allow the content, debtor and legal basis to be determined at the time the claim arises.' Also *see* decision of the Swiss Federal Supreme Court dated 12 May 1987, DSC 113 II 163, para. 2.
537. Decision of the Swiss Federal Supreme Court dated 11 December 1986, DSC 112 II 433, para. 3: 'As was already the case for the High Court, it is also unnecessary for the Federal Supreme Court to comment on these questions if the assignment already proves to be invalid on the basis of article 27(2) CC and article 20(1) CO. There is broad agreement in doctrine and jurisprudence that an assignment of all present and future claims, unlimited in time and subject matter, is immoral and therefore void under these provisions.'
538. Article 170(1) CO.
539. Article 170(2) CO.
540. Article 167 CO.

- Internal assumption of debt: This describes the contractual relationship between the debtor and the third party promising the debtor to answer for the debt, either by satisfying the creditor or by taking the debtor's place with the consent of the creditor (external assumption of debt).[541] An internal assumption of debt does not itself turn the third party into a debtor vis-à-vis the creditor.[542]
- Cumulative assumption of debt: Although the substituting party becomes a debtor vis-à-vis the creditor, the original debtor is not released and remains liable for the debt. Thus, following a cumulative assumption of debt, the creditor has two debtors who are jointly and severally liable. Often, it is a difficult question of interpretation whether the parties intended to conclude a cumulative assumption of debt, a guarantee, or a surety since all three concepts serve as means of security for the creditor.[543]
- External assumption of debt: It extinguishes the debtor's debt vis-à-vis the creditor and gives rise to a new claim of identical content of the substituting party vis-à-vis the creditor. An external assumption of debt requires the creditor's approval.[544]

491 The Swiss Federal Supreme Court describes the interplay between the various types as follows:

> On the other hand, the appellants could be released from their restitution obligation through the debt assumption mechanism. This usually begins with a contract between the debtor and the substituting party, whereby the substituting party promises to release the debtor from his debt to the creditor (internal debt assumption within the meaning of article 175(1) CO). In order for the former debtor to be discharged, a contract must then be concluded between the substituting party and the creditor (external debt assumption within the meaning of article 176(1) CO).
>
> The external assumption of debt is a contract that is not subject to any formal requirements. Article 176(2) CO establishes a rebuttable presumption that the communication to the creditor by the substituting party (or by the debtor as the substituting party's direct representative) of the internal debt assumption agreement constitutes an offer by the substituting party to enter into an external debt assumption agreement with the creditor. The creditor's consent may be tacit (article 176(3) CO), in particular if the offer to take over the debt is advantageous to the creditor; consent is presumed if the creditor accepts – without reservation – a payment from the substituting party or consents to other acts performed by the substituting party as debtor (article 176(3) CO).[545]

541. Article 175 CO.
542. *See* Article 175(2–3) CO regarding modalities of performance for the third party's duty to answer for the debt.
543. *See* hereinabove paras 322–324.
544. Article 176 CO.
545. Decision of the Swiss Federal Supreme Court dated 15 July 2021, no. 4A_486/2020, para. 6.1.

492 If an external assumption of debt is concluded, the creditor has a new debtor. However, the content of the obligation itself remains the same. In particular, the accessory rights remain unaffected by the change of debtor.[546]

493 Although the substituting party has assumed the debt, it may raise all defences against the creditor, be it that such defence arises from the debt itself (e.g., prescription) or the personal relationship with the creditor (e.g., set-off).[547]

V NOVATION OF A CLAIM

494 Novation consists of the contractual agreement of creditor and debtor to let an existing obligation extinguish and to replace it with a new one, i.e., to change the legal basis of the existing debt relationship.[548]

495 According to Article 116(1) CO, novation is not to be presumed. The party asserting novation, therefore, carries the burden of proof that the parties intended for novation to take place. Such intention is often present if parties conclude a settlement agreement.[549]

496 However, there is an exception where parties entertain current accounts (e.g., if parties do not assert claims and counterclaims from mutual business transactions individually, but offset them against each other and regularly draw the balance). Here, there is a presumption of novation if the balance on the account has been drawn and acknowledged.[550]

546. Article 178(1) CO.
547. Article 179 CO.
548. Decision of the Swiss Federal Supreme Court dated 25 March 2009, DSC 135 V 124, para. 4.2.
549. Decision of the Swiss Federal Supreme Court dated 6 November 1979, DSC 105 II 273, para. 3.a: 'A settlement, including a court settlement, is a contract by which a dispute or uncertainty about a legal relationship is settled with mutual concessions. In doing so, the parties often replace an existing legal relationship with a new one within the meaning of article 116 CO. This applies in particular if, in the case of a complex legal relationship, as here, they agree on a balance payment, i.e., both parties waive further claims against each other. In contrast to a mere amendment of the contract, the novation removes the identity of the claim, and defences and weaknesses that were attached to the replaced claims usually cease to exist.' Also *see* herein below para. 746.
550. Article 117(2) CO.

Chapter 8
The Special Part of the Code of Obligations

497 While the previous seven chapters have laid out the general principles of Swiss contract law, this chapter will deal with the rules established by statutory and case law that apply to specific types of contracts.

498 Where such rules exist, they generally take precedence over the general provisions of the Code of Obligations, but parties are usually free to deviate from them anyway. This combination of possible sources of rules governing a contractual relationship results in the following hierarchy:

(1) contractual provisions agreed by the parties (within the permissible limits);[551]
(2) provisions of the special part of the Code of Obligations (Articles 184–551 CO);[552]
(3) provisions of the general part of the Code of Obligations (Articles 1–183 CO);[553] and
(4) contractual provisions deduced from the parties' hypothetical will.[554]

499 Of course, the provisions – whether based on the parties' common will, statute or case law – are subject to interpretation.[555] Only the result of such interpretation constitutes the substantive rules that applies to a specific issue.

500 Given the limited scope of this introductory book, it is not possible to address all types of contracts. Rather, the essential distinction between nominate and innominate contracts will be addressed first (section I) before analysing the contract types which are at the heart of a large number of commercial disputes: sales contracts (section II),

551. *See* hereinabove paras 229 et seqq.
552. *See* hereinabove para. 243.
553. *See* hereinabove para. 243.
554. *See* hereinabove paras 244 et seq.
555. *See* hereinabove paras 35 et seqq. (interpretation of statutory provisions) and paras 207 et seqq. (interpretation of parties' expressions of intent).

contracts for work (section III) and mandate agreements (section IV). Finally, the settlement agreement will be dealt with, as it is the contract a dispute practitioner is most likely to negotiate and draft (section V).

I INTRODUCTION: NOMINATE AND INNOMINATE CONTRACTS

501 The Code of Obligations provides for several types of contracts (e.g., sales contract) for which it sets forth special rules in Articles 184–551 CO.[556] These contract types are referred to as nominate contracts.

502 However, it follows from the principle of freedom of contract that parties may agree on types of contracts not foreseen in the Code of Obligations. Such contracts are referred to as innominate contracts.

A Nominate Contracts

503 When determining the legal regime applicable to a specific contract, the first step is to determine whether the contract in question fulfils the characteristic features of any of the contract types set forth in the special part of the Code of Obligations. This procedure is referred to as (substantive) qualification of a contract.

504 The basis for the legal qualification of a contract is its content.[557] Therefore, as a first step, qualification requires the determination of a contract's content by way of interpretation.[558] Importantly, the parties' denomination of the contract is not decisive when qualifying a contract.[559] Thus, even if the parties title their agreement 'Sales Contract', it may well be qualified as a contract for work in the sense of Articles 363–379 CO if its content lends itself to such qualification.

505 In the second step, the performance obligations of the parties are compared to the characteristic performance obligations of the special part's contract types. The special part of the Code of Obligations sets forth these characteristic obligations in the first provision of each contract type.[560]

506 If there is a match, the contract in question is a nominate contract and subject to the rules set forth in the special part of the Code of Obligations for that contract type.

556. So-called ancillary statutes (*Nebengesetze*) may also contain such special rules (*see, e.g.*, Federal Act on Package Travel).
557. Decision of the Swiss Federal Supreme Court dated 20 December 2017, DSC 144 III 43, para. 3.3.
558. *See* hereinabove paras 207 et seqq.
559. Decision of the Swiss Federal Supreme Court dated 5 September 2003, DSC 129 III 664, para. 3.1.
560. *See, e.g.*, Article 184 CO: 'A contract of sale is a contract whereby the seller undertakes to deliver the item sold and transfer ownership of it to the buyer in return for the sale price, which the buyer undertakes to pay to the seller.'

507 The density with which the special part of the Code of Obligations regulates certain contract types varies. For example, the employment contract (Articles 319–362 CO) is regulated in far greater detail than the mandate agreement (Articles 394–406 CO). Equally, the subject matters addressed with respect to each contract type differ. They may include:

- rules on conclusion of contract;[561]
- rules on agency;[562]
- rules on performance failure and remedies;[563]
- rules on prescription;[564] or
- rules on termination.[565]

508 A nominate contract is subject to both, the provisions of the general part as well as the specific part of the Code of Obligations. This begs the question of how the provisions of the general and the special part interplay with each other.

509 If a specific issue is conclusively governed by the provisions of the special part, these provisions prevail over the general part (principle of *lex specialis derogat legi generali*).[566] However, where the special part does not address an issue, the provisions of the general part remain relevant. Further, in some special scenarios, case law grants a contracting party a choice as to whether to rely on the provisions of the general or the special part.[567]

510 In any case, it is important to remember that (with very few exceptions) the provisions contained in the special part of the Code of Obligations are not mandatory. Thus, the parties' agreement prevails. Only where their agreement is silent and requires supplementation, do the provisions of the special part come into play.

B Innominate Contracts

1 Groups of Innominate Contracts

511 Innominate contracts are generally divided into two groups:

- Mixed contracts (*gemischter Vertrag, contrat mixte, contratto misto*), which contain elements of different types of nominate contracts. An example of this

561. *See, e.g.*, Article 184(3) CO (sales contract).
562. *See, e.g.*, Article 396(2–3) CO (mandate agreement).
563. *See, e.g.*, Articles 197–209 CO (sales contract) or Articles 367–370 CO (contract for work).
564. *See, e.g.*, Article 370 (contract for work).
565. *See, e.g.*, Article 190 CO (sales contract).
566. For example, the issue of accidental damage in relation to an object of a sale is exclusively governed by Article 185 CO leaving no room for application of Article 119(2) CO.
567. For example, if a purchased item is defective, the buyer may invoke either the provisions on warranty of quality (Articles 197 et seqq. CO), the general liability under Article 97 CO or the rules on fundamental error (Article 24 CO), but not both at the same time (*see* below para. 619).

group would be a contract under which a housekeeper lives in a flat (rent contract) in return for providing housekeeping services (employment contract). In order to constitute a mixed contract, the mixture of elements from various nominate contracts must be such that the application of statutory provisions of only one type of contract would not do justice to the nature of the contract in question. In this regard, a mixed contract must be distinguished from a nominate contract which contains only minor important elements that are alien to that nominate contract.

- *Sui generis* contracts (*Vertrag eigener Art, contrat sui generis, contrato atipico*); they are completely new creations. An example of this group is the exclusive distribution contract.

512 Some scholars argue that there is a third group: the compound contracts (*zusammengesetzter Vertrag, contrat composé, contratto composto*). Compound contracts consist of different contracts that are separate from each other, but not entirely independent of each other. They are linked to each other in a way that they form a synallagmatic relationship. The fate of one contract is inextricably linked to that of the other, so that, for example, the rescission of one contract also affects the status of the other.[568]

2 *The Relevance of the Code of Obligations' Special Part for Establishing the Content of an Innominate Contract*

513 Like nominate contracts, the content of an innominate contract is primarily determined by the parties' expressions of intent. This is as long as the parties' agreement does not violate any mandatory provision of the Code of Obligations' general part.

514 As concerns mandatory provisions of the Code of Obligations' special part, their application to innominate contracts is less straightforward. Although systematically their scope of application is limited to the specific type of contract, the Swiss Federal Supreme Court held that they may also apply to innominate contracts which is, however, subject to a case-by-case analysis.[569] It must be assessed whether the rationale that underlies the mandatory nature of a provision (in particular, any intended protection of a weaker party) also applies to the innominate contract in question.[570]

568. Decision of the Swiss Federal Supreme Court dated 19 November 2012, DSC 139 III 49, para. 3.3: 'A compound contract exists if the parties conclude several contracts but they are interdependent. In view of their mutual dependence, it is not appropriate to subject the individual parts of the contract to a different legal fate. Rather, the contractual focus of regulation must be determined for each legal question.'
569. Decision of the Swiss Federal Supreme Court dated 10 June 2002, no. 4C.54/2002, para. 3.2.
570. Decision of the Swiss Federal Supreme Court dated 18 December 2008, no. 4A_404/2008, para. 4.1.3: 'On the other hand, an analogous application is possible and required if and to the extent that a rule of the nominate contracts also fits a legal question to be assessed for the innominate

515 Namely, in the case of a mixed contract, the mandatory provisions of the concerned nominate contracts must be considered. In contrast, *sui generis* contracts will only rarely have mandatory provisions of the special part applied to them.

516 If the innominate contract proves to be incomplete, the contract must be supplemented.[571] Non-mandatory contract law is directly applicable insofar as it is found in the general part of the Code of Obligations. However, the rules of the special part may not apply directly, but they may apply by analogy.[572] Such analogous application is particularly relevant for mixed contracts. Here, a court must determine which of the concerned contract types shall be relied on for a specific issue:

> In each case, it is necessary to determine which rules should apply in view of the particularities of the agreement in question. It will only rarely be possible to subject the agreement entirely to one contract governed by law (nominate contract), since in principle the elements of a nominate contract do not prevail to the point of absorbing all the elements that are foreign to it. It will therefore be necessary to examine precisely what the legal question is and which legal provisions or principles should be used to resolve it. Insofar as the elements of the contract are of a different nature, it is justified to subject them to the rules of various nominate contracts (e.g., employment contract, partnership contract, supply contract, agency contract, lease contract).[573]

517 Where this approach is not feasible because there is a lack of suitable statutory law that could be applied by analogy, the court must fill the gap in the light of the parties' hypothetical will.[574]

---

contract according to the principles of statutory analogy. In doing so, the judge has to examine whether the deviation of the specific contract from the contract type (here, the lease) changes the situation of the need for protection. In each individual case, on the basis of the specific contract, the judge must determine for each arising legal question separately and without a schematic assessment according to which legal provisions of the nominate contracts or according to which legal principles it is to be assessed.'

571. *See* hereinabove paras 241 et seqq.
572. *See, e.g.*, decision of the Swiss Federal Supreme Court dated 26 March 1992, DSC 118 II 157, para. 2.c: 'If, on the other hand, the franchisee is subordinate to the franchisor (so-called subordination franchising), as is typically the case – and also the case here – the question of an analogous application of protective provisions under employment contract law or commercial agency contract law becomes important.'
573. Decision of the Swiss Federal Supreme Court dated 30 May 2005, DSC 131 III 528, para. 7.1.1.
574. Decision of the Swiss Federal Supreme Court dated 23 April 1981, DSC 107 II 144, para. 3: 'The court must supplement contracts that have been validly concluded but do not provide a solution to a problem that has arisen between the parties. In the absence of statutory provisions, he can only do this by looking at what the contracting parties would have agreed in good faith if they had envisaged the unresolved situation; he is inspired by the structure of the contract and its purpose, and takes account of all the circumstances. Where the issue to be resolved relates to an event that was uncertain when the contract was concluded, the hypothetical will of the parties does not correspond to what they would have decided if they had known that the event would occur, but to what they would have agreed if they had envisaged the possibility. The same principles apply to the supplementation of innominate or complex contracts.'

II SALES CONTRACT

518 A sales contract is a contract whereby the seller undertakes to deliver the item sold and transfer ownership of it to the buyer in return for the sale price, which the buyer undertakes to pay to the seller.[575]

A Statutory Basis

519 The sale contract is a nominate contract governed by Articles 184–236 CO which are divided into five chapters:

(i) General provisions (Articles 184–186 CO).
(ii) Sale of chattels (Articles 187–215 CO).
(iii) Sale of real estate (Articles 216–222 CO).
(iv) Specific types of sales (Articles 222–236 CO).
(v) Exchange contract (Articles 237–238 CO).

520 In international sale contracts, the CISG[576] may apply.[577] As Switzerland is a contracting state of the CISG, the CISG forms an integral part of Swiss contract law. The parties may exclude the application of the CISG to their contract.[578] Yet, such exclusion is generally not assumed if the parties' choice of law clause merely states that 'Swiss law' shall apply.[579]

521 Further, the sale of certain objects may be governed by special rules. For example, the sale of ships and aircraft is subject to particular legislation.[580]

B Delimitations

1 Gift/Mixed Gift

522 A gift (Article 239 CO) can be distinguished from a contract of sale by the characteristic of gratuitousness.[581]

575. Article 184(1) CO.
576. United Nations Convention on Contracts for the International Sale of Goods (Vienna, 1980).
577. The scope of application of the convention is set forth in Articles 1–6 CISG.
578. Article 6 CISG.
579. Decision of the Swiss Federal Supreme Court dated 28 May 2019, no. 4A_543/2018, para. 4.1: 'The choice of the law of a contracting state is presumably not an implicit exclusion of the CISG, since according to prevailing case law and doctrine it is part of the national law. Therefore, for an implied exclusion, further indications are necessary that clearly and unambiguously suggest a choice of the non-unified law by opting out of the CISG.'
580. *See* Federal Act on Shipping under the Swiss Flag and Federal Act on the Aircraft Register.
581. Article 239 CO: '... without receiving an equivalent consideration.'

523 A so-called mixed gift exists if a price that is too low (in relation to the objectively reasonable price) is agreed with the intention of making a gift. A disproportionate value of the benefits is not sufficient in itself, a mixed gift also presupposes that the donor/seller intends to benefit the recipient.[582] A mixed gift is an innominate contract (mixed contract) and as such subject to both, the provisions on sales contracts as well as gifts (Articles 239–252 CO).[583]

2 *Contract for Work*

524 A sales contract's delimitation from contracts for work (Article 363 CO) is often controversial when parties agree on the transfer of an object that does not exist at the time of contract conclusion but has yet to be manufactured.

525 If the customer provides the materials required to manufacture the good and the contractor's work is limited to the process of manufacturing, the contract is qualified as a contract for work.

526 However, there are difficulties in differentiating between a sales contract and a contract for work and materials (*Werklieferungsvertrag, contrat de livraison d'ouvrage, contratto die fornitura di un'opera*), which is governed by Articles 363–379 CO. Under such contract, the contractor undertakes to produce the work from materials he has procured himself.

527 If a good is produced with regard to the individual needs of the ordering party, this is a contract for work and materials. In contrast, a standard product manufactured in series is to be qualified as a sales contract for a future object. The decisive element for differentiating between a contract for work and materials and a sales contract for a future object is the customer's influence on the production process.[584]

C Types of Sales Contracts

528 The Code of Obligations distinguishes between sale of chattels (*Fahrniskauf, vente mobilière, comperavendita mobiliare*) and sale of real estate (*Grundstückkauf, vente*

582. Decision of the Swiss Federal Supreme Court dated 2 April 2001, no. 5C.212/2000, para. 4.b: 'The objective element of a gift is the enrichment of the recipient; the subjective element is the donor's will to make a gift (*animus donandi*) and the recipient's will to accept. The parties must agree that the gift is gratuitous. In the case of a mixed gift (*negotium mixtum cum donatione*), it is also a prerequisite that the exchange of performance is based on the donor's intention to benefit or make a donation. The Federal Supreme Court has recently confirmed that in the case of a mixed gift, the subjective characteristic of *animus donandi* is an indispensable requirement, which is why an intention to make a gift may not be inferred solely from the possibly significant disproportion of the considerations exchanged.'
583. *See* hereinabove para. 514.
584. Decision of the Swiss Federal Supreme Court dated 8 February 2019, no. 4A_399/2018, para. 2.2; decision of the Swiss Federal Supreme Court dated 22 January 2003, no. 4C.301/2002, para. 2.1.

immobilière, comperavendita di fondi). The former concerns the sale of objects that are not land, property or a right in rem entered in the land registry.[585] The distinction is important because the statutory regimes differ on some aspects, such as form requirement,[586] warranty[587] and the transfer of risk and benefits.[588]

529 A further distinction is drawn between ordinary sales contracts (*bürgerlicher Kauf, vente civile, vendita civile*) and commercial sales contracts (*Handelskauf, vente commerciale, vendita commerciale*). In an ordinary sales contract, the buyer purchases the object for direct use, whereas in a commercial sales contract, the purpose of the purchase is the selling-on of the object to make a profit. The distinction is relevant, as some statutory provisions only apply to commercial sales contracts, such as Articles 190–191 CO (seller's default) and Article 215 CO (damages calculation).

530 A special type of sales contract is the sale with successive deliveries (*Sukzessivlieferungsvertrag, vente à livraisons successive, vendita con consegne differite*). Such contract is special in that delivery of the objects of purchase takes place in separate instalments and each instalment is paid for separately.

D Formation of a Sales Contract

531 A sales contract is formed by the exchange of mutual expressions of intent covering the essential terms of the contract (*essentialia negotii*).[589] This refers to the seller's obligation to hand over the object of purchase and to transfer ownership of it as well as the buyer's obligation to pay the purchase price.

532 Sales of chattels[590] are not subject to any form requirement.[591] In contrast, sale of real estate is valid only if done in the form of a public deed.[592,593]

533 A special case is the arising of a sale contract by means of a right of pre-emption, purchase or repurchase. Here, a party may unilaterally effect conclusion of a sales contract by exercising such right that the other party has previously granted. Importantly, pre-emption, purchase or repurchase rights for real estate must be granted in the form of public deeds[594] and are subject to the maximum time periods of Article 216a CO.

585. Article 187 CO.
586. *See* Article 216 CO.
587. *See* Article 219 CO.
588. *See* Article 220 CO.
589. *See* hereinabove paras 96 et seqq.
590. *See* hereinabove para. 533.
591. But *see* below para. 538 regarding potential form requirements that apply to the act of transferring ownership.
592. *See* hereinabove para. 149.
593. Article 216(1) CO.
594. Article 216(2) CO.

E The Seller's Main Obligations

1 *Main Obligations: Delivery of the Object of Sale and Transfer of Ownership*

534 Pursuant to Article 184(1) CO, a seller has two main obligations: first, deliver the object of the sale to the buyer and, second, transfer ownership of the object to the buyer.

535 Delivery of the object of sale requires the seller to give the buyer de facto control of the object. This is achieved differently depending on whether the object of the sale is a chattel, real estate or a right.

536 Transferring ownership refers to the legal control of the object of the sale. Transfer of legal control presupposes that the seller has the power to dispose of the object (i.e., that he is the owner of the object or rightfully empowered by the owner to make the sale). Further, the act of transferring legal control may be subject to form requirements irrespective of whether the sale contract was subject to such form requirements.[595] Again, the manner in which transfer of legal control is achieved varies depending on whether the object of the sale is a chattel, real estate or a right.

2 *Modalities of Performing Main Obligations*

537 The object of sale depends on the parties' agreement. The object of sale may be both, movable and immovable objects. Further, rights (such as claims or trademarks),[596] electricity, gas or water may form the object of a sale.[597]

538 There is a general distinction between specific objects of sale (*Spezieskauf, vente d'un corps certain, vendita di una cosa determinata*) and generic objects of sale (*Gattungskauf, vente d'une chose de genre, vendita di une cosa generica*). The former relates to objects that the parties have sufficiently individualised to clarify which exact object is to be delivered. A generic object of sale is, in contrast, only determined by general characteristics (e.g., a phone of a specific brand and with a certain configuration). The seller may then choose which object fulfilling the required characteristics he will deliver in the end.[598]

539 In terms of quality, the purchased object must meet the contractually agreed requirements. If the quality of the delivered item deviates from the promised standard, this constitutes a defect for which the seller is generally liable (warranty of quality).[599]

595. For example, transfer of the ownership in a right (such as a claim) is effected by assignment which is subject to the written form requirement (Article 165(1) CO).
596. Decision of the Swiss Federal Supreme Court dated 15 June 1976, DSC 102 II 339, para. 3.
597. *See* Article 713 CC.
598. Article 71(1) CO.
599. *See* below paras 570 et seqq.

If the parties fail to stipulate any requirements as to the quality of the object of sale, the relevant quality standard is the one that a buyer is entitled to expect in good faith under the circumstances.[600]

540 Unless agreed otherwise, the place of delivery is determined in accordance with Article 74(1) CO resulting in the debtor bearing the burden of collecting the object – either at the seller's place of business or where the object was located at the time of contract conclusion.[601] In the practice of international trade, parties often deviate from this provision by agreeing on an Incoterms rule. The issue of transportation costs is governed by Article 189 CO which the parties may deviate from.

541 Unless agreed otherwise, the seller must deliver the object and transfer ownership immediately after conclusion of the sale contract.[602] The duty to immediate delivery is to some extent relativised by Article 184(2) CO which provides that the parties to a sales contract must perform their respective obligations simultaneously. Therefore, the seller may withhold delivery until the buyer has paid the purchase price.[603]

F The Buyer's Main Obligations

1 First Main Obligation: Payment of Purchase Price

542 The buyer's main obligation consists in paying the agreed purchase price.[604]

543 The price must not necessarily be numerically denominated. 'The price is deemed sufficiently determined where it can be determined from the circumstances.'[605] This is, for example, the case if the parties agreed on a calculation method or referred to an index.[606] Further rules on determination of the purchase price are set forth in Article 212 CO.

---

600. Decision of the Swiss Federal Supreme Court dated 20 May 2014, no. 4A_619/2013, para. 4.1: 'There is a defect within the meaning of article 197 CO when the object delivered deviates from what it should be under the contract of sale, because it lacks a quality which the seller had promised it to have or a quality which the buyer could have expected according to the rules of good faith. The level of expectation depends on the content of the contract, the rules of good faith and the other circumstances of the case in question.'
601. *See* hereinabove para. 294.
602. Article 75 CO. *See* hereinabove para. 296.
603. Article 82 CO. *See* hereinabove para. 298.
604. Articles 184(1) and 211(1) CO.
605. Article 184(3) CO.
606. Decision of the Swiss Federal Supreme Court dated 12 June 2008, no. 4A_24/2008, para. 3.1: 'It is sufficient for the purchase price to be determinable if all the factors necessary to determine the purchase price can be ascertained from the contract itself and there is no need for other evidence to be adduced. It is sufficient if the price can be determined, for example, by means of a calculation method, by a formula, depending on factors external to the contract such as published indices or on the basis of the agreement that the price is to be determined by estimating the market value or the income value at the time of the execution.'

544 The modalities of payment are generally governed by Articles 74 and 84 et seqq. CO, unless parties agree otherwise.[607] There is one exception: in contrast to the default rule of Article 75 CO, payment of purchase price does not immediately become due, but only upon delivery of the purchase object or the seller's offer to make such delivery.[608]

2 Second Main Obligation: Accepting Delivery

545 The wording of Article 211 CO suggests that the buyer has the obligation to accept delivery of the purchase object. Yet, a majority in doctrine argues that it should rather be qualified as an incumbency and thus failure to accept only amounts to a creditor default.[609,610] So far, the Swiss Federal Supreme Court has not followed this approach and (at least implicitly) assumed that Article 211 CO installs an obligation upon the buyer to accept delivery of the purchase object meaning that failure to accept delivery gives the seller the remedies listed in Articles 107–109 CO.[611]

546 The obligation of accepting delivery only arises if the seller has offered delivery at the place and at the time in accordance with the contract. Contrary, a quality issue of the delivered object does not justify refusal of delivery, a buyer is rather restricted to the remedies of Articles 197 et seqq. CO (warranty of quality). Yet, if the object offered for delivery is of an entirely different nature than the owed object (so-called *aliud*), a buyer is not obliged to accept delivery.[612]

G Performance Failure by the Seller

547 While performance failure by the seller may be categorised in the same three groups of breaches that have already been analysed above,[613] the Code of Obligations

607. *See* hereinabove paras 299 et seqq.
608. Article 213(1) CO. *See* decision of the Swiss Federal Supreme Court dated 16 May 2003, DSC 129 III 535, para. 3.2.1: 'For the contract of sale, article 213(1) CO stipulates that the purchase price becomes due upon the transfer of the object of sale into the possession of the buyer, if no other point in time is agreed. Correctly interpreted, this provision is to be understood as a confirmation of the principle that the seller and the buyer must perform their obligations simultaneously – step by step (article 184(2) CO). The seller is therefore not obliged to perform in advance in order to make the purchase price fall due. It is sufficient that he offers his performance.'
609. *See* hereinabove paras 337 et seqq.
610. *See, e.g.*, Honsell, Schweizerisches Obligationenrecht, Besonderer Teil, Berne 2017, p. 50.
611. *See* decision of the Swiss Federal Supreme Court dated 4 June 1985, DSC 111 II 156, para. 2; decision of the Swiss Federal Supreme Court dated 27 June 1984, DSC 110 II 148, para. 1.
612. Decision of the Swiss Federal Supreme Court dated 5 December 1995, DSC 121 III 453, para. 4.a: 'Accordingly, any delivered object that does not have all the generic characteristics agreed by the parties does not constitute the owed object, but another object, an *aliud*. This is the case, for example, if a delivered automobile has an ordinary gearstick instead of the automatic gearbox provided for in the contract or does not correspond to the expressly agreed model. On the other hand, in the case of a generic purchase, there is no other, but a defective object of purchase (*peius*) if the delivered object belongs to the owed type (article 71(1) CO), but does not have the agreed or legally prescribed quality.'
613. *See* hereinabove paras 340 et seqq.

contains several special provisions that amend the remedies available to a buyer in such a situation.

1 Non-performance

548 In general, the same principles as explained for the general part of the Code of Obligations apply to the sales contract.[614]

549 However, the Code of Obligations contains special rules addressing the scenario that a purchase object is destroyed or damaged after the conclusion of contract without such occurrence being attributable to either party (e.g., due to force majeure). Article 185 CO governs which party should bear the risk of such destruction (passing of the risk; *Gefahrenübergang, transfert des risques, trasferimento dei rischi*). Article 185 CO supersedes the standard rule of subsequent impossibility contained in Article 119 CO.[615] However the parties are free to deviate from Article 185 CO, notably by agreeing on an Incoterms rule.

550 Under Article 185(1) CO, the risk generally passes at conclusion of contract to the buyer, unless there are special circumstances present. Such special circumstances are notably deemed present when the time lag between contract conclusion and delivery of the purchase object is not in the interest of the buyer but of the seller.[616] Further, special rules exist for the sale of generic objects and sales subject to a condition precedent.[617]

551 Importantly, if the seller was in default at the time of the accidental destruction, he is deemed responsible for such destruction.[618] The rules on passing of risk do not apply in such cases unless the seller demonstrates that destruction would have occurred even if he had performed in time.[619]

552 A buyer claiming damages for non-performance may resort to the special rule on damages calculation set forth in Article 191(2–3) CO which applies to both, ordinary

614. *See* hereinabove paras 345–348.
615. *See* Article 119(3) CO: 'This does not apply to cases in which, by law or contractual agreement, the risk passes to the creditor prior to performance.'
616. Decision of the Swiss Federal Supreme Court dated 12 March 2002, DSC 128 III 370, para. 4.c: '... the exceptions were designed to deal with cases where the separation in time between the contract conclusion and the act of disposal was not in the interest of the buyer, but solely or predominantly in the interest of the seller. The exceptions recognised so far all seem to be along these lines. With the exception of the cases expressly regulated in paragraphs 2 and 3 of article 185 CO and the specific stipulations mentioned in paragraph 1, it is the double sale of goods, alternative obligations with a right of option for the seller (article 72 CO), the sale of an object not in the seller's possession, or mixed contracts, in particular the sale of a car including the trade-in of a used car.'
617. Article 185(2–3) CO.
618. Article 103 CO.
619. Huguenin, Obligationenrecht, Zurich 2019, N 2476.

and commercial sales contracts.[620] Based on these provisions, a buyer may use the costs of a good faith cover transaction or the market value of the purchase object as the basis for its damage calculation.[621] Yet, he also may calculate the damage according to the usual principles (Article 191(1) CO).[622]

2 *Default in Performance*

553 The seller's default is governed by the general rules on debtor default in Articles 102–109 CO.[623] Only for commercial sales contracts,[624] special rules on seller's default apply.

554 Under Article 190 CO, two presumptions apply. First, an agreed delivery date is deemed to constitute a deadline for performance meaning that debtor default occurs without any need for a formal reminder and that the creditor is not required to grant the debtor a grace period (Article 108(3) CO).[625] Second, it is assumed that the buyer chooses to forego performance (i.e., delivery of the purchase object) but to uphold the contract entitling him to claim damages.[626] The buyer may rebut this presumption by declaring otherwise immediately upon elapsing of the delivery date.[627]

555 Regarding calculation of damages, the buyer may resort to the special rules contained in Article 191 CO.[628]

620. *See* hereinabove para. 534. Although for the ordinary sales contract the Swiss Federal Supreme Court admits the application of Article 191 CO only by analogy, *see* decision of the Swiss Federal Supreme Court dated 8 March 2000, no. 4C.371/1999, para. 2.a.
621. Regarding the relevant time for determining the market value, *see* decision of the Swiss Federal Supreme Court dated 8 March 2000, no. 4C.371/1999, para. 2.a.aa: 'In addition, the decisive time for establishing the damage resulting from non-performance is, in principle, the time when the seller forewent performance or, in the case of a commercial sale, the time fixed for performance.'
622. *See* hereinabove paras 422 et seqq.
623. *See* hereinabove paras 349 et seqq.
624. *See* hereinabove para. 534.
625. *See* hereinabove paras 355 and 375.
626. *See* hereinabove para. 383.
627. Decision of the Swiss Federal Supreme Court dated 24 September 1990, DSC 116 II 436, para. 1.a: 'Under article 190(1) of the Swiss Code of Obligations (CO), when the agreed term expires, the seller is not only in default with the debtor, but ipso jure in "qualified" default within the meaning of article 107 of the CO, with the particularity that article 190(1) CO creates a legal presumption in favour of foregoing performance and damages for non-performance. However, instead of benefiting from such a presumption of waiver of performance, the buyer may demand performance if he declares this immediately after the expiry of the term of performance. The "Fixgeschäft" is then transformed into a "Mahngeschäft". The buyer waives the right to attribute an essential character to the fixed term; article 190 CO therefore ceases to apply to the contract, which is thus subject to the common regime of articles 107 to 109 CO. If he wishes damages for non-performance, the buyer who maintains the requirement of performance must set his debtor an additional period of time and, immediately after the expiry of this period, declare his intention not to uphold the contract and to claim positive damages.'
628. *See* hereinabove para. 557.

3 *Inadequate Performance*

556 A seller's inadequate performance must be assessed differently depending on whether the breach concerns the main obligations or ancillary obligations.

557 If only ancillary obligations are breached, the legal consequences are governed by Article 97 CO.[629] In contrast, an inadequate performance of the seller's main obligations (delivery and transfer of ownership of the purchase object) is governed by special rules in Articles 192–210 CO.

558 These provisions make a distinction as to whether the inadequate performance concerns the legal title to the purchase object (warranty of title) or the quality of the purchase object (warranty of quality). While Articles 192–210 CO provide for special remedies, the general remedy of damages under Article 97 CO remains available to the buyer, albeit with additional conditions attached to it.[630]

4 *Special Case: Breach of Warranty of Title*

a *Warranty of Title*

559 Warranty of title (*Rechtsgewährleistung, garantie pour éviction, garanzia in caso di evizione*) refers to the seller's obligation to transfer the purchased object free from any rights of third parties that could be asserted against the buyer and that already existed at the time the contract is concluded.[631] In practice, breaches of warranty of title are rather uncommon, as Swiss civil law affords a good faith purchaser ample protection against third-party claims.[632]

560 A breach of warranty of title gives rise to the special remedies of Articles 195 and 196 CO.

b *Liability for Breach of Warranty of Title*

561 The provisions on warranty of title (Articles 192–196 CO) are non-mandatory and thus subject to modification by the parties. However, an exclusion of the seller's liability is void if the seller is aware of the third party's rights to the purchase object.[633]

562 Unless agreed otherwise by the parties, the remedies of Articles 195–196 CO are available to the buyer, if:

629. *See* hereinabove paras 385 et seqq.
630. *See* below paras 567 and 613.
631. Article 192(1) CO.
632. *See, e.g.*, Article 714(2) in conjunction with Article 933 CC protecting the purchaser if the seller was entrusted with the purchase object by the owner.
633. Article 192(3) CO.

- third party rights to the purchase object existed at the time of contract conclusion;
- the buyer was not aware of those rights;[634]
- the seller has delivered the purchase object to the buyer;
- the third party has subsequently dispossessed the buyer of the purchase object;[635] and
- the seller is unable to avail himself of the defence of prescription.[636]

563 In contrast, it is irrelevant whether the seller was at fault. Breach of warranty of title entails a strict liability.

c *Remedies for Breach of Warranty of Title*

564 In case of full dispossession of the buyer, the sales contract is automatically (by operation of law) rescinded.[637] No further action is required by the buyer.

565 Upon rescission, the buyer is entitled to claim restitution of the contract price paid to the seller as well as the expenditures and costs listed in Article 195(1) CO. Any additional claim for damages (such as loss of profit) would have to meet the usual requirements of this remedy.[638]

566 In the event of partial dispossession, there is no automatic rescission of the sales contract. The buyer may only claim damages unless he shows that he would not have entered into the contract if he had foreseen such partial dispossession in which case the buyer may declare rescission.[639]

d *Alternative Remedies*

567 The buyer is not bound to proceed with the remedies of Articles 196–197 CO, but may instead choose to claim damages under Article 97 CO if the conditions of that remedy are also met.[640] Further, the buyer may elect to proceed according to Articles

634. Article 192(2) CO.
635. The buyer carries the burden of proof that he was under a legal duty to surrender the purchase object to the third party (Article 194(2) CO). But there are several assumptions in favour of the buyer in relation to court proceedings or settlements leading to a surrender of the purchase object (Articles 193 and 194(1) CO).
636. *See* hereinabove paras 441 et seqq. Also *see* Article 196a CO providing for a prolonged prescription period for objects of cultural heritage. Other purchase object are subject to the ten-year prescription period of Article 127 CO.
637. Article 195(1) CO.
638. Article 195(2) CO. *See* hereinabove paras 397 et seqq.
639. Article 196 CO.
640. Decision of the Swiss Federal Supreme Court dated 21 February 1984, DSC 110 II 239, para. 1.d. Regarding damages under Article 97 CO and the required conditions for the remedy, *see* hereinabove paras 397 et seqq.

23-24 CO and render the sales contract ineffective.[641] The latter option is particularly relevant when the buyer is aware of the risk of dispossession, but dispossession has not yet occurred.[642]

5 *Special Case: Breach of Warranty of Quality*

a *Warranty of Quality*

568 Warranty of quality (*Sachgewährleistung, garantie pour les défauts de la chose vendue, garanzia per i defetti della cosa*) refers to the seller's obligation to deliver the purchased object in the quality owed under the contract. It is generally governed by Articles 197 et seqq. CO. However, if the purchase object consists of a claim (*Forderung, créance, credito*), the warranty of quality is not governed by Article 197 CO, but rather by the special rules on assignment contained in Articles 171-173 CO.[643]

569 Article 197(1) CO distinguishes between express and implied warranties of quality:

570 An *express warranty* (*Zusicherung, qualités promises, qualità promesse*) is a quality or characteristic of the purchase object that the seller has specifically promised to the buyer. Such promise is an expression of intent by the seller which may be given explicitly or implicitly, and which is subject to the usual rules of interpretation.[644] According to case law, any statement pursuant to which the object of sale has a certain, objectively ascertainable characteristic constitutes an express warranty, provided that the buyer may rely on this statement in good faith.[645] The promised quality or

641. *See* hereinabove paras 159 et seqq.
642. Decision of the Swiss Federal Supreme Court dated 25 October 1983, DSC 109 II 319, para. 2: 'The option of a choice is also justified in the case of legally defective performance pursuant to articles 192 et seq. CO. In this case, it even imposes itself, since the buyer would have to wait for the rightful owner's rejection and consequently accept the associated disadvantages for an indefinite period of time if he could only invoke legally defective performance despite a defect in consent.'
643. Decision of the Swiss Federal Supreme Court dated 7 December 1964, DSC 90 II 490, para. 5.
644. Decision of the Swiss Federal Supreme Court dated 23 November 2004, no. 4C.267/2004, para. 2.1: 'An express warranty is a genuine assertion of a specific, objectively ascertainable characteristic. In contrast, non-binding, promotional statements do not fall under the term of express warranty. Whether a statement by the seller is to be qualified as a binding warranty or as mere advertising is to be determined by interpreting the contract.'
645. Decision of the Swiss Federal Supreme Court dated 27 May 2008, no. 4A_480/2007, para. 3.1: 'According to the case law of the Federal Supreme Court, express warranties can cover not only physical but also economic characteristics of the object of sale, such as the interest income of a property or the turnover generated by a restaurant immediately before the sale. An express warranty is not only given if the seller expressly "warrants" or "guarantees" a characteristic. Rather, any statement according to which the object has a certain, objectively ascertainable characteristic is sufficient if the buyer may rely on this statement in good faith. In contrast, non-binding, promotional statements do not fall under the concept of express warranty.'

characteristic must have been relevant in that it was causal for the buyer's decision to purchase the object at all or at least at the agreed terms.[646]

571 The express warranty must be distinguished from the independent guarantee (*selbständige Garantie, garantie indépendante, garanzia indipendente*). An independent guarantee typically concerns elements that relate to the future and are outside of the seller's sphere of influence.[647] By giving an independent guarantee, the seller gives a contractual promise whose breach is governed by Article 97 CO and thus not subject to the further conditions attached to a breach of warranty (e.g., immediate notification and short prescription period of Article 210 CO).

572 Apart from express warranties, there is also an *implied warranty* under Article 197(1) CO. The purchase object must be of a quality and have the characteristics that can be expected in good faith even if not specifically promised by the seller. The level of expectation depends on the content of the contract and the surrounding circumstances.[648] Any deviation from the expected quality or characteristics is referred to as a 'defect' in Article 197(1) CO.[649] Yet, the implied warranty is qualified in that the seller only warrants that there will not be any such defect that would 'materially or legally negate or substantially reduce the value of the object or its fitness for the designated purpose.'[650]

573 So the deviation from the expected quality or characteristics must reach a serious level: 'a significant reduction in the expected purpose or value of the object.'[651] Such level is namely reached if the buyer would not have concluded the sale contract at all or at least not with the same terms, had the buyer been aware of the deviations from the expected quality or characteristics.[652]

646. Decision of the Swiss Federal Supreme Court dated 14 February 2008, no. 4A_417/2007, para. 5.1: 'According to the case law of the Federal Supreme Court, the seller is only liable for expressly warranted characteristics if the express warranty was causal for the buyer's decision to purchase the item at all or under the agreed conditions. Such causality is to be presumed in the case of express warranties which, according to life experience, are generally capable of decisively influencing the buyer in his decision to buy at all or at the specific terms.'
647. Decision of the Swiss Federal Supreme Court dated 30 September 2013, no. 4A_220/2013, para. 4.3.1: 'In contrast, an independent guarantee contract (article 111 CO) exists if the seller promises a future result that goes beyond the contractual quality of the object of sale because it depends substantially on other future factors that – such as the development of the economy – are independent of the properties of the object and lie outside the seller's sphere of influence.'; decision of the Swiss Federal Supreme Court dated 27 June 1996, DSC 122 III 426, para. 4: 'According to Swiss doctrine, the distinction between an express warranty within the meaning of article 197(1) CO and an independent guarantee must be made according to whether the seller promises a presently existing characteristic of the object of sale or a future result that goes beyond the contractual quality of the object of sale.'
648. Decision of the Swiss Federal Supreme Court dated 20 May 2014, no. 4A_619/2013, para. 4.1.
649. However, in practice, the term 'defect' is used to describe a breach of any kind of warranty of quality.
650. Article 197(1) CO.
651. Decision of the Swiss Federal Supreme Court dated 20 May 2014, no. 4A_619/2013, para. 4.1 ('*une diminution notable de l'utilité prévue ou de la valeur de la chose*').
652. *See, e.g.*, Huguenin, Obligationenrecht, Zurich 2019, N 2612.

574 Importantly, in the sale of a company – if structured as a share deal – the implied warranty only extends to the shares of the company, but not the assets of the company.[653] Unless the seller has given an express warranty in regard to the company's assets, he bears no responsibility for the assets of the company. Yet, the buyer might be able to render the contract ineffective based on mistake.[654]

b *Liability for Breach of Warranty of Quality*

575 A seller's liability for breach of warranty of quality is subject to the following requirements:

- breach of warranty of quality;
- buyer had no knowledge of the warranty breach when entering into the sales contract;
- buyer has not subsequently accepted the breach of warranty; and
- the parties have not excluded liability for the breach in question.

576 *Breach of warranty of quality*: A breach of warranty of quality exists if either an express or implied warranty is engaged in that there is a deviation between the status as should be under these warranties and the actual status of the delivered object. The relevant point in time for determining the presence of such deviation is the time of the transfer of risk (Article 185 CO)[655] unless agreed otherwise by the parties.[656]

577 There is generally no breach of warranty of quality if a seller delivers a lesser quantity than agreed (e.g., delivery of only 50 apples, although 100 apples were promised). Rather, the delivery is deemed only to be a partial delivery. The seller's failure to timely make full delivery constitutes a default in performance.[657]

578 *Buyer not aware of breach of warranty*: Under Article 200(1) CO, the seller is not liable for any breach of warranty of which the buyer was aware at the time of entering into the sales contract. The buyer is deemed to be aware of all such breaches that any normally attentive buyer exercising due care when selecting and viewing an object should have discovered (Article 200(2) CO). Thus, if the lack of awareness is solely due to the buyer's own negligence, the seller is not liable for any breach of warranty. Yet,

653. Decision of the Swiss Federal Supreme Court dated 10 November 1981, DSC 107 II 419, para. 1: 'However, the legal warranty does not refer to the assets of the company, but is also given in the case of a sale of all shares only for the existence and scope of the rights sold with them. According to article 197 CO, the seller is only liable for the economic value of the shares if he has given special express warranties for this and the buyer, for his part, complies with the provisions of article 201 CO.'
654. *See* below para. 618.
655. *See* hereinabove para. 555.
656. Decision of the Swiss Federal Supreme Court dated 30 November 1962, DSC 88 II 410, para. 3.a: 'Of course, the warranted characteristics of the object of sale must in principle be present at the time of the passing of benefit and risk. However, the seller is free to warrant the quality for another time or period.'
657. Decision of the Swiss Federal Supreme Court dated 24 October 1961, DSC 87 II 244, para. b.

this does not apply if the seller has given an express warranty, in which case he may not rely on Article 200(2) CO.[658]

579 The Swiss Federal Supreme Court sets a high standard for the buyer's awareness necessary to liberate a seller from his liability under Article 200 CO:

> In terms of content, the knowledge or the implied knowledge must not only include the symptoms of the defect – in this case, therefore not merely the fact of moisture penetration – but its full significance as a sign of a particular defect and its scope, as has already been mentioned. To know or to be able to know the scope of a defect in this sense does not only include the possibility of a more or less clear idea of its technical nature, but also the possibility of knowing how the defect affects the usability of the object, whether it can be cured, what expenses are necessary to remedy it and in particular what is required in terms of work, time and money. Only if it is established that the buyer was able to recognise the full significance and effect of the defect in factual and economic terms, may he be blamed for his negligence in a purely visual inspection to such an extent that it is assumed that he purchased the goods waiving his right to complain about the breach of warranty.[659]

580 Article 200 CO is not mandatory and may thus be deviated from by the parties. The seller bears the burden of proof regarding the seller's awareness or implied awareness of the breach of warranty.

581 *No acceptance of breach of warranty/immediate notification*: After concluding a sales contract, the buyer may approve a breach of warranty and thereby discharge the seller from any liability. Such acceptance is assumed if the buyer after discovering a breach of warranty does not notify the seller thereof immediately.

582 The notification of a breach of warranty (also referred to as 'notice of defect'; *Mängelrüge, avis des défauts, notifica dei difetti*) is a statement by the buyer addressed to the seller in which the former expresses that he considers the delivered object not to conform to the contractually required quality. It is not sufficient for the buyer to merely express his dissatisfaction; the buyer must indicate the specific breaches of warranty.[660] The notice is not subject to any formal requirement unless otherwise agreed by the parties.

---

658. Decision of the Swiss Federal Supreme Court dated 22 February 1955, DSC 81 II 56, para. 2.c: 'If the seller expressly warrants the existence of a certain quality of the purchase object during the contract negotiations, this does, however, relieve the buyer of the duty to observe even a minimum degree of care before the conclusion of the contract, when choosing and viewing the purchase object. He may rely on the seller's express warranties, and the seller cannot subsequently argue against him that a warranty liability does not apply because the buyer could have discovered the absence of the characteristic in question before the conclusion of the contract if he had exercised due care (article 200(2) CO). The negligence of the buyer, which lies in the failure to exercise due care and generally results in the purchase object being deemed to be approved despite its defects, is offset by the seller's express warranty.'
659. Decision of the Swiss Federal Supreme Court dated 9 July 1940, DSC 66 II 132, para. 5.
660. Decision of the Swiss Federal Supreme Court dated 28 May 2002, no. 4C.395/2001, para. 2.1.1: 'The necessary content of the notice of defects is the indication of the extent to which the object of sale is considered defective, i.e., the extent to which it does not comply with the contractually required or expressly warranted characteristics (article 197(1) CO). It is not

583 As regards timing of the notification, Article 201 CO distinguishes between breaches of warranty that a buyer would discover when duly inspecting a purchased good upon receipt (so-called evident defect; *offener Mangel, défaut apparent, difetto apparente*) and breaches that only reveal themselves later (so-called hidden defect; *versteckter Mangel, défaut cache, difetto nascosto*).

584 Evident defects must be notified immediately after receipt of delivery and upon 'customary inspection', which a buyer is required to conduct upon receipt under Article 201(1) CO. The number of days that are still considered to constitute an immediate notification depends on the circumstances of the case, namely the complexity of the issues at stake. In general, a notification made within seven days is deemed timely, unless waiting that long could enlarge the damage.[661] Whether the seven days start running from receipt of delivery or the date when a 'customary inspection' can be expected to be concluded depends on whether the breach of warranty is so obvious that it could be discovered even without inspection.

585 In contrast, hidden defects must be notified immediately, once the buyer has discovered them (Article 201(3) CO). A hidden defect is deemed discovered if a buyer obtains certainty of its existence.[662]

---

sufficient if the buyer expresses his dissatisfaction in general terms without specifically naming the defects. On the other hand, the mere statement of the unfavourable effects, such as "goods are so bad that they cannot be processed", is sufficient. The complaint must be substantiated in terms of content and express that the delivery is not recognised as being in accordance with the contract and that the supplier is held liable. The requirements for the substantiation of the content result from the purpose of the notice. The purpose of the notice is to inform the seller of the nature, extent and grounds of the complaint so that he can decide how to act in view of the liability in question. The information required for this purpose depends on the circumstances.'

661. Decision of the Swiss Federal Supreme Court dated 29 April 2009, no. 4A_82/2008, para. 7.1: 'When assessing whether a notification has been made in a timely manner, the specific circumstances of the individual case, in particular the nature of the defects, must be taken into account. Decisions in other cases are therefore to be used with caution. In principle, the time limit for making a notification of defects should be short if the defect is such that there is a risk that waiting may lead to greater damage. If this is not the case, the Federal Supreme Court considers a seven-day notice period to be reasonable.'; decision of the Swiss Federal Supreme Court dated 8 February 2019, no. 4A_399/2018, para. 3.2: 'In general, however, it can be said that the time limit for giving notice of defects must be short if the defect is such that there is a risk that waiting may lead to greater damage. In cases of a non-progressing defect, case law recognised a period of one week as reasonable whereas notices of defects were judged to be out of time if they were made only after 14 days or 18 days or one month or five weeks.'

662. Decision of the Swiss Federal Supreme Court dated 29 April 2009, no. 4A_82/2008, para. 7.2: 'The period for giving notice of defects begins with the discovery of the defect. According to case law, a defect is only deemed to have been discovered when the purchaser has become aware of it in such a way that he can raise a sufficiently substantiated notification. In the case of defects that gradually become apparent because they grow in extent or intensity, the first signs are not yet sufficient for this. The time limit for giving notice of defects is therefore not already triggered by the discovery of the first traces of defects, provided that the buyer may assume in good faith that these are merely usual phenomena which do not constitute a deviation from the contract. ... . In the case of defects that gradually become apparent over time, discovery may therefore only be assumed when the serious nature of the condition becomes clear and the buyer can grasp the significance and scope of the defects. Their assessment may require the involvement of experts.'

586 If the buyer fails to notify a defect in good time, he is deemed to have accepted the breach of warranty barring any claim for liability under Articles 197 et seqq. CO.[663] Yet, there is an exception to this where the seller has wilfully misled the buyer. In such cases, late notification does not bar the seller's liability.[664]

587 The buyer bears the burden of proof for the timeliness of the notification.[665] However, such proof is only required if the seller raises the issue of late notification, as a tribunal must not examine timely notification ex officio.[666]

588 The provisions of the Code of Obligations on notification of breaches of warranty are non-mandatory. Parties may agree on different rules regarding notification or even completely dispense with the requirement. When parties stipulate a 'warranty period' (*Garantiefrist*) it is a question of interpretation of the specific clause whether it should be construed as also having effect on the notification requirement.

589 *No exclusion of liability*: The seller's warranty of quality is generally of a non-mandatory nature and may thus be excluded by the parties. An exclusion may be all-encompassing, only concern specific defects or only exclude resort to certain remedies.

590 Often, sales contracts contain an exclusion of liability clause (*Freizeichnungsklausel, clause exclusive de responsabilité, clausola di esclusione della responsabilità*), under which a buyer's remedies for breach of warranty of quality are cancelled or limited. When confronted with such a clause, two questions must be answered: first, does the exclusion of liability clause cover the particular breach of warranty of quality at stake; and, second, is the clause valid in relation to that breach of warranty of quality.

591 As to the first question, the scope of the exclusion of liability clause must be determined by applying the usual rules of contract interpretation.[667] There is a general rule that such exclusions are to be interpreted restrictively.[668] In line with this, an exclusion of liability is generally deemed not to cover express warranties made by the seller.[669]

663. Regarding claims based on other legal bases, *see* below paras 615–619.
664. Article 203 CO.
665. Decision of the Swiss Federal Supreme Court dated 12 May 1981, DSC 107 II 172, para. 1.a (concerning a contract for work): 'If the customer wishes to derive rights from article 370(3) CO, he must prove the timeliness of the notification of defects in accordance with the general rule of article 8 CC. This also includes proof of when the defect notified became apparent to him, how and to whom he notified it.'
666. Decision of the Swiss Federal Supreme Court dated 27 January 1981, DSC 107 II 50, para. 2.a.
667. Decision of the Swiss Federal Supreme Court dated 7 December 1999, DSC 126 III 59, para. 5.a: 'Determining the scope of a clause excluding or limiting the seller's liability is a matter of interpreting the contract.'
668. Decision of the Swiss Federal Supreme Court dated 9 November 1965, DSC 91 II 344, para. 2.a: 'However, the statutory warranty regime is non-mandatory law. It can be contractually excluded or limited (except in the case of fraudulent intent on the part of the seller; article 199 CO). However, this must be clearly expressed in the contract as an exception to the statutory regime. Such agreements are therefore to be interpreted restrictively in case of doubt.'
669. Decision of the Swiss Federal Supreme Court dated 25 August 2005, no. 4C.119/2005, 2.3: 'A general exclusion of liability clause does not exclude the seller's liability for expressly

592 Further, a boilerplate exclusion of liability clause is not considered to cover defects that are entirely outside of what a buyer in the situation at stake could have reasonably expected and that have a significant impact on the commercial balance of the transaction.[670] Whether a breach of warranty deprives a buyer of what he was entitled to reasonably expect depends on the following:

> What a buyer should expect depends on the specific circumstances of the individual case. The interpretation essentially depends on the recognisable purpose for which someone has purchased an item. In this respect, defects that make an item largely unsuitable for the intended use are to be assessed differently from defects that make this use more difficult but still allow it. The economic purpose of the purchase contract must therefore be taken into account when assessing whether or not a particular defect is covered by the exclusion of warranty.[671]

593 As to the second question – the validity of an exclusion of liability clause – Article 199 CO sets forth that an exclusion (or even limitation) of liability for breach of warranty is void if the seller has fraudulently concealed the failure to comply with the warranty of quality from the buyer.[672] Fraudulent concealment is affirmed if the seller makes a false statement or fails to make a disclosure about a known defect despite having a duty to do so. Such disclosure duty may arise from a contract or be deduced from a general relationship of trust. The latter may arise in contract negotiations:

> In particular, in contract negotiations, a relationship of trust is affirmed which obliges the parties in good faith to inform each other to a certain extent of facts which may influence the decision of the other party on the conclusion of the contract or its terms. The extent to which the parties have to inform each other is not decided in general terms, but depends on the circumstances of the individual case, namely the nature of the contract, the way in which the negotiations are conducted, as well as the intentions and knowledge of the parties. There is no duty of disclosure if the seller could assume in good faith that the buyer would easily recognise the true facts. As a rule, this is the case if the buyer should have recognised the true facts by paying due attention.[673]

---

warranted characteristics, because the buyer may rely on the seller's express warranties despite such a clause, unless the contract unambiguously expresses that the seller does not wish to be held liable for its representations.'

670. Decision of the Swiss Federal Supreme Court dated 4 January 2011, no. 4A_529/2010, para. 4.1: 'According to case law, an exclusion of liability clause cannot be invoked against defects of the object sold that are totally unrelated to the eventualities that a purchaser must reasonably take into consideration.'; decision of the Swiss Federal Supreme Court dated 9 December 2004, no. 4C.297/2004, para. 4.2: 'For a defect not to be covered by a standardly formulated exclusion clause, it is not sufficient that it is unexpected; it must also significantly impair the economic purpose of the transaction. In this context, it must be determined within the framework of an overall assessment whether the buyer had to expect the defects of a certain type to the existing extent.'
671. Decision of the Swiss Federal Supreme Court dated 6 October 2004, DSC 130 III 686, para. 4.3.1.
672. Article 199 CO.
673. Decision of the Swiss Federal Supreme Court dated 25 February 2013, no. 4A_648/2012, para. 3.

594 It is unclear whether Article 100 CO[674] also – in addition to Article 199 CO – limits the effect of an exclusion of liability.[675] So far, the Swiss Federal Supreme Court has exclusively relied on Article 199 CO when assessing the exclusion of liability clauses in sales contracts, but without explicitly excluding the concurrent application of Article 100 CO.[676]

c *Remedies for Breach of Warranty of Quality*

595 If a seller's liability for breach of warranty of quality is engaged, three remedies become available to the buyer under Articles 205–209 CO. With few exceptions, the buyer may freely choose among the available remedies. Once the buyer has chosen a remedy, he is bound by such choice, as the remedies constitute so-called formative rights. While the buyer may not combine the three available remedies with each other, he may in addition to one of the three remedies also request damages.

596 *Redhibition* (Article 205 CO; *Wandlung, résiliation de la vente, azione redibitoria*): The remedy of redhibition is similar to rescission[677] in that declaring redhibition renders a sales contract void *ex tunc* and transforms the contract into a liquidation relationship. Yet, the conditions for declaring redhibition differ from the remedy of rescission and the liquidation relationship is subject to special rules in Articles 207–208 CO.

597 The remedy of redhibition is available if the seller is liable for a breach of warranty of quality, redhibition is justified by the circumstances[678] and it is still possible to return the purchase object (unless destruction is not due to the buyer's fault).[679] Whether redhibition is justified by the circumstances must be assessed by the tribunal in each individual case. In essence, this additional condition shall prevent a buyer from declaring redhibition for minor defects.[680] Finally, where the sale involves a batch or set of objects, the additional requirements of Article 209 CO must be met.

598 If redhibition is declared, the sales contract becomes void *ex tunc* and is transformed into a liquidation relationship. The details of the liquidation are set forth in Articles 207–208 CO. The buyer must return the goods to the seller together with any

674. *See* hereinabove paras 419–421.
675. *See, e.g.*, Huguenin, Obligationenrecht, Zurich 2019, N 2643 et seqq. (*pro*); Honsell, commentary on article 199, in: Basler Kommentar, OR I, N 1 (*contra*).
676. *See, e.g.*, decision of the Swiss Federal Supreme Court dated 12 November 2004, no. 4C.295/2004, para. 5.2.
677. *See* hereinabove paras 427 et seqq.
678. Article 205(2) CO.
679. Article 207(3) CO.
680. Decision of the Swiss Federal Supreme Court dated 27 August 1998, DSC 124 III 456, para. 4.d.aa: 'Redhibition is justified, for example, if the object of the contract is unusable due to the defect, or if the repair costs or the reduced value are high and the defect cannot be completely eliminated. However, if the buyer can reasonably be expected to uphold the contract and the seller's interests speak against rescinding the contract, a reduction is the only option.'

benefits derived from it in the interim.[681] If the object has been destroyed, the buyer must only return what remains of the object.[682] The seller must return to the buyer the sale price paid together with interest and compensation for legal costs, expenses and the direct damage incurred by the buyer as a result of the delivery of defective goods (regardless of any fault).[683]

599 *Reduction* (Article 205 CO; *Minderung, reduction du prix, azione estimatoria*): By the remedy of reduction, a buyer may claim a reduction of the purchase price.

600 Reduction is always available when the seller is liable for a breach of warranty unless the reduction in value of the purchase object is larger than the purchase price paid. In this scenario, the buyer may only rely on the remedy of redhibition.[684]

601 The reduction in purchase price is subject to a relative calculation method.[685] Accordingly, the purchase price is reduced on the basis of the ratio between the objective value of the defective item and that of the defect-free item. Thus, the price reduction corresponds to the purchase price multiplied by the reduced value (i.e., the difference between the objective value of the defective object of purchase and the objective value of the defect-free object of purchase) divided by the objective value of the defect-free object of purchase. This ensures that the ratio between the negotiated price and the objective value of the purchase object is maintained.

602 The calculation of the reduction is eased by two presumptions: First, it is assumed that the objective value of the defect-free item corresponds to the agreed purchase price; and, second, it is assumed that the reduction in value of the defective item corresponds to the repair costs.[686] The relevant point in time for calculating the reduction is the passing of the risk from the seller to the buyer.[687]

603 *Replacement* (Article 206 CO; *Ersatzleistung, remplacement de la chose vendue, cosegna di altre cose*): By the remedy of replacement, the buyer may demand delivery

---

681. Article 208(1) CO.
682. As per Article 207(3) CO, the buyer may only declare redhibition if the object was destroyed without his fault.
683. Article 208(2) CO. Regarding the term 'direct damage', *see* below para. 606.
684. Article 205(3) CO.
685. Decision of the Swiss Federal Supreme Court dated 26 April 1955, DSC 81 II 207; para. 3.a: 'The CO does not specify how the reduced value is to be determined. According to old Swiss case law and doctrine, which is based on customary law, it is to be determined according to the relative calculation method, i.e., the purchase price is to be reduced to the amount which - at the time of the conclusion of the contract - corresponds to the ratio between the objective value of the item without defects or with the expressly warranted characteristics and its objective value in its actual condition. The formula is based on the experience that the purchase price is often higher or lower than the objective material value; it aims to maintain the contractual proportion between performance and counter-performance.'
686. Decision of the Swiss Federal Supreme Court dated 8 February 2010, no. 4A_601/2009, para. 3.2.5: 'To facilitate the calculation of the reduction according to the so-called relative method, case law has established two presumptions: firstly, the value of the object free of defects is equal to the sale price agreed by the parties; secondly, the reduction in value is equal to the cost of eliminating the defect.'
687. Decision of the Swiss Federal Supreme Court dated 10 December 1991, DSC 117 II 550, para. 4.b.bb.

of other acceptable goods of the same kind. It is available when the seller is liable for a breach of warranty and the contract of sale is for the delivery of generic objects.[688]

604 Article 206(2) CO even entitles a seller to carry out substitute performance if the sale is for delivery of generic objects. If done immediately after receipt of the notification of the breach of warranty (and only then), the buyer must accept the substitute performance and may not rely on the remedies of redhibition or reduction. At the same time, the seller must compensate the buyer for any damage suffered due to the breach of warranty of quality.

605 *Additional remedy of damages*: In addition to the aforementioned remedies, the buyer may claim damages.

606 If the remedy of damages is combined with redhibition, the legal basis is Article 208(3) CO. While the buyer may claim direct damages already under the remedy of redhibition, any indirect damage (also referred to as consequential damages; *Mangelfolgeschaden, dommage consécutif au défaut, danno consecutivo al difetto*) is subject to Article 208(3) CO and thus contingent upon the seller not succeeding in proving that he was not at fault.[689] In this respect, it is important to distinguish between direct and indirect damage. A damage is direct if it is the immediate consequence of a breach of warranty of quality meaning that there is no additional element in the chain of causation.[690]

607 In contrast, if the remedy of damages is combined with reduction or replacement, the legal basis for claiming damages is not Article 208(2) and (3) CO but Article 97 CO.[691] Any compensation for direct or indirect damage is thus subject to the requirements of Article 97 CO, which offers the seller the possibility of proving that he was not at fault.[692]

608 *No remedy of rectification*: In Swiss sales law, there is no statutory remedy of rectification.[693] Thus, a buyer cannot force a seller to repair a defective good. Rather, the buyer must ensure repair and then claim the repair costs from the seller under the remedy of reduction.[694] However, parties are free to deviate from this statutory regime before or after the occurrence of a breach of warranty of quality.[695]

688. *See* hereinabove para. 543.
689. *See* hereinabove paras 415 et seqq.
690. Decision of the Swiss Federal Supreme Court dated 28 November 2006, DSC 133 III 257, para. 3.2: 'According to the above consideration, there is direct damage within the meaning of article 208(2) CO, which was caused directly by the delivery of defective goods within the causal chain and not only by the occurrence of further causes of damage. Where the distinction is to be made in individual cases is a matter for judicial discretion.'
691. Decision of the Swiss Federal Supreme Court dated 26 April 1956, DSC 82 II 136, para. 3.a.
692. *See* hereinabove paras 415 et seqq.
693. Decision of the Swiss Federal Supreme Court dated 28 May 1969, no. 95 II 119, para. 6: 'Contrary to article 368(2) CO for a contract for work, the warranty of defects does not confer on the purchaser a right to have the defects remedied, the purchaser having no option but to choose between an action for redhibition and an action for reduction.' However, this is controversial in doctrine; *see, e.g.*, Huguenin, Obligationenrecht, Zurich 2019, N 2689-2690.
694. *See* hereinabove para. 605.
695. *See* herein below para. 614.

609 The buyer's defences: The general defence of set-off is available.[696]

610 Further, the seller may invoke the *defence of prescription*,[697] which is, however, governed by the special rules in Article 210 CO. In contrast to Article 127 CO, remedies based on a breach of warranty of quality are subject to a shorter prescription period. The claim prescribes two years after delivery of the object to the buyer, even if he does not discover the defects until later unless the seller has assumed liability under warranty for a longer period.[698] If the purchase object has been integrated into an immovable work (such as a building) in a manner consistent with its nature and purpose and has caused the immovable work to be defective, the prescription period amounts to five years.[699] The parties may agree on a reduction or increase of these prescription periods.[700]

611 Importantly, under Article 210(6) CO, a seller is estopped from invoking the defence of prescription under Article 210 CO (but not under Article 127 CO) if he has wilfully misled the buyer. Such wilful misleading is assumed if the seller has given false information about the purchase object or failed to make required disclosures.[701]

612 *Parties' ability to modify remedy regime*: The seller's obligations relating to warranty of quality are of a non-mandatory nature. The parties may therefore in principle cancel, limit or extend the buyer's remedies for breach of warranty of quality.[702] However, any limitation or exclusion of remedies is subject to the rules and limitations regarding the exclusion of liability clauses.[703]

d *Alternative Remedies*

613 *Ordinary remedies of Articles 97–101 CO*: In case of breach of warranty of quality, the buyer may choose between the ordinary remedies of Articles 97–101 CO[704] and the special remedies of Articles 197–210 CO.[705]

---

696. *See* hereinabove para. 449.
697. *See* hereinabove paras 441 et seqq.
698. Article 210(1) CO.
699. Article 210(2) CO.
700. However, in a b2c-context, Article 201(4) CO limits such reductions.
701. Decision of the Swiss Federal Supreme Court dated 7 September 2010, no. 4A_301/2010, para. 3.2: 'The seller acts dishonestly not only when he gives false information about the quality of the object, but also when he conceals certain facts that the law, the contract or the rules of good faith require him to reveal. In particular, there is deceit when the seller knowingly fails to disclose a defect to the buyer – who was unaware of it and could not discover it because it was hidden – even though he knew that it was important to the buyer. The burden of proving deceit lies with the buyer.' Also *see* hereinabove paras 595–596.
702. Decision of the Swiss Federal Supreme Court dated 16 March 2005, no. 4P.271/2004, para. 5.
703. *See* hereinabove paras 594 et seqq.
704. *See* hereinabove paras 391 et seqq.
705. Decision of the Swiss Federal Supreme Court dated 26 November 2010, no. 4A_472/2010, para. 2.1: 'The Federal Supreme Court has accepted the alternative application of articles 197 et seqq. CO and articles 97 et seqq. CO when the seller delivers a defective item. However, the buyer may only bring a general action for damages arising from contractual liability if he complies with the conditions for bringing a special action for defects, i.e., the duty to inspect and notify

614 However, the ordinary remedies are only available for breach of warranty of quality if the buyer has no approved the defect (e.g., by failing to make immediate notification).[706] Further, the ordinary remedies are subject to the prescription regime of Article 210 CO.[707]

615 If a buyer decides to rely on the general remedy of damages under Article 97 CO, the seller's fault becomes relevant. If the seller succeeds in proving that the breach of warranty of quality occurred without his fault, he must not pay any damages. In this context, fault does not concern the breach of warranty of quality itself, but rather the seller's decision to enter into the contract with knowledge of the breach of warranty of quality or negligent disregard thereof.[708]

616 *Rendering the sales contract ineffective due to defects in consent*: According to established case law,[709] in the event of a breach of warranty of quality, the buyer has the choice whether to rely on the remedies of Articles 197–210 CO or to render the sales contract ineffective due to defects of consent within the meaning of Articles 23–31 CO.[710] In particular, avoidance on the grounds of intentional deception is permissible as an alternative to the warranty of quality. However, the buyer must decide between one of these options. In particular, if he relies on the warranty of quality (e.g., by requesting a reduction of the purchase price from the seller), he simultaneously approves the contract in accordance with Article 31 CO and thus foregoes any further rights he may have on the basis of a defect in consent.[711] In practice, a buyer will try to rely on Articles 23–31 CO if he has failed to immediately notify the seller of a breach of warranty.[712]

(article 201 CO) and the prescription period (article 210 CO).' However, some scholars reject the alternative availability of the remedies (*see, e.g.*, Honsell, Schweizerisches Obligationenrecht, Besonderer Teil, Berne 2017, p. 131).

706. Decision of the Swiss Federal Supreme Court dated 26 November 2010, no. 4A_472/2010, para. 2.1. Also *see* hereinabove paras 586 et seqq.
707. Decision of the Swiss Federal Supreme Court dated 19 February 2007, DSC 133 III 335, para. 2.
708. Decision of the Swiss Federal Supreme Court dated 26 November 2010, no. 4A_472/2010, para. 3.2: 'For the seller to be liable, he must be at fault. This is the case where the seller knew or ought to have known of the existence of the defect and failed to disclose it to the buyer. This constitutes a breach of a duty ancillary to the contract. ... The seller is therefore presumed to be at fault, and can only escape liability if he proves that he exercised all the care that could reasonably be expected of him. The proof required under article 97(1) CO is subject to strict requirements. If the seller has reason to suspect the existence of a defect, in particular because the buyer has made a complaint, the seller has a duty in principle to check. If he fails to examine all the circumstances giving rise to his doubts, he cannot exonerate himself from liability.'
709. Decision of the Swiss Federal Supreme Court dated 14 December 2000, DSC 127 III 83, 1.b. However, some scholars reject the alternative availability of Articles 23–31 CO (*see, e.g.*, Schwenzer/Fountoulakis, Schweizerisches Obligationenrecht – Allgemeiner Teil, Bern 2020, N 39.41).
710. Also *see* hereinabove paras 159 et seqq.
711. Decision of the Swiss Federal Supreme Court dated 14 December 2000, DSC 127 III 83, 1.b.
712. Decision of the Swiss Federal Supreme Court dated 10 November 1981, DSC 107 II 419, para. 1: 'By contrast, avoidance on the grounds of mistake does not depend on the special requirements of the warranty of quality, even if the mistake relates to an essential characteristic of the purchased item; in this case, it is generally sufficient for the buyer to invoke the mistake within the period specified in article 31 CO, regardless of whether he has inspected the item and immediately notified the seller of any defects.'

617 *Remedies for torts*: A buyer may also rely on remedies for torts if the requirements of Article 41 CO are fulfilled.[713] However, the buyer must not have approved the breach of warranty in the sense of Article 201 CO.[714]

H Performance Failure by the Buyer

618 If the buyer fails to pay the purchase price, he is in default. While the buyer's default is generally subject to the rules of Articles 102–109 CO, Articles 214–215 CO set forth certain special rules that take precedence.

619 Article 214 CO establishes two separate payment delay regimes depending on the time at which the purchase price must be paid.[715] A distinction is drawn between a buyer who must pay the purchase price before delivery (prepayment sale) or at the same time as delivery (cash sale) and the buyer who may pay the purchase price after receipt of the purchase object (sale on credit). Regardless of such distinction, a seller may claim default interest.[716]

620 In a *cash or prepayment sale*, the buyer's default in paying the purchase price entitles the seller to 'withdraw from the contract without further formality.'[717] Thus, the seller is no required to set a grace period in the sense of Article 107(2) CO.[718] But, he must notify the buyer immediately of his decision to withdraw from the contract.[719] If he fails to do so, he has foregone his right under Article 214(1) CO and, if he wants to rescind the contract, must set a grace period.[720] Withdrawal from the contract under

713. Decision of the Swiss Federal Supreme Court dated 16 March 1964, DSC 90 II 86, para. 2: 'According to established case law, a buyer who has suffered damage as a result of the delivery of a defective item is not only entitled to contractual claims under articles 97 et seq. and 197 et seqq. CO, but under certain conditions he can also invoke the provisions on liability in tort (articles 41 et seqq. CO). For such a concurrence of claims to exist, it is first and foremost necessary that the breach of contract for which the seller is responsible also constitutes a breach of a general principle of the legal order by unnecessarily endangering life and limb or other legal interests of the buyer or third parties. This first condition would undoubtedly be fulfilled here: The fire caused by the defect in the purchased item damaged the claimant's property and was likely to endanger him or third parties personally.'
714. Decision of the Swiss Federal Supreme Court dated 21 May 1941, DSC 67 II 132, para. 2: 'But we need to go a step further and accept that approval of the defective item under article 201(2) CO excludes even an action for compensation for damage caused by an unlawful act.'
715. Regarding determination of such time, *see* hereinabove para. 549.
716. Article 213(2) in conjunction with Article 104 CO.
717. Article 214(1) CO.
718. *See* hereinabove paras 373 et seqq.
719. Decision of the Swiss Federal Supreme Court dated 10 February 1970, DSC 96 II 47, para. 2: 'However, they had to notify him of their withdrawal "immediately" (article 214(2)), i.e., as soon as they could reasonably be expected to do so in the ordinary course of business and in the particular circumstances of the case. They did so on 7 October 1959. Their declaration was made in good time. They did not delay it speculatively, and the claimant suffered no disadvantage from the lapse of only six days. In particular, it has not been established that he had made preparations for performance in the meantime and would have been disadvantaged as a result.'
720. Decision of the Swiss Federal Supreme Court dated 14 June 1960, DSC 86 II 221, para. 11.c: 'He forfeited this right because he failed to notify the company immediately in accordance with

Article 214(1) CO gives the seller the same special remedies of Article 107 CO at his choice.[721] The seller may thus maintain the contract and demand positive damages or rescind the contract and demand negative damages.

621 In a *sale for credit*, the seller does not have the right to rescind the sales contract, unless the seller has reserved such right in the contract.[722] Such reservation may, for example, take the form of a retention of title clause.[723]

622 Article 215 CO sets forth two rules for the calculation of damages in case of buyer's default. While the wording of Article 215 indicates that these rules only apply to commercial sales, it is generally acknowledged that they also apply to ordinary sales.[724]

623 The first rule addresses the case where the seller, after rescinding the sales contract, sells the purchase object to a third party for a lower price. Article 215(1) CO specifies that the seller may claim the price difference as positive damages.

624 The second rule relates to purchasing objects for which a market or stock exchange price exists. Here, the seller is entitled to claim as positive damages the difference between the contractual purchase price and the market price at the time of performance without needing to sell the object.[725]

625 Finally, as regards a buyer's second main obligation, failure to accept delivery of the purchase object entitles the seller to proceed in accordance with Articles 107–109 CO.[726]

I Peculiarities of the Sale of Real Estate

626 Generally, Articles 197–215 CO also apply to the sale of real estate.[727] Yet, Articles 216–220 CO contain some special rules that take precedence where the purchase object is real estate.

article 214(2) CO. However, this does not mean that he has also lost the right to proceed in accordance with articles 107 et seqq. CO.'

721. *See* hereinabove paras 376 et seqq.
722. Article 214(3) CO.
723. Decision of the Swiss Federal Supreme Court dated 22 September 1964, DSC 90 II 285, para. 2: 'However, contrary to the claimant's opinion, article 214(1) CO is not applicable to the present case. Since the purchase price was to be paid "within 10 days after assembly", this was neither a prepayment nor a cash purchase, but a sale on credit. According to article 214(3) CO, the seller can only withdraw from the contract in the event of default by the buyer if he has expressly reserved this right. The lower court is of the opinion that the claimant is barred from invoking article 214(3) CO because the necessary reservation of the right of rescission is lacking. This view is incorrect. According to established case law and doctrine, if a reservation of title is agreed, the seller's unilateral right of withdrawal must always be deemed to be included, even if this has not been specifically emphasised. This applies even if the retention of title has been agreed but not registered and ownership of the item has therefore been transferred to the buyer.'
724. Huguenin, Obligationenrecht, Zurich 2019, N 2533.
725. Article 215(2) CO.
726. *See* hereinabove para. 550.
727. Article 221 CO.

627 Notably, pursuant to Article 216(1) CO, the form requirement of public deed applies.[728] Such form requirement also applies to pre-contracts as well as an agreement conferring a right of pre-emption, purchase or repurchase in relation to real estate.[729]

628 Further, there are special provisions on warranties for quality regarding the size of the plot of land[730] and on the passing of benefits and risks.[731]

III CONTRACT FOR WORK

629 A contract for work is a contract whereby the contractor (*Unternehmer, entrepreneur, appaltatore*) undertakes to produce a work (*Werk, ouvrage, opera*) and the customer (*Besteller, maître de l'ouvrage, committente*) undertakes to pay the contractor for that work.[732]

A Statutory Basis

630 The contract for work is a nominate contract governed by Articles 363–379 CO which are divided up into three chapters:

- Definition (Article 363 CO).
- Contractor's and customer's obligations (Articles 364–374 CO).
- Termination (Articles 375–379 CO).

631 In international contracts for work, the CISG may apply.[733] Under Article 3(1) CISG, '[c]contracts for the supply of goods to be manufactured or produced are to be considered sales unless the party who orders the goods undertakes to supply a substantial part of the materials necessary for such manufacture or production.' Thus, contracts may qualify as contracts for work under Swiss law, but simultaneously constitute sales contracts under the CISG.

B Delimitations

632 The delimitation of a contract for work from a *sales contract* can give rise to controversy when parties have agreed on the transfer of an object that does not exist at the time of contract conclusion but has yet to be manufactured.[734]

---

728. *See* hereinabove para. 149.
729. Article 216(2) CO.
730. Article 219 CO.
731. Article 220 CO.
732. Article 363 CO.
733. *See* hereinabove para. 524.
734. *See* hereinabove paras 529 et seqq.

633 Further, the contract for work must be distinguished from the mandate agreement (Articles 394–406 CO). The former entails a duty to deliver a specific result, whereas the latter only entails a duty to act diligently in furtherance of a goal (best-efforts).

634 The distinction between the two can be difficult, as both contract types require one party to work towards a certain goal. By interpreting the contract one must determine whether a specific result is owed. Such promise may only be inferred if there are objective criteria to examine whether the specific result has been achieved.[735] This issue must be assessed on a case-by-case basis considering the specific obligations agreed on by the parties.[736]

C Formation of a Contract for Work

635 A contract for work is formed by the exchange of mutual expressions of intent covering the essential terms of the contract (*essentialia negotii*).[737] This refers to the contractor's obligation to carry out and deliver a work and the customer's obligation to pay the work price.

636 The object of the contract is the work, i.e., the result of an activity, not the activity as such. The work may be tangible or intangible (e.g., intellectual work in the form of an expert report). A work may consist not only of creating a new thing but also of modifying, enlarging, improving, renovating or giving new characteristics to an existing object.

637 The work price must not be fixed in the contract. It is sufficient that the parties have agreed on the contractor generally being entitled to some form of remuneration. Where the price was not fixed in advance or fixed only as an approximate amount, it is determined according to the value of the work produced and the expenses incurred by the contractor.[738]

735. Decision of the Swiss Federal Supreme Court dated 11 May 2001, DSC 127 III 328, para. 2.c: 'Technical expert reports in particular regularly lead to a result that can be checked according to objective criteria and qualified as correct or incorrect. The correctness of the result of the expert report can therefore be objectively guaranteed and can be promised as a success. In principle, there is nothing to prevent the applicability of the law on contracts for work with regard to such expert reports. However, if there are no objective criteria for assessing the correctness of the result of the expert report, this can neither be guaranteed by the expert nor checked by the customer. In this case, the objective accuracy of the result cannot be promised as a work. The expert thus does not owe a successful outcome in the sense of the objective correctness of the result, but only - but still - a diligent action in the interest of the contractual partner and with regard to a certain outcome, the occurrence of which, however, cannot be guaranteed. The contract thus fulfils the characteristics of a mandate agreement.'
736. Decision of the Swiss Federal Supreme Court dated 25 November 2010, no. 4A_252/2010, para. 4.1.
737. *See* hereinabove paras 96 et seqq.
738. Article 374 CO.

638 Contracts for work are not subject to any form requirements. However, where the contract for work is the result of a public tendering process, public law may impose form requirements.[739]

639 Often, complex contracts for work contain a reference to a detailed set of rules issued by an industry-specific association. Prominent examples are the SIA 118 General Terms and Conditions for Construction Works issued by the Swiss Society of Engineers and Architects or the Conditions of Contract issued by the International Federation of Consulting Engineers (FIDIC). Technically, these sets of rules are considered to constitute general terms of conditions (GTCs), which only become an integral part of the contract if properly incorporated.[740]

D The Contractor's Main Obligations

640 The contractor's main obligation is the production and delivery of a work.[741]

641 In terms of quality, the work must meet the contractually agreed requirements. If the quality of the delivered work deviates from the promised standard, this constitutes a defect for which the seller is generally liable (warranty of quality).[742] The notion of warranty of quality is the same in sales contracts as in contracts for work.[743]

642 Delivery of the work consists of the handover of the completed work to the customer.[744] For there to be delivery, the work does not have to be free of defects. A defective work can therefore also be delivered, regardless of the type of defect.[745]

739. *See, e.g.*, Article 29(1) of the Swiss Federal Ordinance on Public Procurement requiring the contract for work after the award to be concluded in writing.
740. Decision of the Swiss Federal Supreme Court dated 4 December 2001, no. 4P.209/2001, para. 3.a. Regarding incorporation of general terms and conditions, *see* hereinabove paras 253 et seqq.
741. Article 363 CO.
742. Decision of the Swiss Federal Supreme Court dated 10 June 2014, no. 4A_173/2014, para. 5.2: 'The object of performance is defective if it deviates from the contract, if it lacks an expressly warranted characteristic or a characteristic that is assumed and presupposed according to the principle of trust. Consequently, whether or not a defect is present is assessed solely on the basis of the specific content of the contract.' As to liability, *see* below paras 671 et seqq.
743. Swiss Federal Supreme Court dated 8 May 2007, no. 4C.130/2006, para. 7.3. As to the notion of warranty of quality under sales law, *see* hereinabove paras 573–579.
744. Decision of the Swiss Federal Supreme Court dated 11 September 2007, no. 4A_51/2007, para. 4.5: 'Delivery within the meaning of this provision is understood to mean the handover of the completed, albeit possibly defective, work to the customer with the intention of fulfilling the contract. The distinction between unfinished and defective work can be difficult. The decisive factor in this respect is whether the contractor has expressed that the work has been completed. This is to be assumed in any case if the contractor sends the final invoice to the customer, which is why the latter is then obliged in good faith to fulfil his obligations to check and give notice of defects.'
745. Decision of the Swiss Federal Supreme Court dated 25 November 2010, no. 4A_252/2010, para. 5.4.2: 'Completion must be distinguished from the absence of defects in the work. A work can have a defect and still be complete. The absence of defects in the work is not a prerequisite for its delivery and acceptance. The defectiveness of the work does not prevent delivery and acceptance, regardless of the nature of the defects.'

However, the customer will then be entitled to special remedies for breach of warranty of quality.[746]

643 Generally, the contractor is obliged to carry out the work in person or to have it carried out under his personal supervision,[747] which is a deviation from the general rule of Article 68 CO.[748] Yet, Article 364(2) CO specifies that this does not apply where the nature of the work is such that his personal involvement is not required. In any case, the customer may (even after conclusion of the contract) permit the contractor to rely on subcontractors – it may do so explicitly or implicitly. However, if a contractor is obliged to carry out the work in person or at least supervise it and fails to do so, this will result in the debtor's default.[749]

644 Unless otherwise required by agreement or custom, the contractor is obliged to supply the resources, tools and machinery necessary for producing the work at his own expense.[750] As regards the materials necessary for the work, the parties are free to agree either on provision by the customer or the contractor.[751] If the customer provides the materials, Article 365(2–3) CO installs certain duties on the contractor regarding proper handling of the materials and notification of any defects discovered in the materials.

645 Finally, the contractor has a general duty of care under Article 364(1) CO. Courts have deduced ancillary duties of information[752] as well as duties to protect the work from damage[753] and to not incur unnecessary costs[754] from this general rule.

746. *See* below paras 680 et seqq.
747. Article 364(2) CO.
748. *See* hereinabove para. 281.
749. Decision of the Swiss Federal Supreme Court dated 25 January 1977, DSC 103 II 52, para. 4: 'If a contractor breaches this obligation incumbent on him to personally carry out or manage the production work, this can only be taken by the customer as grounds for rescission in accordance with articles 107 to 109 CO.'
750. Article 364(3) CO.
751. *See* Article 365 CO. If the contractor supplies the necessary materials, the contractual relationship qualifies as a contract for work and materials (*see* hereinabove para. 531).
752. Decision of the Swiss Federal Supreme Court dated 5 June 2003, DSC 129 III 604, para. 4.1: 'The duty of care is an expression of the duty of loyalty, resulting from the relationship of trust existing between customer and contractor. Duties to inform and advise have been deduced from the duty of care; they are based on the idea that the contractor, in his capacity as a specialist, must advise the customer and inform him of any circumstances that are important for the performance of the work. Thus, to prevent damage, the contractor may be required to inform the customer about the appropriate use of the work; for example, the installer of a central heating system will have to indicate precisely the quality of water to be used. Generally speaking, if it is foreseeable that the work will be used in a way that is inappropriate or contrary to its intended purpose, and if this could be dangerous, the owner must be made aware of this if he is not supposed to be aware of the risk.'
753. Decision of the Swiss Federal Supreme Court dated 31 March 2004, no. 4C.337/2003, para. 2.1: 'In addition to this general duty, the contractor is bound by certain ancillary duties, including the duty to protect, which essentially consists of the contractor's obligation to take all necessary measures to protect the customer or third parties from dangers to their property. In particular, the contractor must take all necessary steps to prevent the item entrusted to him for repair from being stolen. The ancillary obligation arises from the contractual relationship of trust between the parties, with the debtor required to do everything necessary for the proper performance of the main obligation and the achievement of the purpose assigned to the performance. However, according to case law, the duty of loyalty of the employee or the contractor, provided

E The Customer's Main Obligations

646 The customer's main obligation is the payment of the price for the work. The price is generally determined in one of two ways: a flat rate (*Festübernahme, forfait, a corpo*) or by the value of the works. Where parties have failed to specify the work price in the contract, the price will be determined by the value of the works.[755]

647 Flat rate prices consist of a firm commitment by the contractor to complete the work at a specified price regardless of the actual costs incurred. There are two forms of flat rates: lump-sum prices and unit prices.

648 The lump sum price is a single sum for the entire work which is due regardless of the activity actually carried out and the costs incurred. Yet, the contractor is in this constellation required to carry out only the steps necessary for completion of the work.[756]

649 The unit price is an individual sum for each delivery of materials and each service (unit) necessary to complete the work. The price is then fixed at completion of the work depending on the number of units actually carried out.[757] However, only the quantities necessary for completion of the work when acting with due care entitle the contractor to remuneration.[758]

for in particular in article 321a(1) CO and article 364(1) CO, does not generally place the latter in the position of guarantor, which would result in an obligation to perform any act that could prevent damage to the employer or the customer.'

754. Decision of the Swiss Federal Supreme Court dated 6 March 1970, DSC 96 II 58, para. 1.
755. Article 374 CO.
756. Decision of the Swiss Federal Supreme Court dated 22 June 2005, no. 4C.90/2005, para. 3.2: 'If the remuneration is fixed in advance as part of a contract for work, the customer must pay the full price even if the completion of the work requires less labour than was planned (article 373(3) CO in conjunction with 373(1) CO). Such a price agreement is binding (*pacta sunt servanda*). According to unanimous doctrine, the lump sum price is a fixed price in the sense that it is unchangeable and independent of the actual construction costs of the work, the quantities of work performed, expenses and labour; ... . The reasons why the construction costs of the work ultimately turn out to be lower is – as explained – irrelevant. In the case of a lump-sum price agreement, the contractor, as the claimant rightly emphasises, only has to provide those services that are necessary to complete the agreed work.'
757. Decision of the Swiss Federal Supreme Court dated 8 July 2005, no. 4C.88/2005, para. 2: 'The unit price is a flat rate method of remuneration under article 373 of the Swiss Code of Obligations. It involves fixing the amount due on the basis of the units required to complete the work; as in the case at hand, this may be a price per square metre. The number of units determining the remuneration is established either by means of an actual quantity measurement, revealing what the contractor has actually done, or by means of a theoretical quantity measurement based on the plans for the work.'
758. Decision of the Swiss Federal Supreme Court dated 8 July 2005, no. 4C.88/2005, para. 2: 'In the case of remuneration based on a unit price, this [the duty of due care] implies in particular that the contractor carries out the work without exceeding a reasonable number of units; similarly, if the contractor carries out his work in quantities greater than those agreed, he cannot obtain remuneration for the whole. According to the case law, as long as the customer has not expressly or tacitly recognised the contractor's invoice, he may contest the basis of calculation and argue that the expenses claimed by the contractor are excessive.'

650 Despite the firm commitment characteristic of a flat rate price, Article 373(2) CO foresees an adjustment mechanism. Where completion of the work is prevented or seriously hindered by extraordinary circumstances that were unforeseeable or excluded according to the conditions assumed by both parties, the court may at its discretion authorise an increase in the price or the termination of the contract. Courts are rather reluctant when dealing with Article 372(2) CO and apply a high threshold, especially to the condition of undue hindrance.[759] Also, if the contractor does not notify the customer in a timely manner of the existence of such circumstances, he forfeits his right to demand an adjustment of the price mechanism.[760]

651 Further, if the plans of the work are amended (change order), the contractor is generally entitled to an increase of the flat rate price.[761] If the parties fail to agree on such a price, the default rule of Article 374 CO applies and the contractor charges the additional work due to the change order on the basis of the value of the works, even if the contract for work itself is subject to a flat rate price.[762]

652 However, parties are free to deviate from Articles 373 and 374 CO. Often, contracts for work contain special rules dealing with price adjustments and increases in production costs.

653 If the price is calculated at the value of the works, the basis is costs plus fees. Thus, the contractor must prove the costs, which he incurred in carrying out the work, and then may add a reasonable fee as a profit margin and compensation for his risk.

654 Payment of the price of the work is due only upon delivery.[763] Thus, unless agreed otherwise, no advance payments are owed. The delivery consists either of the physical

759. *See, e.g.*, decision of 28 November 1978, DSC 104 II 314, para. b: 'Extraordinary circumstances within the meaning of this provision are circumstances which the contractor need not expect because they are not foreseeable in the normal course of events or which both parties did not anticipate according to their common understanding. They may already exist when the contract is concluded (e.g., geological conditions) or only occur subsequently (e.g., an extraordinary increase in wages, interest rates or material prices), i.e., according to these examples they may not only be of a natural but also of an economic nature. … . This also applies to the condition of undue hindrance, which is expressed in the higher production costs of the work and must therefore be assessed primarily on the basis of the reciprocal performance. What is required is a blatant, obvious disproportion between the value of the services provided by the contractor and the consideration promised by the customer.'

760. Decision of the Swiss Federal Supreme Court dated 27 June 1990, DSC 116 II 315, para. 3.

761. Decision of the Swiss Federal Supreme Court dated 27 May 2010, no. 4A_183/2010, para. 3.2: 'The firm nature of the flat rate price (in this case, the initial price of CHF 100,000 for site installation) is not absolute. Article 373(2) CO provides for a first exception where … . A second exception occurs when there is a change in the order in relation to the object of the contract initially agreed; the firm price agreed by the parties is, in fact, decisive only for the work planned at the time, without qualitative or quantitative changes. In principle, changes to the order entitle the contractor to a price increase for additional work carried out.'

762. Decision of the Swiss Federal Supreme Court dated 17 April 2000, no. 4C.409/1999, para. 1.c.cc: 'In the event of a change order, the contractor is in principle entitled to additional remuneration. Unless otherwise agreed, the price of modifications must be determined in accordance with article 374 CO, i.e., on the basis of the value of the materials used and the work performed. Furthermore, it is not necessary for the customer to have ordered the additional work for it to be charged to him; it is sufficient for him to have accepted it.'

763. Article 372 CO.

handover of the work or, if no physical handover is possible (e.g., a building), the declaration of the contractor that his work is completed.[764] Payment becomes even due if the work suffers from defects. However, the customer is entitled to (partially) retain payment under Article 82 CO until the contractor has remedied the defects after being requested to do so.[765]

F Performance Failure by the Contractor

655 While performance failure by the contractor may be categorised in the same three groups of breaches that have already been analysed above,[766] the Code of Obligations contains several special provisions that amend the remedies available to a customer in such a situation.

1 Non-performance

656 In general, the same principles as explained for the general part of the Code of Obligations apply to the contract for work.[767]

657 However, the Code of Obligations contains special rules addressing the scenario that the work is destroyed or damaged after conclusion of contract without such occurrence being attributable to either party (e.g., due to force majeure). Article 376 CO governs which party should bear the risk of such destruction. This provision supersedes the standard rule of subsequent impossibility contained in Article 119 CO.[768] However, the parties are free to deviate from Article 376 CO.

658 Under Article 376(1) CO, if the work is destroyed by accident prior to completion or delivery, the contractor is not entitled to payment for work done or expenses incurred, unless the customer is in default on acceptance of the work. Thus, the contractor generally carries the risk of destruction of the work. However, Article 376(2) CO sets forth that the loss of materials is borne by the party that supplied them. Further, Article 376(3) CO contains an exception if the destruction is due to a defect in the materials supplied or in the construction site designated by the customer or as a result of the method of production that he prescribed.

764. Decision of the Swiss Federal Supreme Court dated 25 August 2003, no. 4C.85/2003, para. 7.2: 'According to article 372(1) CO, the price of the work is due at the time of delivery. Delivery within the meaning of this provision is the handing over by the contractor to the customer of a completed work that has been carried out in accordance with the contract in each of its parts. It does not matter whether or not the work is defective. From the contractor's point of view, acceptance corresponds to delivery. This is done by hand-over or by express or tacit notice from the contractor to the customer. If partial deliveries and payments have been agreed, the price for each part of the work is payable when that part is delivered (article 372(2) CO).'
765. Gauch, Der Werkvertrag, Zurich 2019, N 2366–2410.
766. *See* hereinabove paras 340 et seqq.
767. *See* hereinabove paras 345–348.
768. *See* Article 119(3) CO: 'This does not apply to cases in which, by law or contractual agreement, the risk passes to the creditor prior to performance.'

659 Further, Article 378 CO contains special rules for impossibility that is attributable to the customer.[769]

2 *Default in Performance*

660 The contractor's default is governed by the general rules on debtor default in Articles 102–109 CO.[770] But, Article 366(1) CO sets out a specific rule regarding delay in carrying out the work.

661 A default in carrying out the work (*Herstellungsverzug, demeure pour l'exécution de l'ouvrage, ritardo nell'esecuzione dell'opera*) must be distinguished from the default in delivering the work. Article 366(1) CO solely concerns the former and enables the customer to take action against the contractor even before the delivery date.

662 Article 366(1) CO covers three different forms of delay:

- Delay in beginning production: Unless agreed otherwise, the customer may demand the contractor to immediately commence production of the work.[771] But, if the parties have agreed on a specific delivery date, this is to be understood – in the absence of other indications – as giving the contractor the freedom to decide when to begin production, as long as he can meet the delivery date.[772]
- Delays of ongoing production in breach of contract: This covers failure to meet agreed-upon intermediate deadlines (milestones) or delays in relation to a binding work programme.
- Foreseeable delay in relation to delivery: At one point, a contractor may be so far behind schedule that there is no longer any prospect of him completing the work on time.

663 If there is a delay in the sense of Article 366(1) CO, the customer must send a formal reminder (Article 102(1) CO) and set the contractor a final grace period (Article 107(1) CO, subject to Article 108 CO).

664 The remedies available to the customer under Article 366(1) CO are the usual ones for debtor default.[773]

769. *See* below para. 705.
770. *See* hereinabove paras 349 et seqq.
771. Article 75 CO.
772. Gauch, Der Werkvertrag, Zurich 2019, N 674.
773. *See* hereinabove paras 371 et seqq. Regarding the question whether a customer may rescind the entire contract for work if such contract concerns a multitude of deliverables that can be separated from each other, *see* decision of the Swiss Federal Supreme Court dated 30 March 2015, DSC 141 III 106, para. 16.2.

3 Inadequate Performance

665 A contractor's inadequate performance must be assessed differently depending on whether the breach concerns the main obligations or ancillary obligations.

666 If only ancillary obligations are breached, the legal consequences are governed by Article 97 CO.[774] In contrast, an inadequate performance of the contractor's main obligations (carrying out and delivery of the work) is governed by special rules in Articles 367–371 CO. These special rules are exclusive in the sense that there is no room for the general remedy of damages under Article 97 CO or the remedies for debtor's default.[775]

4 Special Case: Breach of Warranty of Quality

a Warranty of Quality

667 Warranty of quality refers to the contractor's obligation to deliver the work in the quality owed under the contract. It is generally governed by Articles 367 et seqq. CO. These provisions are non-mandatory and may be deviated from by the parties.[776]

668 The notion of warranty of quality is the same in sales contracts as in contracts for work.[777] Thus, the work must comply will all express and implied warranties:

> The work is defective within the meaning of article 367(1) CO if it does not possess the qualities agreed – expressly or tacitly – by the parties, or the qualities that the customer could have expected according to the rules of good faith. With regard to the first type of defect, we should not limit ourselves to what has been expressly stated, but should seek, in accordance with the general rules of interpretation, what the parties intended in each specific case. As for the expected quality, this refers, on the one hand, to the material used – which must not be of below-average quality (*see* article 71(2) CO) – and, on the other hand, to the properties necessary or customary for the agreed use.[778]

b Liability for Breach of Warranty

669 A seller's liability for breach of warranty of quality is subject to the following requirements:

774. *See* hereinabove paras 385 et seqq.
775. Decision of the Swiss Federal Supreme Court dated 27 October 2014, no. 4A_387/2014, para. 4.2.
776. But limitations apply to an exclusion of liability, *see* below para. 679.
777. Decision of the Swiss Federal Supreme Court dated 8 May 2007, no. 4C.130/2006, para. 7.3. As to the warranty of quality in sales law, *see* hereinabove paras 573–579.
778. Decision of the Swiss Federal Supreme Court dated 8 May 2007, no. 4C.130/2006, para. 3.1.

- breach of warranty of quality;
- breach of warranty of quality not attributable to the customer;
- the customer has not subsequently accepted the breach of warranty; and
- the parties have not excluded liability for the breach in question.

670 *Breach of warranty of quality*: A breach of warranty of quality exists if either an express or implied warranty is engaged in that there is deviation between the status as should be under these warranties and the actual status of the delivered work.

671 The relevant point in time for determining the presence of such deviation is the time of delivery. However, if a breach of warranty of quality already crystallises before actual delivery, the customer must not await actual delivery but may proceed in accordance with Article 366(2) CO. Where during the production of the work it becomes evident that, through the fault of the contractor, the work will be defective, the customer may set the contractor a grace period within which to take remedial action and notify him that any failure to do so will result in the hire of a third party to take such remedial action at the risk and expense of the contractor.

672 *Breach of warranty of quality not attributable to the customer*: The contractor may not be held liable for the breach of warranty of quality if the customer is at fault for such breach due to having given instructions concerning production of the work that were contrary to the express warnings of the contractor or for any other reason.[779] The warning of the contractor must be explicit and not just a mere statement that the contractor would prefer to proceed in another manner than instructed.[780] Further, there is no liability for the breach of warranty of quality if such breach can be traced back to defective materials provided by the customer.[781]

673 *No acceptance of breach of warranty/immediate notification*: After delivery, the customer may approve a breach of warranty and thereby discharge the seller from any liability. Such approval is assumed if the customer after discovering a breach of warranty does not notify the seller thereof immediately.[782]

674 The notification of a breach of warranty (*Mängelrüge, avis des défauts, notifica dei difetti*) in a contract for work follows largely the same rules as under the sales contract.[783] Article 370 CO also distinguishes between evident and hidden defects.

779. Article 369 CO.
780. Decision of the Swiss Federal Supreme Court dated 6 June 1990, DSC 116 II 305, para. 2.c.bb: 'According to article 369 CO, the contractor's warranty of quality generally only ceases to apply if the customer adheres to his instructions despite an express warning (*avis formula, espresso parere*). According to the case law of the Federal Supreme Court, an express warning can only be assumed if there is a clear expression of intent by the contractor from which the customer must conclude that the contractor rejects responsibility for the prescribed execution. … . A general reservation by the contractor that he would proceed differently in technical terms or that he would have preferred a different subcontractor does not constitute a warning.'
781. Article 365(2) CO.
782. Article 370 CO.
783. *See* hereinabove paras 586–593.

675 Evident defects are deemed approved if not immediately raised after the initial inspection or if a customer even fails to conduct such inspection. Under Article 367(1) CO, the customer is required to inspect the condition of the delivered work as soon as feasible in the normal course of business. In contrast, hidden defects must only be notified once actually discovered.[784]

676 If the customer fails to notify a defect in good time, he is deemed to have accepted the breach of warranty barring any claim for liability under Articles 368 et seqq. CO. Yet, there is an exception to this where the contractor has wilfully concealed the breach of warranty from the customer. In such cases, late notification does not bar the seller's liability.[785]

677 *No exclusion of liability*: The seller's warranty of quality is generally of a non-mandatory nature and may thus be excluded by the parties.[786] An exclusion may be all-encompassing, only concern specific defects or only exclude resort to certain remedies. However, the limits of Article 100 CO apply to exclusions of liability.[787] Whether the limits of Article 199 CO[788] apply by analogy is controversial in doctrine.[789]

c *Remedies for Breach of Warranty*

678 If a contractor's liability for breach of warranty of quality is engaged, three remedies become available to the customer under Article 368 CO. The customer may freely choose among the available remedies. Once the customer has chosen a remedy, he is bound by such choice, as the remedies constitute so-called formative rights.[790] While the customer may not combine the three available remedies with each other, he may in addition to one of the three remedies also request damages.

679 All remedies under Article 368 CO only become available after delivery of the work. A customer wishing to take action in view of an impending breach of warranty of quality may, however, proceed in accordance with Article 366(2) CO.[791]

680 *Redhibition* (Article 368(1) CO; *Wandlung, résiliation du contrat, azione redibitoria*): The remedy of redhibition also exists in sales law, albeit in a slightly different form.[792] Aside from the breach of warranty of quality, there is one additional requirement. The remedy of redhibition is only available in cases of serious defects, i.e., when

784. Article 370(3) CO.
785. Article 370(1) CO.
786. Decision of the Swiss Federal Supreme Court dated 4 September 2001, no. 4C.82/2001, para. 2.b.
787. *See* hereinabove paras 419–421.
788. *See* hereinabove para. 598.
789. Huguenin, Obligationenrecht, Zurich 2019, N 3155, with further references.
790. Decision of the Swiss Federal Supreme Court dated 10 January 1983, DSC 109 II 40, para. 6. However, if the contractor fails to remedy the defect in the work despite being requested to do so, the customer may declare redhibition despite having chosen the remedy of repair before (decision of the Swiss Federal Supreme Court dated 1 April 2010, DSC 136 III 273, para. 2.4).
791. For details on Article 366(2) CO, *see* below para. 687.
792. *See* hereinabove paras 601–603.

a customer has no use for the work delivered or cannot reasonably be expected to accept it. A work is only deemed unusable if it is completely useless and the defect cannot be remedied.[793] Whether a customer can be expected to accept a work is a question of balancing the interests of the contractor with those of the customer.[794]

681 Redhibition is not available despite such serious defects, in three scenarios. First, there is no remedy of redhibition if the work has been produced on the customer's land or property which by its nature cannot be removed without disproportionate detriment.[795] Second, if the customer uses the work despite being aware of the defect, he forfeits the remedy of redhibition.[796] Third, a customer may not rely on the remedy of redhibition if he is responsible for the destruction or significant deterioration of the work.[797]

682 If redhibition is declared, the contract for work becomes void *ex tunc* and is transformed into a liquidation relationship.[798] The customer must return the work to the contractor together with any benefits derived from it in the interim. The contractor must return to the customer the price paid together with interest.

683 *Reduction* (Article 368 CO; *Minderung, reduction du prix, azione estimatoria*): By the remedy of reduction, a customer may claim a reduction of the price. However, this remedy is not available if the work is entirely worthless. In such a case, the customer is limited to the remedy of redhibition. Same as in sales law, the reduction in price is subject to a relative calculation method.[799] There is a presumption that the reduced value of the work corresponds to the costs of repairing the defects.[800]

793. Decision of the Swiss Federal Supreme Court dated 19 August 2002, no. 4C.126/2002, para. 2.1.
794. Decision of the Swiss Federal Supreme Court dated 11 April 1972, DSC 98 II 118, para. 3.a: 'Whether redhibition is permissible or merely a reduction in the price of the work depends on the mutual interests, which must be weighed against each other according to the principles of equity. However, this balancing of interests leads to the redhibition of the contract in this case, as the work was unusable for the customer due to production in breach of the contract and as the manufacturer did not make use of the opportunity offered to it to subsequently repair the containers.'
795. Article 368(3) CO. Decision of the Swiss Federal Supreme Court, no. 4A_177/2014, para. 4.1: 'In the case of works which are constructed on the customer's land and which by their nature can only be removed with disproportionate disadvantages, the customer is only entitled to the rights mentioned in the second paragraph of article 368 CO (article 368(3) CO), i.e., redhibition is not permitted. Whether the contractor is facing such disadvantages depends on the circumstances of the individual case, in particular on the value of the work in connection with the property and the reduction in value that it would suffer in the event of separation. In principle, a disadvantage for the contractor is not disproportionate if the defective work is unusable for the customer within the meaning of article 368(1) CO.'
796. Decision of the Swiss Federal Supreme Court dated 19 August 2002, no. 4C.126/2002, para. 2.1.
797. Article 207(3) CO in analogy.
798. Decision of the Swiss Federal Supreme Court dated 27 October 2014, no. 4A_387/2014, para. 4.1; decision of the Swiss Federal Supreme Court dated 19 August 2002, no. 4C.126/2002, para. 2.1.
799. *See* hereinabove para. 606. Decision of the Swiss Federal Supreme Court dated 6 June 1990, DSC 116 II 305, para. 4.a.
800. Decision of the Swiss Federal Supreme Court dated 5 June 1985, DSC 111 II 162, para. 3.c: 'Thus, in the absence of any indication to the contrary, the court may also rely on the presumption that the depreciation corresponds to the cost of restoration, each of the interested

684 *Rectification* (Article 368(2) CO; *Nachbesserung, réparation de l'ouvrage, reparazione dell' opera*): By the remedy of rectification, a customer may request the contractor to remedy any defects in the work so that the final product corresponds to the status as contractually owed. The remedy is available in case of breach of warranty of quality if, one, rectification is objectively possible and, two, does not cause excessive costs to the contractor. The costs of rectification are deemed excessive if they are disproportionate to the benefit that rectification of the defect would bring to the customer.[801] The contractor bears the burden of proof in regard to such disproportionality.[802]

685 Failure by the contractor to execute necessary repair works is a case of debtor's default governed by Article 102–109 CO. Under Article 107 CO, the customer may thus either continue to insist on rectification, demand compensation for non-fulfilment (of the rectification) or rescind the contract. In addition, he may rely on Article 366(2) CO by analogy and take charge of completing the rectification of the work at the risk and expense of the contractor (so-called performance by substitution;[803] *Ersatzvornahme, exécution par substitution, esecuzione sostitutiva*) – be it by hiring a third party or by doing the necessary work himself.[804] Once rectification is completed, the customer has a claim for compensation for the costs of such rectification works regardless of any fault of the contractor.[805] Either way, the customer must set the contractor a grace period before proceeding under Article 107 CO or Article 366(2) CO. In order to rely on Article 366(2) CO, the customer must, in addition, threaten the contractor with performance by substitution.[806]

---

parties being free to establish that it would be less – the repair costing more than the depreciation – or greater – the repair leaving a depreciation factor.'

801. Decision of the Swiss Federal Supreme Court dated 9 July 1985, DSC 111 II 173, para. 5: 'According to this doctrine, there must be a disproportion between the anticipated rectification costs and the benefit that the rectification of the defect brings to the customer; costs and benefits must be weighed against each other. Contrary to the opinion of the defendant and the assessment made by the Court of Appeal, the ratio of the rectification costs to the construction costs or to the agreed remuneration for the work is not decisive. When weighing up the costs and benefits, not only economic but also non-economic interests can be taken into account on the part of the customer. In addition to the costs for the actual rectification of defects, the rectification costs also include the associated costs for preparatory and restoration work as well as the consequential costs of rectifying defects, which include, for example, costs for relocating and rehousing residents. Since the exclusion of the right to repair in the event of excessive costs as an application of the impracticality of specific performance is intended to protect the contractor from unreasonable demands, it is sufficient for the right to repair to lapse if the customer's benefit can no longer reasonably justify the costs associated with the repair.'
802. Decision of the Swiss Federal Supreme Court dated 24 February 2004, no. 4A.265/2003, para. 3.2.
803. *See* hereinabove para. 396.
804. Decision of the Swiss Federal Supreme Court dated 28 July 2000, no. 4C.159/1999, para. 5: 'Like the remedy of rectification, the claim for reimbursement of the costs of substitute performance is independent of the contractor's fault for the defect; the only requirement is that the customer is not responsible for the defect himself.'
805. Decision of the Swiss Federal Supreme Court dated 28 July 2000, no. 4C.159/1999, para. 5.
806. Article 366(2) CO: '... and notify him that any failure to do so will result in the hire of a third party to take such remedial action or to complete the work at the risk and expense of the contractor.'

686 *No remedy of replacement*: In contrast to the sales contract, there is no remedy of replacement in a contract for work, unless agreed on by the parties. A request by the customer that the work be replaced is rather interpreted as a declaration of redhibition.[807]

687 *Additional remedy of damages:* In addition to the aforementioned remedies, liability for breach of warranty of quality entitles the customer to damages. However, this requires that the contractor was at fault. Despite the wording of Article 368 CO, case law assumes that it is not the customer who must prove the contractor's fault, rather – as is the general rule under Article 97 CO[808] – it is up to the contractor to prove that he was not at fault.[809]

688 The claim for damages supplements the aforementioned remedies to the extent that it also covers the consequential damage caused by the breach of warranty of quality.[810] For this remedy to be available, it is not necessary that the customer actually relied on any of the other afore-mentioned remedies.[811] If the customer relies on redhibition, he may only claim negative damages (e.g., costs related to conclusion of contract or inspection of the work).[812]

689 *Alternative remedies*: In contrast to sales law, the customer may not rely on the ordinary remedies of Articles 97–101 CO.[813] Yet, he may rely on remedies for torts if the requirements of Article 41 CO are fulfilled.

690 *The customer's defences*: The general *defence of set-off* is available.[814] Further, the seller may invoke the *defence of prescription*,[815] which is, however, governed by the

807. Decision of the Swiss Federal Supreme Court dated 11 April 1972, DSC 98 II 118, para. 2: 'In a letter dated 7 August, she then asked the defendant to remove the tanks and replace them with new ones. The claimant thus decided in favour of redhibition within the meaning of Art. 368 para. 1 CO. Admittedly, contrary to the differing opinion of BECKER, it could not demand that the defendant supply new tanks. However, this does not alter the fact that the claimant's request to remove the two tanks immediately, the claimant refused to accept the defective work.'
808. *See* hereinabove paras 413–418.
809. Decision of the Swiss Federal Supreme Court dated 10 November 1981, DSC 107 II 438.
810. Decision of the Swiss Federal Supreme Court dated 7 October 2005, no. 4C.106/2005, para. 3.1: 'He is also entitled to damages if the contractor is at fault, but only to the extent that the damage cannot be compensated by reduction, redhibition or rectification. The claim for damages therefore only exists for consequential damages, which are caused by the defect, but go beyond it.'
811. Decision of the Swiss Federal Supreme Court dated 20 February 2004, no. 4C.297/2003, para. 2.1: 'However, it cannot be inferred from this that a customer who merely claims damages – without exercising one of the remedial rights provided by law – is entirely deprived of his warranty rights. In a situation of this kind, however, the customer will only be entitled to claim compensation for the consequential damage due to the defect ("Mangelfolgeschaden"); in other words, he will not be able to obtain through an action for damages the equivalent of a reduction in the price of the work or reimbursement of the costs of repair that he would have been able to claim under article 368(2) CO, 1st or 2nd hypothesis.'
812. Gauch, Der Werkvertrag, Zurich 2019, N 1874–1875.
813. Decision of the Swiss Federal Supreme Court dated 27 October 2014, no. 4A_387/2014, para. 4.2.
814. *See* hereinabove paras 449.
815. *See* hereinabove paras 441 et seqq.

special rules in Article 371 CO which largely coincide with the rules of Article 210 CO.[816]

691 *Parties' ability to modify remedy regime*: The contractor's obligations relating to warranty of quality are of a non-mandatory nature. The parties may therefore in principle cancel, limit or extend the customer's remedies for breach of warranty of quality.[817] However, any limitation or exclusion of remedies is subject to the rules and limitations regarding the exclusion of liability clauses.[818]

G Performance Failure by the Customer

692 Customer's failure to timely pay the price is governed by the general rules on debtor's default in Articles 102–109 CO.[819] There are generally no special rules that supersede these provisions. There is no room for an application of Article 214 CO by analogy.[820]

693 Yet, case law permits the contractor to deviate from Article 109 CO in one aspect. If the contractor has already begun with the execution of the work before declaring rescission, he must be given the opportunity to allow the withdrawal to take effect only for the future (*ex nunc*), meaning that he may claim remuneration for the work completed up to that point in time.[821]

694 If the work in question concerns the supply of material and labour or labour alone on a plot of land for buildings or other works, for demolition work, for scaffolding, for securing excavations or the like, on that plot of land, the contractor has a right to the creation of a statutory lien. The specific conditions of such lien (especially the time limit of four months upon completion of the works) are set forth in Articles 837 and 839 CC.

695 As regards the customer's defence of prescription, Article 128(3) CO foresees that payment claims for work carried out by craftsmen prescribe within only five years upon becoming due. For all other claims for payment of price, the prescription period is ten years under Article 127 CO.

---

816. *See* hereinabove paras 615–616.
817. Decision of the Swiss Federal Supreme Court dated 6 June 1990, DSC 116 II 305, para. 3.a.
818. *See* hereinabove para. 682.
819. *See* hereinabove paras 360 et seqq.
820. Gauch, Der Werkvertrag, Zurich 2019, N 1274.
821. Decision of the Swiss Federal Supreme Court dated 9 June 2010, no. 4A_603/2009, para. 2.2: 'Under article 107 CO, the contractor may rescind the contract – with effect "*ex nunc*" when the work has already begun – if the customer does not perform his main obligations in due time, in particular if he does not pay the price of the work or advance payments after having been given formal notice to do so. Furthermore, in accordance with articles 91 and 96 CO, which govern creditor default, the contractor also has the right to rescind the contract if the customer breaches his duty to cooperate, for example if he does not carry out the preparatory work required of him.'

696 A contractor's failure to keep within a previously provided estimate as to the price of the work does generally not entitle the customer to withhold payment. However, in serious cases, the customer might have a right to rescind the contract with effect *ex tunc*, even if the work has already been delivered.[822] Further, for construction work carried out on a plot of land, a disproportionate exceeding of an estimate may entitle the customer to reduce the price to be paid.[823] Finally, failure to notify the customer of a cost overrun may constitute inadequate performance (violation of general duty of care) by the contractor and thus entitle the customer to damages – which in turn could be used for a set-off defence.[824]

H Termination of a Contract for Work

697 As explained hereinabove, a contractor's performance failure may give rise to the remedies of rescission or redhibition putting an end to contract for work. In addition to that, Articles 375, 377 and 379 CO foresee other grounds for termination of a contract for work.

698 Under Article 375 CO, the customer may rescind the contract if the contractor disproportionately exceeds his cost estimate without the costumer contributing to such overrun. An excessive cost overrun is generally assumed when a threshold of 10%–20% is surpassed, although the individual circumstances of each case must still be considered.[825] If the work is carried out on a plot of land, rescission is only available if the work has not yet been completed.[826]

699 Further, Article 377 CO provides a customer with a termination right that he may exercise at any point in time and without any cause. Yet, he must pay the contractor for work already completed and indemnify him in full. Such indemnity includes loss of profit due to the early termination.[827] The indemnity is due even if termination is a reaction to a breach of contract by the contractor unless the breach is of such nature as

822. Article 375(1) CO. *See* below para. 704.
823. Article 375(2) CO.
824. *See* hereinabove para. 670.
825. Decision of the Swiss Federal Supreme Court dated 31 March 2009, no. 4A_577/2008, para. 3.1: 'According to an empirical standard (rule of thumb) developed by the doctrine and case law, exceeding the cost estimate is excessive beyond a margin of tolerance of approximately 10%. This rule is not absolute, however, and the judge's assessment will always depend on the particulars of the case in question; for example, the Federal Court accepted a margin of tolerance of 20% in a case where the owners could hardly rely on a very accurate estimate since it was not based on a detailed statement of the cost of the work. The decisive criterion for determining the permissible overrun in a particular case is commercial fairness, as inferred from article 24(1)(4) CO.'
826. Article 375(2) CO.
827. Decision of the Swiss Federal Supreme Court dated 27 October 1970, DSC 96 II 192, para. 5: 'The "full indemnity" owed by the customer under article 377 CO consists of the positive damages corresponding to the contractor's interest in full performance of the contract; it therefore includes the loss of profit.'

to give rise to important reasons for termination.[828] Article 377 CO is non-mandatory and may thus be deviated from by the parties.[829]

IV MANDATE AGREEMENT

700 A mandate agreement is a contract whereby the mandatee undertakes to conduct certain business or provide certain services.[830] It is the fallback contract for all kinds of services that are not covered by another type of contract in the special part of the Code of Obligations.[831] Examples of mandate agreements are the contracts between a lawyer and his client, a doctor and his patient or a bank and its customer.

A Statutory Basis

701 The mandate agreement is governed by Articles 394–406 CO which are divided into four chapters:

- Definition (Article 394 CO).
- Formation (Article 395 CO).
- Effects (Articles 396–403 CO).
- Termination (Articles 404–406 CO).

B Delimitations

702 A mandate agreement must be distinguished from a contract for work. Whereas the former only entails a duty to act diligently in furtherance of a goal (best efforts), the latter entails a duty to deliver a specific result.[832]

703 Further, the delimitation of a mandate agreement from an employment contract (Articles 319–362 CO) can give rise to controversy. Both, a mandatee and an employee, are bound to follow instructions from their contracting partner. The distinctive factor is their general level of subordination.[833] An employee is integrated into the employer's

828. *See* hereinabove paras 469 et seqq. Decision of the Swiss Federal Supreme Court dated 10 September 2002, no. 4C.387/2001, para. 6.2.
829. Gauch, Der Werkvertrag, Zurich 2019, N 582.
830. Article 394(1) CO.
831. Article 394(2) CO.
832. *See* hereinabove paras 637–638.
833. Decision of the Swiss Federal Supreme Court dated 19 July 2017, no. 4A_10/2017, para. 3.1: 'An employment contract is distinguished above all from other contracts for the provision of services, in particular from a mandate agreement, by the existence of a subordinate relationship, which makes the employee dependent on the employer from a personal, organisational, temporal and, to a certain extent, economic point of view. The employee is subject to the employer's supervision, orders and instructions; he or she is integrated into the work organisation of others and given a specific place within it. Formal criteria, such as the title of

organisation. In contrast, a mandatee is independent and may decide for himself when and where he carries out his services, subject to any other agreement or the nature of the respective contract. Further, a mandatee is only subject to his contracting partner's instructions as far as they concern the assigned business and services.[834] An employer's power of instruction is more comprehensive.[835]

C Formation and Content of the Mandate Agreement

704 As required for every contract, there need to be mutual expressions of intent. While under the general rule of Article 6 CO, silence does not amount to acceptance of an offer,[836] Article 395 CO stipulates a special rule for mandate agreements:

> A mandate is deemed to have been accepted where it has not been declined immediately and relates to business which is conducted by the mandatee by official appointment or on a professional basis or for which he has publicly offered his services.

705 The term 'professional basis' includes lawyers, medical doctors, architects and banks. A public offering of services is namely assumed when they have formed the object of public advertisement. Although Article 395 CO speaks of a duty to 'immediately' decline an offer, doctrine awards the recipient of an offer a short time period to examine the offer and underlying documentation.[837]

706 While remuneration of the mandate is presumed in practice, it is not an objectively essential term (*essentialia negotii*) of the mandate agreement.[838] The provisions of Articles 394–406 CO also cover the furnishing of services for free.

707 With conclusion of a mandate agreement, the mandator automatically authorises the mandatee to carry out such legal transactions on his behalf as required for performance of the mandate agreement.[839] This entails an authorisation for the mandatee to act as a direct or indirect agent in the sense of Articles 32 et seqq. CO.[840]

---

the contract, the declarations of the parties or the social security deductions, are not decisive. Instead, substantive criteria relating to the way in which the work is actually performed must be taken into account, such as the degree of freedom in the organisation of work and time, whether or not there is an obligation to report on the activity and/or to follow instructions, or the identification of the party bearing the economic risk. In principle, instructions that are not limited to simple general guidelines on how to carry out the task, but that influence the purpose and organisation of the work and establish a right of control for the entitled party, indicate the existence of an employment contract rather than a mandate agreement.'

834. Article 397 CO.
835. Article 321d CO.
836. *See* hereinabove para. 93.
837. Huguenin, Obligationenrecht, Zurich 2019, N 3228.
838. Article 394(3) CO.
839. Article 396(2) CO.
840. *See* hereinabove paras 119 et seqq. Decision of the Swiss Federal Supreme Court dated 2 June 1992, DSC 118 II 313, para. 2.a: 'It fails to recognise that the authorisation for direct or indirect agency derived from article 396(2) CO is limited to the legal acts necessary for the performance of the mandate.'

Yet, such general authorisation is insufficient for the legal transactions listed in Article 396(3) CO (e.g., conclusion of a settlement agreement or sale of real estate). For such transactions, the law requires the mandatee to have received special authority from the mandator. Such special authorisation may be given by including a clause to that effect in the mandate agreement. In any case, the mandator may ratify an unauthorised act by the mandatee.[841]

D The Mandatee's Obligations

1 Duty to Perform Business Entrusted to the Mandatee

708 The mandatee is obliged to perform the business entrusted to him in a diligent and faithful manner.[842] The scope of the mandate depends primarily on the content of the mandate agreement and, lacking such specification, is secondarily determined by the nature of the business to which it relates.[843] Further, the mandator can specify the scope of the mandate by giving specific instructions, which the mandatee must generally follow.[844]

709 While the mandatee is obliged to strive towards certain goals, he does not carry a duty to obtain specific results.[845] The level of required diligence is determined in accordance with the rules applicable to employment contracts (i.e., Articles 321a and 321e CO).[846] However, these rules must not be applied blindly to mandate agreements, but rather with certain amendments to accommodate for the special relationship inherent to a mandate agreement, in which the mandator usually seeks support from a person with special skills:

> Article 398(1) CO refers for the degree of care of the mandatee to that of the employee in the employment relationship (article 321e(2) CO), whereby this reference is to be understood to mean that the mandatee is not liable for the same – less strict – care as the employee, but according to the same rule. The standard

841. *See* hereinabove para. 138.
842. Article 398(2) CO.
843. Article 396(1) CO.
844. Article 397(1) CO.
845. Decision of the Swiss Federal Supreme Court dated 9 February 2007, DSC 133 III 121, para. 3.1: 'Article 398(2) CO makes the mandatee liable to the mandator for the diligent and faithful performance of the mandate. Paragraph 1 of this provision refers to the rules governing employee liability in employment relationships, i.e., article 321e CO. This provision states that the employee is liable for the damage he causes to the employer intentionally or through negligence (para. 1) and determines the degree of diligence required (para. 2). In his capacity as mandatee, the doctor is responsible for the diligent and faithful execution of the mandate. While it is inherent in the medical profession for doctors to use their knowledge and skills to obtain the desired result, this does not mean that they must achieve this result or even guarantee it, as the result as such is not one of their obligations. The extent of the doctor's duty of care is determined according to objective criteria. The requirements that must be met in this respect cannot be fixed once and for all; they depend on the particularities of each case, such as the nature of the intervention or treatment and the risks involved, the margin of discretion, the time and resources available, and the doctor's training and abilities.'
846. Article 398(1) CO.

of care is therefore based on the skills, expertise and characteristics of the mandatee of which the client was or ought to have been aware. Whether a breach of the lawyer's duty of care has occurred must always be assessed on the basis of the specific case.[847]

710 Based on this, the Swiss Federal Supreme Court describes the mandatee's duty of diligence as follows:

> The mandatee is liable to the mandator for the faithful and diligent execution of the business entrusted to him (article 398(2) CO). The degree of diligence is determined according to objective criteria. The degree of diligence required is that which a conscientious mandatee in the same position would exercise in the performance of the business entrusted to him. Higher requirements are to be placed on the mandatee who carries out his activity professionally for remuneration. A distinction must be made according to the type of mandate and the special circumstances of the individual case must also be taken into account. If there are generally accepted rules of behaviour and practices for a particular profession or trade, these can be used to determine the level of diligence. In principle, the mandatee is not liable for the success of his activity. Rather, liability is based on careless or unfaithful execution of the mandate that is harmful to the client.[848]

711 In contrast to the general rule of Article 68 CO, there is a presumption that the mandatee is obliged to perform his obligations personally.[849] But he may be authorised (explicitly or implicitly) by the mandator to delegate (parts of) the business entrusted to him to a third party.[850] The mandatee may also call in auxiliary persons (Article 101 CO) for lower-level tasks.[851]

2 *Duty of Trust*

712 The duty of trust (*Treuepflicht, devoir de fidélité, dovere di fedeltà*) obliges the mandatee to protect the interests of the mandator at all times.[852] This namely includes duties to advise the mandator on relevant risks, to warn the mandator if his instructions are impractical or unreasonably risky,[853] to act with discretion and respect the confidentiality of certain matters and to avoid any conflicts of interest.[854]

847. Decision of the Swiss Federal Supreme Court dated 1 November 2016, no. 4A_380/2016, para. 4.1.
848. Decision of the Swiss Federal Supreme Court dated 5 March 2014, no. 4A_364/2013, para. 6.1.
849. Article 398(3) CO.
850. Article 398(3) in conjunction with Article 399 CO.
851. Importantly, the liability of the mandatee for auxiliary personnel is governed by Article 101 CO, not by the less strict provisions of Article 399(2) applicable in case of delegation.
852. Article 398(2) CO.
853. Decision of the Swiss Federal Supreme Court dated 30 January 1989, DSC 115 II 62, para. 3.a: 'The duty of loyalty means in particular that the mandatee must advise and inform the mandator. By providing regular advice, the mandatee must assist the mandator in choosing the appropriate measures. If he receives instructions that run counter to the interests of the customer, he must advise against them. The scope of the duty to inform is everything that is of importance to the customer. As a specialist, the mandatee must also inform the mandator about

3 *Duty to Render Accounts and Return*

713 Under Article 400(1) CO, the mandatee is obliged to give an account of his activities under the mandate and to return to the mandator anything received for whatever reason as a result of such activities. He must perform this obligation at the mandator's request, which may be made at any time. Two separate duties follow from Article 400(1) CO: (i) rendering of accounts (*Rechenschaftsablagepflicht*, *devoir de présenter des comptes, dovere di conteggio*); and (ii) returning of anything received (*Herausgabepflicht, devoir de restituer, dovere di restituzione*).

a *Duty to Render Accounts*

714 The duty to render accounts shall enable the mandator to monitor the mandatee's activities.[855] It forms the prerequisite and basis of the duty to return benefits and finds its limits in the principle of good faith.[856]

715 It is not clear from the law what information the mandatee must provide specifically, which documents he must submit and how far his duty extends in general. This depends above all on the nature of the mandate, the special agreements between the parties as well as the transactions or services that the mandatee has to perform. In general, however, it can be said that the duty of rendering accounts is limited to matters relating to the contractual relationship.[857] Yet, the mandatee must inform the contractual partner fully and truthfully. He must provide the mandator with all documents that relate to the business conducted in his interests. This includes all activities undertaken by the mandatee (contracts and correspondence with third parties and the mandator).[858] Importantly, the mandatee must also report on issues that might give rise to a damages claim against him.[859]

716 When rendering accounts the mandatee must make sure that he presents the information to the mandator in an easily understandable and comprehensible manner.[860]

the appropriateness of the assignment and the instructions, the costs and risks as well as the chances of success without being requested to do so.'

854. Huguenin, Obligationenrecht, Zurich 2019, N 3269-3271.
855. Decision of the Swiss Federal Supreme Court dated 26 March 1984, DSC 110 II 181, para. 2.
856. Decision of the Swiss Federal Supreme Court dated 19 November 2012, DSC 139 III 49, para. 4.1.2.
857. Decision of the Swiss Federal Supreme Court dated 19 November 2012, DSC 139 III 49, para. 4.1.3.
858. Decision of the Zurich Commercial Court dated 27 September 2021, no. HG 190051, para. 5.2.1.
859. Decision of the Swiss Federal Supreme Court dated 17 April 2012, DSC 138 III 425, para. 6.4: 'The claim to rendering of accounts under article 400 CO is not excluded even if the mandatee could thereby be exposed to claims for damages. Accordingly, the fact that the respondents are also requesting the information in order to be able to check whether they wish to take legal action to assert claims for damages does not give the appellant an overriding legitimate interest in refusing to provide information.'
860. Decision of the Zurich Commercial Court dated 27 September 2021, no. HG 190051, para. 5.2.1.

b *Duty to Return*

717 The mandatee must return everything he has received from the mandator in the course of performing the mandate, everything he has created himself and everything he has received from third parties. The prerequisite for the duty to return is an internal connection with the specific mandate. This includes, in particular, indirect benefits and benefits from third parties that accrue to the mandatee in the course of the performance of the mandate.

718 The duty to return includes assets (including indirect benefits such as commissions and retrocessions from third parties).[861] It also covers all documents (including correspondence and contracts) that relate to the business conducted in the interests of the mandator. A bank, for example, must hand over account and custody account statements to the client.[862] Yet, purely internal documents such as preparatory studies, notes, drafts, collections of materials and own accounts are not subject to the duty to return, but might still be subject to the rendering of accounts.[863]

E The Mandator's Obligations

1 *Duty to Pay Remuneration*

719 Article 394(3) CO leaves it to the parties to agree on a remuneration. If the mandatee acts in a professional capacity, a duty to pay a remuneration is presumed.[864]

720 If parties fail to agree on the amount of the remuneration, it is determined in accordance with custom. If no such custom can be identified, the tribunal must fix the remuneration by taking into account all relevant circumstances, such as the difficulty of the tasks to be completed, the time required to perform the tasks and the mandatee's experience.[865]

861. Decision of the Swiss Federal Supreme Court dated 10 January 2012, DSC 138 III 137, para. 5.3.1: 'In addition to the assets that the mandatee receives directly from the mandator for the performance of the mandate, the duty to return also applies to indirect benefits that the mandatee obtains as a result of the performance of the mandate. The mandatee should neither gain nor lose from the mandate – apart from any fee. He must therefore surrender all assets that are intrinsically linked to the performance of the mandate. If, for example, an asset is sold at a higher price than specified by the mandator, the latter is entitled to the advantage.'
862. Decision of the Swiss Federal Supreme Court dated 19 November 2012, DSC 139 III 49, para. 4.4.
863. Decision of the Swiss Federal Supreme Court dated 19 November 2012, DSC 139 III 49, para. 4.1.3.
864. Decision of the Swiss Federal Supreme Court dated 28 September 1956, DSC 82 IV 145, para. 2.a.
865. Decision of the Swiss Federal Supreme Court dated 9 February 2009, DSC 135 III 259, para. 2.2: 'Admittedly, it has been disputed whether custom, to which article 394(3) CO refers, can not only determine the onerous nature of the contract, but also lead to the fixing of the amount of the fees. However, there is no need to go back over the consideration of custom, which has already been accepted in case law and which is supported by recent doctrine. If there is no

721 The mandator may reduce the remuneration if the mandatee has not performed the mandate properly. Although an explicit legal provision on reduction is lacking – in contrast to the law on sales contracts or the contracts for work – case law admits that the mandator may draw on the remedy of reduction.[866] A complete cancellation of the mandatee's remuneration is, however, exceptional and only justified where the inadequate performance by the mandatee amounts, in essence, to non-performance.[867]

2 *Reimbursement of Expenses*

722 Under Article 402(1) CO, the mandator is obliged to reimburse the mandatee for expenses incurred in the proper performance of the mandate plus interest. The parties may, however, deviate from this default rule.[868]

723 Only expenses that were objectively necessary and reasonable for performing the mandate form part of the mandatee's claim of reimbursement.[869] A mandatee must thus prove the existence of the expense, its necessity and its reasonableness.[870]

3 *Release from Obligations*

724 The mandator is obliged to release the mandatee from obligations vis-à-vis third parties entered into in the course of the mandate.[871] The mandatee should generally not suffer any loss of assets as a result of his activities in the interests of the mandator. While cash expenditures are covered by the obligation to reimburse expenses, the duty

custom, the court sets the remuneration taking into account all the relevant circumstances, it being emphasised that it must be objectively proportionate to the services rendered.' Also *see* decision of the Swiss Federal Supreme Court dated 18 February 1975, DSC 101 II 109, para. 2.

866. Decision of the Swiss Federal Supreme Court dated 2 October 2017, no. 4A_89/2017, para. 5.2.2: 'In the event of inadequate performance, the mandatee's entitlement to fees remains, but the amount of the agreed fee (*Honorarforderung*) may be reduced in order to restore the balance of the contractual services. This is because the remuneration payable to the mandatee represents consideration for the diligent work he carries out in the matter entrusted to him, and if he fails to act with the requisite diligence, he is not entitled to claim compensation under article 394(3) CO and the parties' agreement, to the full fees agreed, i.e., to the remuneration that would be fairly due to a diligent attorney. The mandator's right to a reduction exists even where the fees have been fixed as a lump sum.'
867. Decision of the Swiss Federal Supreme Court dated 2 July 1998, DSC 124 III 423, para. 4.a: 'After assessing the case law and the opinions of legal scholars, it must be concluded that the mandatee, even in the event of inadequate performance of the mandate, is entitled to fees for the activity he has carried out in accordance with the contract. It is only where the inadequate performance of the mandate is tantamount to total non-performance, proving useless or unusable, that the mandatee may lose his right to remuneration; the same applies where the mandatee's remuneration itself constitutes the damage caused by the inadequate performance.'
868. Decision of the Swiss Federal Supreme Court dated 20 July 2015, no. 4A_429/2014, para. 6.2.5.
869. Decision of the Swiss Federal Supreme Court dated 4 February 2015, no. 4A_424/2014, para. 2.
870. Decision of the Swiss Federal Supreme Court dated 1 July 2011, no. 4A_128/2011, para. 3.2: 'Any unjustified expenses and disbursements are not covered by the consensus of the mandate, which is why the mandator may refuse to reimburse unnecessary or excessive expenses.'
871. Article 402(1) CO.

to release from obligations concerns debt obligations entered into by the mandatee towards a third party in his own name, but in the interest of the mandator.[872]

725 As for the reimbursement of expenses, only debt obligations entered into that were necessary and reasonable may form part of the mandator's duty to release.

726 The release occurs, at the choice of the mandator, either by making direct payment to the third-party creditor, by assuming the mandatee's debt obligation (external assumption of debt[873]) or by making a corresponding payment to the mandatee (who may then use the money received to pay his debt).

F Performance Failure

727 In general, performance failures in mandate agreements are subject to the rules of the general part of the Code of Obligations.[874]

1 Performance Failure by the Mandatee

728 Performance failure by the mandatee entitles the mandator to damages.[875] The legal basis of this remedy is Article 97(1) CO in conjunction with Article 398(2) CO.[876] In contrast, Article 398(1) CO does not form the basis of the remedy, but only defines the level of diligence owed.

729 The question of whether parties may exclude or limit a mandatee's liability for damages has not yet been clarified by the Swiss Federal Supreme Court. There is an argument for denying an exclusion or limitation considering that the mandatee's duty to diligence is an indispensable characteristic of the mandate. However, the prevailing doctrine – upholding the parties' autonomy and the principle of freedom of contract – permits an exclusion or limitation of liability within the restrictions imposed by Article 100 CO.[877]

730 Apart from damages, a mandator may request reduction of the remuneration.[878] If the remuneration has already been paid to the mandatee, any claim for repayment would be subject to the rules of unjust enrichment (Articles 62–67 CO) and thus a shorter prescription period of three years.

872. Decision of the Zurich Commercial Court dated 27 May 2014, no. HG120079, para. 3.3.1.
873. *See* hereinabove para. 493.
874. *See* hereinabove paras 340 et seqq.
875. As to the remedy of damages, *see* hereinabove paras 397 et seqq.
876. *See* decision of the Swiss Federal Supreme Court dated 20 June 2016, no. 4A_45/2016, paras 2.2 and 2.4.
877. Huguenin, Obligationenrecht, Zurich 2019, N 3268a, with further references.
878. *See* hereinabove para. 725.

731 In regard to the mandatee's duty to return, performance failure will consist of a debtor's default.[879] However, there is a defence against such default. The mandatee may claim a right to withhold returning if the mandator has not yet paid the remuneration owed.[880] As long as the mandatee invokes such right, there is no debtor's default.

2 *Performance Failure by the Mandator*

732 Since the mandator's obligation will mostly be for payment of money, performance failure will mainly take the form of debtor's default.[881]

733 However, if the mandator has breached any other obligation under the mandate agreement, he is liable to the mandatee for the damage arising from such breach.[882] The usual rules of the remedy of damages apply.

G Termination of a Mandate

734 Under Article 404 CO, either party may terminate by notice the mandate agreement for whatever reason at any point in time. As regards the exercising of the termination right, the general rules on termination by notice apply.[883] The mandate agreement is terminated with effect *ex nunc*.

735 The termination right of Article 404 CO is considered to be of mandatory nature and may thus not be deviated from.[884] The rationale of this rule and its mandatory character lies in the distinctive position of trust that a mandatee holds. Once the relationship of trust between the parties has been damaged, there is no point in trying to maintain the contract.

879. In this regard, *see* hereinabove paras 349 et seqq.
880. There are three potential bases for such right to withhold returning (*see* decision of the Swiss Federal Supreme Court dated 21 November 1996, DSC 122 IV 322, para. 3). However, there is no right to withhold returning of objects (namely, documents) that cannot be liquidated and turned into cash.
881. In this regard, *see* hereinabove paras 349 et seqq.
882. Article 402(2) CO. Yet, if the mandate is performed for free, the rule of Article 422 CO applies, which is more favourable for the mandatee.
883. *See* hereinabove paras 460 et seqq.
884. Decision of the Swiss Federal Supreme Court dated 6 July 2011, no. 4A_141/2011, para. 2.2: 'According to established Federal Supreme Court case law, the right to terminate the contract at any time pursuant to article 404(1) CO is of a mandatory nature and may neither be waived nor restricted by contract. The Federal Supreme Court expressly confirmed this case law in DSC 115 II 464, para. 2. Since this decision, it has always clearly and unequivocally upheld the mandatory nature of article 404 CO.' But there are several scholars heavily criticizing the Federal Supreme Court's case law.

736 The termination right even exists if parties agree in the mandate agreement on a fixed term. Further, the parties may not hinder any party from exercising his termination right by imposing penalties on the terminating party.[885]

737 The right of cancellation is only limited to the extent that it shall not be exercised at an inopportune time. In such a case, the terminating party must compensate the other party for the resulting damage.[886]

738 The term 'at an inopportune time' is interpreted rather widely. From the Swiss Federal Supreme Court's case law, two requirements may be deduced: first, the terminated party must not have given just cause for the termination and, second, the termination must be disadvantageous for the terminated party with regard to the time and the dispositions he has made.[887]

739 In any case, the terminating party must not pay any compensation if he can show good cause[888] for the termination.[889] In contrast, where termination is exclusively due to economic considerations, rather than to aspects relating to the trust among the parties, a termination at an inopportune time is assumed.[890] Further, if the terminating party disregards contractually agreed notice periods or a fixed term, the termination is presumed to be made at an inopportune time.[891]

740 Under Article 404(2) CO only negative damages may be claimed. Thus, generally, no loss of profit will be due.[892] However, if a mandatee is able to prove that he rejected another mandate in order to accept the mandate in question, he may still claim loss of profit.[893]

741 Parties may agree on liquidated damages or penalties that apply in case of termination at an inopportune time. The Swiss Federal Supreme Court does not consider such clauses invalid, as they do not restrict the right to terminate at any time, but merely deal with the consequences of terminating at an inopportune time which the law frowns upon.[894] The usual rules on contractual penalties apply.[895]

---

885. Decision of the Swiss Federal Supreme Court dated 23 May 1978, DSC 104 II 108, para. 4.
886. Article 404(2) CO.
887. Decision of the Swiss Federal Supreme Court dated 12 June 1984, DSC 110 II 380, para. 3.b.
888. *See* hereinabove para. 469.
889. Decision of the Swiss Federal Supreme Court dated 29 July 2008, no. 4A_237/2008, para. 3.2.
890. *See* decision of the Swiss Federal Supreme Court dated 13 December 1983, DSC 109 II 462, para. 4.c (referring to the lower court's reasoning).
891. Gehrer/Giger, commentary on Article 404 CO, in: Huguenin et al. (eds), Handkommentar zum Schweizer Privatrecht, N 14, with further references.
892. Decision of the Swiss Federal Supreme Court dated 15 November 2004, no. 1P.58/2004, para. 4.4.
893. Honsell, Schweizerisches Obligationenrecht, Besonderer Teil, Berne 2017, p. 340.
894. Decision of the Swiss Federal Supreme Court dated 6 July 2011, no. 4A_141/2011, para. 2.4: 'According to the case law of the Swiss Federal Supreme Court, it is then permissible to provide for a contractual penalty in the event of termination at an inopportune time within the meaning of article 404(2) CO. For example, the Federal Supreme Court has deemed article 8.1 of the SIA standard 102 (1969), according to which the architect is entitled to the fee for the work performed as well as a fee supplement [of 15%] if the customer withdraws the mandate from the architect through no fault of the architect, to be effective in the event of untimely termination.'

V SETTLEMENT AGREEMENT

742 'With the settlement agreement, the parties settle a dispute or uncertainty about a legal relationship with mutual concessions.'[896] The settlement agreement constitutes an innominate contract which is governed by the general part of the Code of Obligations.

A Formation of the Settlement Agreement

743 The settlement agreement is not subject to any form requirement by law,[897] even if the disputed contractual relationship itself was subject to such requirement.[898] However, a form requirement applies if the settlement agreement contains within it a transaction that is subject to such form requirement (e.g., as part of a settlement agreement the parties transfer property in a plot of land).

744 Importantly, and contrary to other legal systems, the mere opening of settlement discussions does not interrupt any prescription periods that might be running in respect of the disputed claims. Only with conclusion of the settlement agreement, does a new prescription period of ten years start running for the claims arising under the settlement agreement.[899]

745 The provisions of the Code of Obligations on defects in consent (Articles 23- 31 CO)[900] cannot be applied without some amendments to the special nature of the settlement agreement. A party may only claim a fundamental error under Article 24(1)(4) CO if the alleged error concerns the uncontentious basis of the settlement agreement.[901]

B Effects of the Settlement Agreement

746 A settlement agreement does not automatically entail novation of the claims at dispute.[902] In line with Article 116(1) CO, novation is not presumed but must be clearly

895. *See* hereinabove paras 432 et seqq.
896. Decision of the Swiss Federal Supreme Court dated 4 December 2003, DSC 130 III 49, para. 1.2.
897. Article 11 CO.
898. Decision of the Swiss Federal Supreme Court dated 17 November 1980, DSC 106 II 222, para. 2.
899. Article 127 CO in conjunction with Article 135(1) CO.
900. *See* hereinabove paras 159 et seqq.
901. Decision of the Swiss Federal Supreme Court dated 4 December 2003, DSC 130 III 49, para. 1.2: 'Consequently, only those circumstances that have been taken by both parties, or by one party recognisably for the other, to form the basis of the settlement as established facts can be considered as relevant under article 24(1)(4) CO. If, on the other hand, the mistake relates to a dubious point that has just been settled and, according to the parties' intention, should have been definitively settled as a result (so-called *caput controversum*), the reliance on mistake is excluded; otherwise, the very issues for which the parties concluded the settlement would be reopened.'
902. Decision of the Swiss Federal Supreme Court dated 15 May 2012, DSC 138 III 570, para. 2.1.

agreed between the parties to the settlement, which must be proven by the party invoking it. However, in the case of a complex legal relationship, the agreement on a balance payment usually leads to novation.[903]

747 A settlement agreement usually follows the purpose of putting an end to the parties' dispute. Thus, it entails parties waiving asserted claims (to some extent). The scope of such waiver is presumed to be wide:

> The aim of ending a dispute or uncertainty about a legal relationship can generally only be achieved if all issues relating to the dispute or uncertainty are settled. This concern must be taken into account in the interpretation, even if the scope of a settlement of disputes or differences of opinion may vary. Therefore, if questions are not expressly regulated that are closely related to the dispute settled and the answering of which is necessary to resolve the dispute, it can generally be assumed that they should not be excluded from the settlement by the parties in the absence of an express reservation. According to the presumed intention of the parties, it is therefore generally justified to assume that such questions are answered analogously in the settlement.[904]

748 Often, a settlement agreement explicitly reiterates the purpose of ending the dispute among the parties with a so-called settlement clause (*Saldoklausel, clause pour solde*) by which the parties confirm that upon performance of the settlement agreement, they have no further claims against each other on any grounds whatsoever.[905] The scope of a settlement clause is subject to the usual rules of contract interpretation. There is a general presumption that such a clause should cover all disputes of which the parties were or ought to have been aware at the time of conclusion.[906]

749 If arbitral or court proceedings are pending at the time of conclusion of the settlement agreement, the parties have generally two options:

750 One, to have the settlement agreement (or at least parts of it) recorded by the court or arbitral tribunal (e.g., in the form of a consent award). This act gives the settlement agreement the same effects as a judgment or arbitral award.

751 Two, to have the claimant withdraw his claim in the pending court or arbitral proceedings without informing the court or arbitral tribunal about the content of the settlement agreement. This could, however, lead to a cost order against the claimant, which should be taken into account when determining the terms of the settlement agreement.

903. *See* hereinabove para. 497.
904. Decision of the Swiss Federal Supreme Court dated 18 March 2015, no. 4A_596/2014, para. 3.1.
905. *See, e.g.*, decision of the Swiss Federal Supreme Court dated 12 February 2015, no. 4A_523/2014, para. A: 'After execution of this agreement all claims against A.________ are fully settled.'
906. Decision of the Swiss Federal Supreme Court dated 7 May 2019, no. 4A_482/2018, para. 2.5.3.

www.ingramcontent.com/pod-product-compliance
Lightning Source LLC
LaVergne TN
LVHW020638300926
849161LV00004B/742